Commitment
to
Partnership

Explorations of the
Theology of Marriage

D0851890

Commitment
to
Partnership

Explorations of the
Theology of Marriage

William P. Roberts, Editor

Paulist Press
New York / Mahwah

Library of Congress Cataloging-in-Publication Data

Commitment to partnership.

  1. Marriage—Religious aspects—Catholic
Church—Congresses. 2. Catholic Church—
Doctrines—Congresses. I. Roberts, William P.
BX2250.C57   1987   261.8′3581   87-2341
ISBN 0-8091-2868-3 (pbk.)

Published by Paulist Press
997 Macarthur Boulevard
Mahwah, New Jersey 07430

Printed and bound in the
United States of America

Contents

Acknowledgements

I wish to thank the eight speakers who participated in this three day marriage symposium and whose papers appear in this volume. I am also grateful to the four hundred and fifty persons whose active presence made this symposium a dynamic event.

Special thanks are due to the organizations whose financial support made the symposium possible. A major grant was provided by the University of Dayton Fund for Christian Humanism. This grant was matched by gifts from the Marianists at the University of Dayton, the New York Province Marianist Sharing Fund, and the following University of Dayton Schools and Departments: School of Education, College of Arts and Sciences, Department of Religious Studies, Department of Sociology and Anthropology, and the Center for the Study of Family Development.

My appreciation also goes to Robert Hamma, editor at Paulist Press, for his interest and guidance in the publication of this book, to Carol Ann Cannon and Joanne Miller for their help in preparing the manuscript, and to my wife Challon for her advice and support throughout the entire project.

William P. Roberts

Foreword

Canon lawyers, diocesan family life personnel, theologians and religious educators were among the four hundred and fifty persons from across the United States and four other countries who gathered on March 13–15, 1986 in the Kennedy Union Ballroom on the University of Dayton campus to participate in a symposium entitled "Marriage in the Catholic Church: A Contemporary Evaluation."

The purpose of the symposium was to examine the present teaching and practice of the Roman Catholic Church regarding marriage in light of the history of the tradition and in light of contemporary biblical, theological and psychological studies. Are there assumptions that need reexamination? Are there new ways of formulating the tradition that can address in a more fully Christian way the urgent pastoral needs of millions of Catholics? Is it possible, while being faithful to the tradition, to bridge the growing gap that exists between the official hierarchical positions regarding marital and sexual issues and the sense of the faithful (*sensus fidelium*)?

To achieve the purpose of the symposium, eight internationally recognized scholars from various disciplines were invited to present papers on some of the most significant aspects of the meaning of Christian marriage. The presenters were also asked to enter into dialogue with one another.

The eight chapters of this book contain the papers prepared for the symposium. Each chapter begins with a precis of the paper, written by the author. All except the last end with a summary that I have composed of some of the main points raised in the responses that followed the presentation.

The book has been divided into three main parts. In Part One, Biblical and Theological Investigations, Pheme Perkins situates the New Testament teaching on marriage in the context of the world of the first century, while Theodore Mackin, S.J. and Bernard Cooke examine the notions of the sacramentality of marriage and of indissolubility, respectively.

Part Two deals with Ethical and Canonical Issues. Lisa Sowle Cahill treats the community and the couple as the parameters in an ethical consideration of Christian marriage. Peter Huizing, S.J. describes the shift of the Church's understanding of marriage that is represented in the Vatican II doc-

1

ument, *Gaudium et spes*. He then points to the implications this has for church law.

In Part Three, Pastoral Reflections, Rosemary Haughton examines the meaning of marriage in light of women's new consciousness. Jack Dominian integrates the psychological and spiritual aspects of Christian marriage. Chapter 8 contains the reflections that Raymond A. Lucker, as the final speaker, was asked to make, from an episcopal perspective, in response to the preceding papers.

In the epilogue I treat some of the main issues and questions emerging from the symposium that need to be further reexamined and addressed by the Church as we move toward a new millennium. Only through honest and open dialogue in the Spirit of Christ between Church officials, scholars, pastoral experts and married couples can we hope to proclaim the full meaning of the good news about Christian marriage. In this way married couples can be helped to achieve the fullness of Christian holiness in their marriages and thus promote the kingdom of God's unity and love in a terribly torn world.

William P. Roberts

Part One
Biblical and Theological Investigations

1.

Marriage in the New Testament and Its World

Pheme Perkins

This chapter describes the New Testament teaching on sexuality, marriage and divorce from three perspectives. First, the Jewish and pagan cultural presuppositions that are operative in the New Testament world are described. Second, the New Testament perceptions of what is the "ideal," especially in relationship to its inherited Jewish traditions and the sayings of Jesus, are discussed. Third, the pastoral mediation forged by the Paul tradition in various concrete situations of marriages between Christians and pagans, of Christian widows, etc., is discussed. These three steps are crucial to our contemporary reflection on the formation of Christian teaching about marriage.

John Macquarrie rightly observes that marriage differs from other Christian sacraments because it is not a specifically Christian relationship but a natural one common to all human societies. Its incorporation into the sacramental system acknowledges that a special commitment which requires the support of grace lies at the heart of marriage.[1] Understanding of the legal and cultural presuppositions about marriage and divorce operative in the first century requires "unlearning" a long tradition of religious/sacramental treatment of marriage. Not only did the legal patterns for marriage contracts and the presuppositions about relationships vary from one area to the next,[2] but marriage was primarily a relationship between the contracting families and not of some larger legal or religious community at all.[3] The primary purpose of contractual agreements is to provide for peaceful relationships between husband and wife, stipulate conditions for the disposition of property, and ensure the rights of any children born to the couple.

Our investigation of marriage in the New Testament and its world will begin with a survey of the legal and social presuppositions about marriage and divorce, especially as they are evident in the papyri. Following this section, we will look at the evidence for reflection on the significance of marriage that might expand or challenge common presuppositions in three areas: (a) expansion of special restrictions on the marriage of priests or kings to the community of the "elect" in the Dead Sea Scrolls; (b) negative mythologizing of the emergence of sexuality in heterodox Jewish exegesis of Genesis; (c) philosophic criticism of the social ties and obligations created by marriage in Cynic and Stoic philosophers.

We can then see how these developments are reflected in the special setting of emerging Christian communities. Jesus' divorce logion and its tradition-history appropriates the question about the special status of marriage within an elect community of the "righteous" for both Jewish-Christian and Gentile Christian converts. The Pauline assumption that remaining unmarried is preferable for those Christians able to do so needs to be assessed in the context of philosophic and gnosticizing critique of marriage as a cultural institution. The emergence of an ascetic rejection of marriage within Christianity is linked to apocryphal traditions bearing the authority of Thomas and of Paul as early as the late first century and is well established by the mid-second century. Finally, we can also see the reaction to such ascetic trends in the regulations about widows (and women generally) in the pastoral epistles and the symbolic exaltation of marriage as ecclesial symbol in Ephesians. This investigation shows that while Christians presumed that being "in Christ" should find expression in a challenge to the assumptions and behavior of their time with regard to marriage and sexuality, they were by no means agreed about the form(s) in which such difference should be expressed.

I.   Legal and Social Context of Marriage

With the exception of particular concerns that governed the marriages of members of priestly families (e.g. a priest could not marry a divorced woman—Lev 21:7), prohibitions against marriage to a Gentile and against re-marriage to a former spouse who had been married to someone else in the interim, Jewish legal arrangements are much like those of their non-Jewish counterparts. Marriage contracts stipulate the property which the wife brings with her to the marriage and sometimes exclude some of it from his use; the amount either of her dowry or the "bride price" to be settled on her in the event of divorce or her husband's death; property which is to be restricted to the wife's offspring as heirs and not to other offspring the husband may have; the duty of the husband to provide for the wife—particularly in the matter of clothing; her obligations not to "dishonor" the husband; procedures and penalties in the case of divorce for violation of some part of the contract.[4]

Both Jewish and non-Jewish contracts prohibit the husband from taking another woman as wife, or even as concubine. Such provisions appear to be aimed at ensuring that the rights of the wife and her offspring to inheritance are intact.[5] Throughout the Roman period one finds evidence for relationships between persons of divergent status that are not considered marriage. Tombstones show that men might have a wife and concubine together, while sexual relationships between a woman and someone other than her husband were considered a serious offense of adultery. Similarly, it was considered "fornication" for a lower class male to have extra-marital sex with a woman of the aristocratic class. Women of that class who married males of lower class lost their status. But tombstone inscriptions give evidence that some had on-going relationships with men of lower class origins.[6] A number of laws enacted under Augustus sought to curb adultery and divorces made to facilitate more advantageous political alliances, though the impact of such legislation is not at all clear.[7] Even after marriage, women usually remained part of their paternal family, and like all members of the family were under the jurisdiction of its oldest adult male, while their children belonged to their father.[8]

Aramaic evidence suggests that in Jewish circles marriage was a matter of formal agreement. Only the statement from the side of the husband is preserved, "She is my wife and I am her husband, from this day and forever." Whether the young age at which girls were first married made development of a similar form for the woman unlikely or whether there was a parallel formula for the wife, we do not know.[9] Similarly, the divorce formula, here of a Jewish woman divorcing her husband, simply states the intention of the parties, "I have come to hate Eshor, my husband."[10]

Although marriages were usually celebrated with some form of feasting, it is the contractual agreement of the parties and not any further ceremony that makes the marriage.[11] In some instances, presumably because of the death or absence of a girl's father, one finds the mother acting as the agent in her daughter's marriage and also issuing the invitation to the wedding celebration:

> Herais invites you to the marriage of her children, at home, tomorrow, the fifth, starting at the ninth hour [= 3 PM].[12]

The following contract (92 B.C.) represents many of the features of contracts in this period:

> In the twenty-second year of the reign of Ptolemy also called Alexander, the god Philometor, the priesthood of the priest of Alexander and the other priests as listed in Alexandria, the eleventh of the

month Mecheir at Cerceorsiris in the district of Polemon in the Arsinoite nome.

Philiscus, son of Apollonius, Persian of the Epigone, acknowledges to Apollonia (also known as Cellauthis), daughter of Heraclides, Persian, with her brother Apollonius as guardian, that he has received from her 2 talents and 4,000 drachmas in copper coinage as her dowry agreed to by him. Apollonia is to remain with Philiscus, obeying him as a wife should her husband, owning their property in common. Philiscus is to provide everything necessary, both clothing and whatever else is appropriate for a wedded wife, whether he is at home or away, according to the standard of their common resources.

It shall not be lawful for Philiscus to bring home for himself another wife in addition to Apollonia nor to maintain a female concubine nor a little boyfriend nor to beget children by another woman while Apollonia is alive nor to dwell in another house over which Apollonia has no rights, nor to throw her out, nor insult her or treat her badly, nor to alienate any of their common property to defraud Apollonia. If he is shown to be doing any of these things or not providing her with the necessities and clothing and other things as written, Philiscus is to pay the dowry of 2 talents and 4,000 drachmas of copper in full to Apollonia immediately.

And in the same way, it shall not be lawful for Apollonia to be absent for a night or a day from the house of Philiscus without the knowledge of Philiscus, nor to have intercourse with another man nor to ruin the common household nor to dishonor Philiscus in whatever brings dishonor to a husband.

And if Apollonia of her own free will wishes to separate from Philiscus, Philiscus is to return the dowry unaltered within ten days from the day the demand is made. If he does not return it, as written, he is to forfeit one and a half times the amount of the dowry to her immediately.[13]

Other contracts also deal with the disposition of the property in the event of death of one or both parties:

If one of them experiences something mortal and dies, the property that is left shall belong to the survivor and to the children that they will have in common. But if they do not have children in common, or if they are born and die before they grow up, and both parents survive them after the death of either one of them—if Arsinoe should die first, Menecrates is to return the entire dowry to Olympias, her mother, if she is alive; if she is not, then to Arsinoe's closest relatives.[14]

II.   Challenges to Common Practices and Presuppositions

Just as the legal arrangements in the papyri often serve to protect the inheritance of property within the woman's family, so the Roman nobility and the elite of other cities in the empire often enforced marriages within their own class. Those who violated such restrictions lost their privileged status. The post-exilic Jewish community strengthened its own boundaries by prohibiting marriage with Gentiles. Such divisions were given expression in a Hellenistic Jewish "romance," *Joseph and Aseneth*. The first part of the story describes the lovely Egyptian maiden's conversion to Judaism through the agency of an angelic visitor who initiates her with a mystic meal. Joseph had refused to eat with any of the Egyptians, even those sympathetic to Judaism and to have anything to do with Aseneth, since he would not kiss the mouth which worshiped idols (*Jos. Asen.* 8:5). After her conversion, Aseneth breaks with her ancestral religion and calls upon Jacob as father (22:3). This tale apparently serves a double function: not only does it encourage the proselyte to Judaism, but it also shows the Jewish community the importance of such fidelity to its own boundaries.[15]

Though *Jos. Asen.* would have reminded its readers of the popular erotic romances in which the chaste hero and heroine are finally united after numerous adversities, its emphasis on the religious conversion of the heroine makes her marriage to Joseph a religious event. Joseph is not allied to a powerful Egyptian family through marriage but to a beautiful heroine whom his fidelity to Yahweh has rescued from a life of idolatry and sin. This theme is stressed in the psalm of thanksgiving and confession with which Aseneth brings the first section of the book to its close:

I have sinned, Lord, I have sinned; before you I have sinned much. I was prospering in my father's house, and was a boastful and arrogant virgin. I have sinned, Lord, I have sinned; before you I have sinned much. And I have worshipped strange gods who were without number, and eaten bread from their sacrifices. . . . I have sinned, Lord, I have sinned; before you I have sinned much, until Joseph the Powerful One of God came. He pulled me down from my dominating position and made me humble after my arrogance, and by his

beauty he caught me, and by his wisdom he grasped me like a fish
on a hook, and by his spirit, as by bait of life, he ensnared me, and
by his power he confirmed me and brought me to the God of the ages
and to the chief of the house of the Most High, and gave me to eat
bread of life, and to drink a cup of wisdom, and I became his bride
forever. (*Jos. Asen.* 21:12–13, 21)

A second approach to "sacralizing" marriage so as to distinguish the
"righteous" from the immorality of their milieu is evident in the Essene legislation concerning marriage and divorce. The Essenes perceived their legislation prohibiting divorce and remarriage as well as extending the forbidden
degrees of kinship to include the commonly accepted marriage of uncles and
nieces to distinguish them from the "snares of Beliar" that have entrapped
other Jews:[16]

And in all those years Belial will be unleashed against Israel; as God
said through the prophet Isaiah, son of Amoz, "Terror and pit and
snare are upon you, O inhabitant of the Land." (Isa 24:17) The interpretation of it: The three nets of Belial about which Levi, son of Jacob, spoke, in which Belial has ensnared Israel. He set them before
them as three kinds of "righteousness": the first is unchastity; the
second, wealth; the third, defilement of the sanctuary. Whoever rises
out of one gets caught in another; . . . [they] have been caught in
unchastity in two ways: by taking two wives in their lifetime,
whereas the principle of creation is "male and female he created
them," (Gen 1:27) and those who entered the ark, "two by two went
into the ark." (Gen 7:9) And concerning the prince it is written, "He
shall not multiply wives for himself." (Deut 17:17) . . . Moreover
they defile the sanctuary, since they do not keep separate according
to the Law, but lie with her who sees "the blood of her flux." (Lev
15:19) And they take (as wives) each one, the daughter of his brother
and the daughter of his sister, whereas Moses said, "You shall not
approach your mother's sister; she is your mother's kin." (Lev
18:15) The regulation for incest is written for males but it applies
equally to women; so if a brother's daughter uncovers the nakedness
of her father's brother, whereas she is his kin . . . (CD 4:13–18;
4:20–5:2,6–11)

Before its incorporation into the *Damascus Document,* some scholars think
that this section served as an exhortation to non-Essenes.[17] In order to be part
of the community of the elect, it is necessary to reject what most would have

considered legitimate understandings of the law in regard to marriage and divorce.

The *Temple Scroll,* which expands legislation from the Torah to guarantee the sacral holiness of the whole community, presumes that the prohibition of polygamy in Deuteronomy 17:17 is a prohibition of divorce:

> And he shall not take in addition to her another wife, for she alone shall be with him all the days of her life; and if she dies, he shall take for himself another (wife) from his father's house, from his clan. (11 QTemple 57:17–19)

The combination of this legislation and the exhortatory material in CD suggests that the Essenes intended its prohibition to apply to all the righteous and not just to the king as in Deuteronomy 17:17. Their legislation presumes that the true intention of the law must be followed within the community and that that intention prohibits divorce and has a stricter definition of purity and incest than was commonly accepted.

While the material we have examined presumes that marriage within the appropriate limitations of religion, permitted degree of kinship and permanence is God's intent for humanity, mythologizing of Genesis traditions within some Jewish circles raised questions about sexual desire itself. Much mythological speculation was attached to the story of the sons of God and daughters of men in Genesis 6. The sins of the watchers are the subject of 1 Enoch 6–10. They defile themselves by sleeping with the women; they reveal sins to the women, and they beget the giants who fill the earth with bloodshed and unrighteousness (1 Enoch 9:8–10):[18]

> And the angels the children of heaven, saw and lusted after them and said to each other, "Come let us choose wives among the children of men and beget children for ourselves . . ." (1 Enoch 6:1–2)

> [The giants] brought catastrophe upon the whole earth. They consumed all the acquisitions of men. And when men could no longer sustain them, the giants turned against them and devoured humanity. And they began to sin against the birds, beasts and reptiles, and fish and to devour each other's flesh and drink the blood. Then the earth laid accusation against the lawless ones. (1 Enoch 7:3–6)

> And 'Asa'el taught men to make swords, and knives, and shields, and breastplates, and made known to them the metals (of the earth) and the art of working them, and bracelets, and ornaments, and the use of antimony, and the beautifying of the eyelids, and all kinds of

costly stones, and all coloring tinctures. And there arose much god-
lessness and they committed fornication, and they were led astray
and became corrupt in all their ways . . . (1 Enoch 8:1–3)

Other versions of the legend were apparently unable to conceive angelic beings
lusting after women, so the initial sin of lust is shifted to the women (*T. Reub.*
5:6–7). In a fragment of the *Genesis Apocryphon* from Qumran, Lamech, sus-
picious of the appearance of his newborn son Noah, accuses his wife of having
conceived the child through illicit union with one of the angels (1 QapGen II,
1–16). The leader of the fallen angels, Azazel, is often equated with the Satan/
snake of Gen (e.g. *Apoc. Abr.* 23). *2 Apoc. Bar.* 56:5, 10–14 makes the sin
of the fallen angels parallel to the transgression of Adam.

As the myth finds extensive elaboration in gnostic circles, sexual desire
itself becomes the snare which keeps humanity imprisoned in the world of
death. In a work heavily indebted to Jewish apocryphal traditions, *Apocalypse
of Adam,* Adam and Eve lose their eternal knowledge, which flees into the
heavenly seed of Seth, and the lower god creates an evil generation by seducing
Eve and awakening sexual desire in Adam. These motifs are all connected to
the fall of Adam/Eve:

Then the god who created us, created a son from himself [and] Eve,
[your mother], for [. . .]. I knew a sweet desire for your mother.
Then the vigor of our eternal knowledge was destroyed in us, and
weakness pursued us. Therefore the days of our life became few. For
I knew I had come under the authority of death. (*Apoc. Adam* 66,
25–67, 14)

Mythological interpretations of the Genesis materials such as this have
their ethical counterparts in ascetic traditions which condemn all forms of desire for their role in entrapping humans in the perishable body. The encratite
Thomas traditions of eastern Syria gave striking expression to this view as in
the following piece of apocalyptic wisdom preaching employed by the gnostic
author of *Thomas the Contender:*

O the bitterness of the fire that burns in the bodies of men and in
their marrow, burning in them night and day, burning in the limbs
of men and [making] their minds drunk and their souls deranged [and
moving] them within males and females [by day and] night and moving them [with] a [movement that moves] secretly and visibly. For
the males [move; they move upon the females] and the females upon
[the males. Therefore it is] said, "Everyone who seeks the truth from
true wisdom will make himself wings so as to fly, fleeing the lust

that scorches the spirits of men.'' And he will make himself wings
to flee every visible spirit. (*Th. Cont.* 139,33–140,5)

However, mythologizing of the Genesis tradition is not the only ancient
source for condemnation of sexual desire and its effect upon the soul. The philosophic tradition, rarely so radically hostile, was also convinced that only
those who freed themselves from its effects could achieve wisdom. Since the
Cynic philosophers challenged all social conventions and their associated pleasures, they rejected marriage outright as an unnecessary entrapment in the concerns of a deluded humanity:

> One should not wed nor raise children, since our race is weak and
> marriage and children burden human weakness with troubles. There-
> fore, those who move toward wedlock and rearing of children on
> account of the support these promise, later experience a change of
> heart when they come to know that they are characterized by even
> greater hardships. But it is possible to escape right from the start.
> Now the person insensitive to passion, who considers his own pos-
> sessions sufficient for patient endurance, declines to marry and pro-
> duce children. But life will become devoid of people. For from
> where, you will ask, will the succession of children come? I only
> wish that dullness would leave our life, and that everyone would be-
> come wise! For now, perhaps only the one persuaded by me will go
> childless, while the world, unconvinced, will beget children. But
> even if the human race should fail, would it not be fitting to lament
> this as much as one would if the procreation of flies and wasps should
> fail? For this is what people say who have not observed the true na-
> ture of things.[19]

Most philosophers would assume that sexuality and marriage are necessary for
the procreation of children but that the soul of the philosopher must be above
any of the passions of the body in order to attain truth. Thus, Philo insists that
the soul has nothing to do with the passions of the body when united to the
divine Logos or Wisdom (e.g. Spec. Leg. 2:30; Leg. All. 3:152).[20] However,
God had to give humans sexual desire so that they would produce children
(Abr. 137).

The first century stoic, Musonius Rufus, departed somewhat from the tradition that rearing children was the chief end of marriage. He argued that
though it was a noble end of marriage it was possible without marriage. Therefore, he concludes that mutual companionship and love are required:

> But in marriage there must be above all perfect companionship and
> mutual love of husband and wife, both in health and sickness and

under all conditions, since it was with desire for this as well as for having children that both entered upon marriage. Where, then, this love for each other is perfect and the two share it completely, each striving to outdo the other in devotion, the marriage is ideal and worthy of envy, for such a union is beautiful. But where each looks only to his own interests and neglects the other, or, what is worse, when one is so minded and lives in the same house but fixes his attention elsewhere and is not willing to pull together with his yoke-mate nor to agree, then the union is doomed to disaster, and though they live together, yet their common interests fare badly; eventually they separate entirely or they remain together and suffer what is worse than loneliness.[21]

Musonius considers procreation of children the only reason for sexual relationships between husband and wife. Anything else reduces the human being to the level of an animal:

Not the least part of the life of luxury and self-indulgence lies also in sexual excess; for example, those who lead such a life crave a variety of loves, not only lawful but unlawful ones as well, not women alone but also men. . . . Men who are not wanton or immoral are bound to consider sexual intercourse justified only when it occurs in marriage and for the sake of begetting children, since it is lawful but unjust when it is mere pleasure-seeking even in marriage. . . . There must be sheer wantonness in anyone yielding to the temptation of shameful pleasure and like swine rejoicing in his own vileness. In this category, too, belongs the man who has relations with his own slave maid, a thing which some people consider blameless, since the master has it in his power to use his slave as he wishes. In reply, I have just one thing to say . . . let him consider how he would like it if his wife had relations with a male slave. Would it not seem completely intolerable if a woman had a husband and had relations with a slave, but even if a woman without a husband should have? And yet surely one will not expect men to be less moral than women, or less capable of disciplining their desires.[22]

In response to the Cynic arguments that the philosopher should not marry, Musonius argued that the philosopher can only fulfill his obligations to teach and lead others by assuming those obligations toward family and city that all men have:

The philosopher is the teacher and leader of men in all things which are appropriate for men according to nature, and marriage is manifestly in accord with nature. For what other reason did the creator divide humanity into two sexes and implant in each a strong desire for the other? Is it not plain that he wished the two to be united and live together, and by their common efforts to devise a way of life in common and to produce and raise children so that the race might never die? . . . It would be each man's duty to take thought for his own city, and to make his home a rampart for its protection. But the first step toward making his home a rampart is marriage. Therefore, whoever destroys marriage destroys the home, the city and the whole human race. . . . It is clear that it is fitting for a philosopher to concern himself with marriage and having children. And if this is fitting, how can the argument that marriage is a handicap for a philosopher ever be sound? For manifestly the study of philosophy is nothing else than to search out by reason what is right and proper and by deeds to put it into practice.[23]

These examples show that the first century contained a number of possibilities for evaluating the ideal of marriage in human life. In one way or another, these ideals all imply a break with a group's experience of the legal and social realities of marriage in their environment. *Jos. Asen.* uses the "ideal love" of the romantic novel and the religious symbols of a sacred banquet to exalt the conversion of a prospective spouse to Judaism. Essene legislation insists upon a stricter interpretation of forbidden degrees of kinship and rejects divorce. Neither view would have been shared in the larger Jewish community, or in the non-Jewish world. But, for the Essene, the world outside the sect is dominated by sin. In the apocryphal Jewish traditions whose interpretations of Genesis were incorporated into gnostic myths, sexuality, sin and death are all linked together. Salvation can only be mediated through a radical break with the body and its passions. The philosophic dispute over the appropriateness of marriage represents a more moderate concern with the passions, but it also brings out the potential distraction of the familial and social responsibility entailed by marriage itself. The Cynic philosophers reject all such artificial human concerns. Musonius argues from the other side that the philosopher must set an example of appropriate human conduct in all areas, sexuality, marriage and civic responsibility.

III.   Jesus' Divorce Logion

Sayings opposing divorce are a fixed part of the Jesus tradition (Mt 5:31–32; 19:3–9; Lk 16:18; Mk 10:2–12; 1 Cor 7:10–11). There is no doubt that a version of the saying against divorce goes back to Jesus himself.[24] The earliest

form of the saying is likely to have been addressed to the male in the third
person without the exception made in the Matthean versions (Mt 5:32; 19:9).
It is more difficult to decide whether the conclusion to the saying followed
Matthew 5:32, the one who divorces his wife "makes her an adulteress," or
Luke 16:18, the one who divorces his wife and marries someone else "com-
mits adultery." The Lucan variant is also evident in Matthew 19:9 which likewise makes divorce and remarriage an act of adultery by the man. The second
version is a more logical legal conclusion from the tradition, such as that represented by the Essenes, which prohibited adultery. The man becomes an adul-
terer by divorcing his wife and marrying another. The former reflects the more
common view that adultery is primarily attached to the extra-marital sexual
relations by the wife. In either case, Jesus' saying departs from what one might
expect in a legal ruling on the issue by its interest in the effect of the husband's
action on the status of the wife.[25]

The Dead Sea Scrolls evidence shows that, while most Jews permitted
divorce and only sought to regulate its conditions, first century sectarian Judaism did prohibit it outright. Further, CD, like the pronouncement story in
Mark 10:6 (Mt 19:6), found the grounds for its position in Genesis. Both Jesus'
saying and the Essene legislation presume that their teaching reflects the intent
of God for humanity, which is to be realized in a community that lives out of
a different eschatological perspective than the rest of Israel. Only those whose
life is shaped by the standards of the sect can expect salvation from God.

The Matthean texts have cast both of Jesus' sayings into a form which
makes his teaching sharply antithetical to the prescriptions of the Mosaic law.
Matthew 5:32 is cast in the antithesis pattern used throughout this section. Matthew 19:3–9 heightens the rejection of Mosaic legislation found in the Markan
source (Mk 10:2–9) by making the challenge to Mosaic legislation (Deut 24:1–
4) the subject of a second exchange between Jesus and the Pharisees.[26] At the
same time, these texts would seem to be closer to Pharisaic discussion than to
the eschatological radicalism of Jesus or Qumran by introducing the question
of possible "grounds" for a divorce.[27] However, the particular reason given,
porneia (sexual immorality), should not be understood as "liberalizing" Jesus' saying. The word is not equivalent to "adultery" as some earlier interpretations used to hold. Rather, as the Essene texts suggest, it introduces the
question of marriages which are "sexually immoral," that is, within degrees
of kinship that are considered incestuous.[28] Acts 15:28–29 and 21:25 use *porneia* to prohibit such marriages among Gentile converts. The difficulty addressed by the Matthean exception would presumably have arisen with
converts to early Jewish-Christian communities whose marriages were "incestuous" by the standards of their new community. Guelich has argued that
Matthew 5:32 stems from the pre-Matthean Jewish-Christian tradition. He suggests that that community was particularly concerned to show that Jesus' teach-

ing did not violate the holiness of the law as might have appeared to be the case if either incestuous or adulterous relationships had been allowed to stand.[29]

Mark 10:11–12 reformulates the tradition so that it applies in the more urban and Hellenized environment where a divorce might as easily be initiated by the wife as well as the husband. A similar assumption is evident in 1 Corinthians 7:13. Dealing with Gentile churches, neither Mark nor Paul has any concern to guard community sentiments about marriages that might be perceived as counter to the will of God.[30] The affirmation that divorce was only permitted because of human "hardness of heart" (Mk 10:5) performs a function similar to that of the "snares of Belial" in the Essene texts. It designates certain human accommodations as sinful or a representation of human life during a time of separation from God. However, Mark's ethical perspective is shaped by the conviction that Jesus' coming has changed the times. The Christian now lives between that old age and the full realization of salvation. In that situation, it is possible to recreate marriage according to its original intention.[31]

IV. Ascetic Trends Within Christianity

The Pauline appeal to Jesus' saying follows directly upon a discussion of whether or not a man ought to engage in any form of sexual relations. 1 Corinthians 7:1 refers to a slogan being repeated at Corinth, "It is good for a man not to touch a woman." The reply in verses 2–3, that marriage was established "on account of *porneia*," reflects conventional Jewish ethics. Unlike the pagans, whose lives were marked by idolatry and sexual immorality, the Jews worshiped the true God and kept themselves from all forms of illicit sexual behavior through monogamous marriage.[32] However, Paul himself is sympathetic to and even advocates the ascetic position that it is preferable to remain celibate (vv. 6–8). Marriage is presented as a divinely established institution for those whom God has not given the gift to remain unmarried, since it alone provides an expression of human sexual desire that is not "lust" or *porneia* (v. 9).[33]

Anxious to read twentieth century values into the Pauline text, Christian commentators often stress the mutuality of sexual obligation in 1 Corinthians 7:4–5 as evidence for the influence of a new Christian vision of person.[34] Musonius argued, as we have seen, that mutuality is the chief end of marriage. He included their "bodies, and even their lives" among the goods that husband and wife hold in common. Jewish legal arrangements often stipulated sexual relationships as part of the contract. Failure to maintain regular sexual relationships could increase the amount owed the wife in case of divorce, or decrease it if the fault lay with the wife.[35] Murphy-O'Connor, rightly insisting

that the whole discussion must be understood in terms of problems created by
the ascetic position, observes that Paul's sole purpose in referring to the
"debt" owed one's spouse is to counter problems created when one partner
wishes to suspend sexual relations for ascetic reasons.[36]

The prohibition of divorce, which Paul is able to ground by appeal to a
saying of the Lord, in vv. 10–11 is aimed at another possibility raised by the
ascetics: Christians who wish to lead a life of celibacy should free themselves
from the obligations of marriage by divorcing their spouses. If one retains the
passive translation of the verb *choristhenai* ("be separated") in v. 10,[37] then
the situation envisaged is one in which an ascetically inclined husband divorces
his wife. Verse 11c repeats the injunction that a husband is not to divorce his
wife. The initial passive verb may have implied that wives should not agree to
such an action, though, as we have seen, divorce did not require the consent
of the other party or the proof of particular grounds in court. If the husband is
divorcing his wife for ascetic reasons, then the possibility of his remarriage is
not envisaged. Paul has not quoted the saying of Jesus in his appeal to the
Lord's authority. His formulation in vv. 10b–11b suggests that he may be ad-
dressing himself to a particular situation in Corinth, perhaps mentioned in the
letter referred to in verse 1.[38]

Paul's subsequent treatment of divorce in the case of marriages between
Christians and non-Christians (vv. 12–16) shows that he understands the injunction to remain unmarried or be reconciled to her husband to be limited to
the case in which both parties are Christian. It also indicates that quite unlike
the Jewish Christian tradition in Matthew, Paul does not envisage a situation
in which a Christian must divorce a non-Christian spouse. Paul's slogan, "God
has called you to peace," reflects a sentiment that we saw expressed in Musonius: marriage aims at the harmonious, communal life of the couple. The
Christian has no reason to divorce a non-Christian who is willing to live with
him or her. On the other hand, a Christian divorced by a non-Christian spouse
may remarry (7:15). Murphy-O'Connor protests that Paul is not drawing a distinction between applicability of Jesus' teaching to situations in which both
parties are Christian over against one in which a non-Christian spouse obtains
a divorce. In neither case does Paul employ a mode of legal reasoning which
begins with the prohibition of divorce. Instead, he suggests, Paul has drawn
his conclusions in both instances on the merits of the particular situations. In
the first case, he can also invoke the Lord's authority as a supporting argument.[39]

The ascetic motivation of the first instance precludes the possibility that
the husband will remarry. It also leaves open the possibility that the community, schooled by Paul's general discussion of asceticism and marriage in 1
Corinthians 7, may even exercise some persuasive influence toward the reconciliation of the couple(s) in question. The situation of the Christian/non-

Christian is quite different. The non-Christian is not part of the community. Nor is he or she likely to have remained unmarried.[40] Thus, the fact that the spouse is non-Christian does change several variables in the situation. The non-Christian's marriage to another party rules out the possibility of reconciliation with his or her Christian partner. The Christian would then be forced to remain "unmarried" until the death of the non-Christian party.

Paul consistently argues against the view that sexual asceticism is "commanded," which would be the case for a Christian deprived of the possibility of reconciliation with a divorced spouse. Persons who do not have the "calling" to a celibate life should marry. Doing so in no way jeopardizes their salvation (7:25–28a,36). Paul's explanation of his preference for those Christians who can to remain unmarried in vv. 28b–38 shows something of the ambiguity into which his preference for remaining unmarried while refusing to accept sexual asceticism as a norm for all Christians has led him. We have already seen that Cynic preachers lamented the cares, obligations and false values to which a married person is subject. Paul suddenly casts a similar argument in Christian form by insisting on the shortness of time before the end and suggesting that concern to please one's spouse takes away from the single-minded devotion to the affairs of the Lord possible for the unmarried.[41] Exegetes continue to dispute the question of whether eschatology or service to the Lord is the primary motive for preferring celibacy in this passage.[42] It is more likely that neither can be preferred over the other. Paul frequently marshals collections of arguments, without any consistent ordering, to support positions of which he appears unsure.[43] Paul also typically brings such passages to a conclusion with a simple statement or ruling that in no way encompasses the complications of the situation and the argument that has gone before it. 1 Cor 7:39–40 performs that function in this section. Christian widows are free to remarry—as long as it's a fellow Christian. However, it would be better if they remained unmarried.[44]

It is frequently the Paul of the simplified conclusions who becomes the influential force in the development of the tradition. The ascetic, anti-marriage posture, which Paul struggles to moderate, played an important role in Christian churches as the apocryphal acts demonstrate. The Paul of the legends in the second century *Acts of Paul and Thecla* sponsors the break-up of engagements and independent households of women apparently headed by wealthy widows. The tales of Paul and Thecla may have been circulated among such communities of Christian women.[45] The Thecla legend continued to be repeated in the fourth century where its anti-marriage message is clearly perceived as freeing Christian women from the kind of obligations that had been lamented by the Cynics. The encomium on Thecla by pseudo-Chrysostom provides a striking example:

Thecla had nothing in common with the earth, no connection with marital necessities, such as bearing up against a fornicating bridegroom, depriving oneself of the authority for making personal advancements, preparing food, being the object of jealousy when dressed up, being spat upon before giving birth as though she were not a married woman, and after giving birth finding herself facing legal charges on behalf of the children. And should a female be born, her husband is angry because it is not male. And should a male be born, her husband is angry because the child was not good-looking. And if both are good-looking, her husband is angry because the pain of caring for them is greater than the benefits.

Virginity even reverses the curse of Eve since the woman is not subject to a husband and does not bear children:

For the text that reads, ''Your turning shall be to your husband, and he shall rule over you,'' is powerless with respect to those not lorded over by husbands. The passage, ''she shall bear children in sorrows,'' does not apply to those who live as virgins, for she who does not bear children is outside the sentence of terrible labor pains. [46]

Archaeological remains as well as literary references attest to the popularity of the cult of Thecla among Christians of Asia Minor. She was clearly seen as a patroness for the groups of Christian virgins which constituted an established part of the Christian community by the fourth century. [47] The Manichaean teacher Faustus used the existence of Christian virgins, the rejection of marriage in the various apocryphal acts, Paul's preference for the unmarried state and the teaching of Paul to Thecla as arguments against the praise of marriage and hostility to Manichaean asceticism among orthodox Christians. [48]

V. Countering the Ascetic Trend

Further evidence for the influence of an ascetic reading of Christianity comes from the counter-positions of the pastoral epistles. Just as the Musonius appealed to the obligations of citizenship and the household to support the appropriateness of marriage for the philosopher, so the pastorals invoke the picture of the Christian as ''good citizen'' and Christianity as the source of a ''household ethic'' in which each person fulfills his or her appropriate role. [49] The pastorals oppose an unspecified group of opponents who are said to ''take prisoner'' women of the Church

> who make their way into households and make prisoners of war of weak women, burdened with sins and swayed by various impulses, who will listen to anybody and can never arrive at knowledge of the truth. (2 Tim 3:6–7)

The teaching of the opponents included an ascetic strain which involved both celibacy and food prohibitions:

> Now the Spirit expressly says that in later times some will depart from the faith by giving heed to deceitful spirits and doctrines of demons, through the pretentions of liars whose consciences are seared, who forbid marriage and enjoin abstinence from foods which God created to be received with thanksgiving by those who believe and know the truth. (1 Tim 4:1–3)

In the *Acts of Paul,* the apostle is pictured as a vegetarian, who never drank alcohol. 1 Timothy 5:23 seems to explicitly reverse such a prohibition, "No longer drink only water, but use a little wine for the sake of your stomach." Thecla's position as apostle and teacher in the *Acts of Paul* is directly associated with her virginity. The conflict over women teaching in the churches of the pastoral epistles is addressed by binding them to the home and claiming that child-bearing (not virginity) is the Christian woman's salvation from the curse pronounced against Eve:

> Let a woman learn in silence in all submission. It is not right for a woman to teach or have authority over a man, but to be silent. For Adam was fashioned first, then Eve. And Adam was not deceived, but the woman was led astray into transgression. But she will be saved through child-bearing, if she continues in faith and love and holiness with modesty. (1 Tim 2:11–15)

Since the author speaks of the "sneak attacks" by which the false teachers are gaining a following among the women, it would appear that the prohibition against their teaching and having authority over men is aimed at stopping the spread of false teaching within the community. But their appeal also seems to be connected with the asceticism which sponsored the break with the roles of wife and mother in the Thecla stories.[50] Viewed against the background of a controversy over the ascetic/non-ascetic interpretation of the Pauline tradition, the elaborate rules for enrolling women as widows, with a special "office" in the community (1 Tim 5:3–16), take on a different hue. While insisting upon the obligation of Christians to care for widows with no other means of support, the author wishes to reduce the numbers of such persons by insisting that families must provide for their own widowed members, and to restrict the "office" of widow. Not only must such women be over sixty and have raised their family in an exemplary manner so that they can teach younger women to do likewise, they must also have only been married once (a restriction also applied to bishops and deacons).[51] Bassler has argued that the circle of widows included young women who had never been married but had vowed themselves to a life of chastity (1 Tim 5:12).[52] The requirement that younger widows marry and bear children (v. 14) not only counters the ascetic renunciation, it also reinforces Christian conformity with the "household ideals" of the larger culture.[53]

Ascetic trends within the Pauline churches are not limited to the pastoral epistles. Nor should they be considered simply a women's issue. Colossians and Ephesians offer hints of other examples of a gnosticizing asceticism. Colossians 2:8,16–23 warns the recipients against a false "philosophy" whose precepts involved food, drink, observance of certain festivals, self-abasement (fasting and perhaps sexual abstinence), and worship of angels. The nature of this religious group is disputed. It appears to have involved a syncretism of philosophic (pythagorean?), Jewish (concern with elemental spirits and festivals appears in Galatians 4:3,8–10; worship of angels suggests apocalyptic heavenly visions) and perhaps gnosticizing developments (ascent to heaven; use of the word *pleroma*). The author's response is to invoke the traditional language of sin and forgiveness and a Christology which envisages Christ as the cosmic image of God. The community, which forms the body of Christ, already shares the heavenly reality of Christ, his *pleroma*. They are to manifest that heavenly life in the ethical conduct of their lives as Christians.[54] Part of the paraenesis of the letter employs the genre of household-code to describe the proper order of persons within the household. Brief injunctions to wives/ husbands and children/parents are followed by a longer warning to slaves that they must show genuine obedience to their masters. The masters, also under a heavenly master, must treat their slaves fairly (3:18–4:1).[55] In each case, the obedience of the subordinate party is matched by an obligation of the superior to be loving, not use harsh treatment and act justly.

When this household code is taken over in Ephesians, the section on wives/husbands is considerably expanded (5:22–33; cp. Col 3:18–19). The epistle's ecclesiology, Christ as head of a cosmic body, the Church, is used to expand both sides of the injunction. It explains the manner in which wives are "subject" to their husbands as the Church is to Christ (vv. 22–24, 33b—cp. v. 21). And, in an even more extended fashion, the analogy specifies how husbands are to "love their wives" (vv. 25–33a). The idea that the husband should not treat the wife as a master does a subordinate but as the soul cares for the body was a philosophical topos which appears in Plutarch (*Praec. Conjug.* 142E). Ephesians connects that topos with the image of the Church as body and bride (cf. 2 Cor 11:2) of Christ. Such "marriage" imagery has parallels in Old Testament descriptions of Israel as the bride of Yahweh, mythic and cultic references to a "sacred marriage," and gnostic myths of the heavenly union between the Savior and Wisdom as the foundation of a "marriage" between the soul and its heavenly counterpart. None of these examples has the same structure as Ephesians. Ephesians emphasizes the self-sacrifice of Christ which makes the bride pure and holy. This modification of the image is in line with the letter's ecclesiology. Christ's death on the cross brought into being the "new man" forged out of the reconciliation of the two opposed groups, Jew and Gentile (Eph 2:11–22).[56]

Ephesians 5:31 adds the citation of Genesis 2:24, a passage which appears elsewhere in the New Testament as part of the argument against divorce (Mk 10:7–8; Mt 19:4) and in Paul's warning against Christians using prostitutes (1 Cor 6:16). Philo of Alexandria allegorized this passage to speak of the mind's turn away from God to entanglement with sense-perception and passions. When the proper subordination of sense-perception (passions) to Mind is restored, then "there will be flesh no more, but both of them will be Mind." Such a conversion is necessary for true love of God (*Leg. All.* 2:49–50).[57] Ephesians understands the Genesis text as a reference to the "great mystery," the union between Christ and the Church.

Some versions of the Old Latin and the Vulgate translated the Greek "mysterion" into Latin as "sacramentum." This translation facilitated the understanding of this passage as evidence for the "sacramental character" of Christian marriage. Though Ephesians does not speak of "sacrament" in the terms of later theology, its incorporation of marriage into a cosmic ecclesiology grounded in the relationship between Christ and the Church as the body that he purified, redeemed and sustains does separate Christian marriage from its secular counterparts.[58] The injunctions of the household code are divorced from a concern with the good order of society. They are subsumed under the greater mystery by which Christians participate in the reality of the heavenly Christ (cf. 1:22–23; 3:9–10; 4:8–10,13–16).

Gnostic sources, especially those from Valentinian schools, have ritualized and mythologized marriage into an image of the "bridal chamber," the opposite of secular human marriage. In *Exegesis on the Soul* (CG II 6 132,23–133,10), the soul which had been lost in prostitution to the body is united with her heavenly savior:

> But then the bridegroom, according to the Father's will, came down to her into the bridal chamber, which was prepared. And he decorated the bridal chamber. For since that marriage is not like fleshly marriage, those who are to have intercourse with each other will be satisfied with that intercourse. And as if it were a burden, they leave

behind them the annoyance of physical desire, but they do not [separate from] each other, but this marriage [. . .] but [once] they unite [with one another], they become a single life. Wherefore the prophet said concerning the first man and first woman, "they will become one flesh" (Gen 2:24). For they were originally joined to one another when they were one with the Father before the woman led astray the man who is her brother. This marriage brought them back together again and the soul has been joined to her true love, her real master, as it is written, "for the master of the woman is her husband" (Gen 3:16; Eph 2:23).

Here the soul's conversion reverses the involvement with the body and passions that Philo's allegory holds separates a person from God.

The original unity of the Mind with God presumed in Philo appears in gnostic texts as the primal unity of the soul with its heavenly counterpart. The *Tripartite Tractate* (CG I 5) speaks of "Church" as a heavenly aeon linked to the kisses of Father and Son (58,19–59,1). It also uses the image of the Savior's incarnation as "self-giving" on behalf of those who must be gathered out of this world into the divine pleroma (123,17–22; 125,1–5). They are members of the "body" of the Savior which is manifested as a "sound" body when the pleroma is restored (123,13–27).

A ritual of the "bridal chamber" forms the culmination of the gnostic sacramental system in the *Gospel of Philip* (CG II 3). The inequality evident in worldly marriage is overcome by the gnostic:

Whereas in this world the union is one of husband with wife—a case of strength complemented by weakness—in the aeon the form of the union is different, although we refer to them by the same names. (76,6–9)

The gnostic "bridal chamber" is not a matter of defilement, darkness or desire as earthly marriage is:

Indeed marriage in the world is a mystery for those who have taken a wife. If there is a hidden quality in the marriage of defilement, how much more is the undefiled marriage a true mystery! It is not fleshly but pure. It belongs not to desire but to the will. It belongs not to the darkness or the night but to the day and the light. . . . Bridegrooms and brides belong to the bridal chamber. No one shall be able to see the bridegroom with the bride unless [one become] one. (82,4–10,23–26)

Although *Gos. Phil.* insists that the "bridal chamber" is not like defiled marriage, it is still possible that this rite represented a sacralization of marriages between members of the sect.[59]

Additional support for the possibility that some gnostic groups had sacralized marriage in a ritual form is provided by a fragmentary work, *Testimony of Truth* (CG IX,3), which attacks both orthodox Christians and a number of other gnostic sects among them the followers of Basilides and Valentinus. This work demands a radical asceticism. Sexual passion shows that persons are not of the seed of the Son of Man but belong to the condemned seed of Adam:

> neither any [pleasure] nor desire, nor [can they] control them. It is fitting that they should become undefiled, in order that they might [show] to every[one] that they [are from] the [generation of the] Son of Man, since it is about [them] that the Savior bore witness. But [those that are from] the seed [of Adam] are manifest by their [deeds which are] their [work]. They have not ceased [from desire which is wicked . . .]. . . . the day when they will beget [children]. Not only that, but they have intercourse while they are giving suck. (67,1–37)

Members of an unnamed gnostic group are condemned because they marry and beget children (58 and 59, fragmentary).

The polemic of *Testim. Tr.* shows the same tension between ascetic rejection of marriage and the desire to affirm marriage but separate the practices of the religious group from the secular realities of marriage that we have traced in the Pauline tradition. The groups which developed a ritual of the "bridal chamber" seem to have viewed the rite as a way of recognizing the necessity of an "ascetic conversion" from the worldly relationships grounded in passion. The attack on those who marry and beget children shows that sexual relationships between husband and wife were permitted in some groups. But gnostic sacramentalism lifts those relationships out of the realm of darkness and passion, since they are the "image" of the spiritual reality in which the gnostic soul is united with its heavenly counterpart.

VI. Concluding Comments

Although the legal and social reality of marriage was perceived as a private contractual arrangement, marriage was the cornerstone of every individual's place in the larger world. Philosophic writings often saw in the management of the household the microcosm of a person's responsibilities to the larger community. The "household codes" represent a popularization of

philosophic descriptions of "good order." Others, like the Cynics, rejected
marriage, its involvement with passions and other cares. This rejection formed
a protest against the power of the larger society and its values over individuals.
We have seen that this pattern emerges within Christian circles. Paul prefers
the "unmarried" state, since it makes complete devotion to the Lord possible.
The ascetic interpretation of the Pauline tradition in the apocryphal acts appears to have led groups of Christian women to reject the common pattern of
remarriage after the death of a spouse or to renounce marriage altogether.

Yet, as the Essene examples and Jesus' divorce logion indicate, asceticism is not the only avenue by which a religious group may use marriage to
distinguish itself from the surrounding culture. It is also possible to insist on
a vision of marriage itself, which differs from the common ethos. The rejection
of divorce was grounded in the perception of marriage as a permanent relationship between husband and wife that was not created and dissolved simply
by the intent of the contracting parties. Paul's "exception" in the case of divorce by a non-Christian spouse does not violate the spirit of the critique of
divorce, since Paul supports the permanence of marriage from the side of the
Christian spouse. Paul's criticism of the Corinthian ascetics also protected
marriage against dissolution on religious grounds. Paul might not have agreed
with the Jewish-Christian "exception" that is reflected in the Matthean versions of the divorce saying, though 1 Corinthians 7 does not speak to that situation. But the exception in Matthew applies to a limited situation that only
arises in a Jewish Christian context. It is not a "liberalizing" of the position
posited in the Jesus tradition.

Finally, we see the beginnings of a third route to distinguishing Christian
marriage from its cultural milieu in creating a "sacral" character for marriage
by linking it to the fundamental religious symbols of the tradition. *Jos. Asen.*
provides an example of such a possibility within a Jewish community that
sought to counter assimilation to a surrounding culture. Where "sacralization"
is pressed in opposition to ascetic opponents as in the pastorals and Colossians,
the process seems to have been little more than using the power of religious
symbols to reinforce the conventional rules of the household code, though Colossians shows a concern for the obligations of the superior party that is unusual
in that context. But the incorporation of the household code into a larger vision
of the Church as the "beloved" bride/body of Christ in Ephesians opens up
the door for a qualitatively new perception of marriage. It participates in and
reflects the new reality of grace which is the heart of salvation. As the gnostic
examples show, ritual enactment of such a vision of marriage can also be perceived to lift it above the conventions of the legal and social world.

The first century legal context for marriage was established in the contractual agreements that preceded it. Such issues as use of common property,
divorce and inheritance are, at least in principle, established there. Much of

our legal activity is concentrated on divorce, the point at which marriages dissolve. For many persons failure of a marriage is further complicated by additional religious sanctions, which were the by-product of the religious institutionalization of marriage that accompanied its sacralization. In the first century, the "difference" to be expressed in Christian marriage was not embodied in patterns of "sacral law." Further, the three dimensions in which that difference was expressed—(a) asceticism and the critique of false cultural values; (b) support for marriage as a permanent relationship in the face of the arbitrariness of the legal/contractual definition of marriage; (c) sacralization of marriage as participation in the new reality of salvation—continue to exist in uneasy tension with one another. Each expresses an important dimension in the Christian experience of marriage as it emerges in the New Testament.

Notes

1. J. Macquarrie, *In Search of Humanity* (New York: Crossroad, 1985).

2. See R. Geiger, "Die Stellung der geschiedenen Frau in der Umwelt des Neuen Testaments," *Die Frau im Urchristentum* (Quaestiones Disputatae 95; ed. G. Dautzenberg et al; Freiburg: Herder, 1983) 138. S. Pomeroy (*Women in Hellenistic Egypt* [New York: Schocken, 1984] 85), argues that this variability made the development of detailed marriage contracts such as we find in the papyri all the more pressing.

3. J.A. Crook, *Law and Life of Rome, 90 B.C.–A.D. 212* (Ithaca: Cornell, 1967) 99.

4. See Z.W. Falk, "Jewish Private Law," *The Jewish People in the First Century. Vol. I* (ed. S. Safrai & M. Stern; Philadelphia: Fortress, 1974) 507–518; H.J. Wolff, "Hellenistic Private Law," *Jewish People*, 538–541; N. Lewis, *Life in Egypt under Roman Rule* (New York: Oxford, 1983) 54–56; Pomeroy, *Hellenistic Egypt*, 89–95.

5. Pomeroy, *Hellenistic Egypt*, 95–96; for a similar provision in a Jewish marriage contract, see J.A. Fitzmyer, "A Re-study of an Elephantine Aramaic Marriage Contract (AP 15)," *A Wandering Aramean. Collected Aramaic Essays* (Missoula: Scholars, 1979) 244.

6. Crook, *Law*, 101–103.

7. Crook, *Law*, 104–106; J.P. Hallett, *Fathers and Daughters in Roman Society. Women and the Elite Family* (Princeton: Princeton University, 1984) 238–243.

8. Crook, *Law*, 107–113; Hallett (*Fathers and Daughters*, 243–262), observes that despite the woman's lack of social and legal power within the husband's family, Roman women maintained very close relationships with their sons, on whom they often relied for support. She suggests that the close-

ness in age between mothers and sons, the longer period before sons married, and the frequent absence of the father all contributed to such relationships.

9. Fitzmyer, "Aramaic Marriage Contract," 253.

10. Fitzmyer, "Aramaic Marriage Contract," 263.

11. Whether or not a marriage was consummated was also irrelevant to its legal validity (Crook, *Law,* 101).

12. Lewis (*Life,* 43) argues that this Egyptian invitation is to the wedding of a brother and sister. This practice appears to have spread to the peasantry by Roman times and eventually led to an explicit prohibition of the practice among Romans: "Romans are not permitted to marry their sister or their aunts, but marriage with brothers' daughters has been allowed" (ibid, 44).

13. Pomeroy, *Hellenistic Egypt,* 87f, (P. Tebtunis I 104).

14. Pomeroy, *Hellenistic Egypt,* 89 (P. Geneva I 21.15–21).

15. See discussion of this writing in J.J. Collins, *Between Athens and Jerusalem. Jewish Identity in the Hellenistic Diaspora* (New York: Crossroad, 1983) 211–218.

16. See discussion of these texts in J.A. Fitzmyer, "The Matthean Divorce Texts and Some New Palestinian Evidence," *To Advance the Gospel* (New York: Crossroad, 1981) 92–96.

17. Fitzmyer, "Divorce Texts," 94.

18. See the extensive discussion of this tradition in G. Stroumsa, *Another Seed: Studies in Gnostic Mythology* (NHS 24; Leiden: Brill, 1984) 17–34.

19. Diogenes #47; A. Malherbe, *The Cynic Epistles* (SBLSBS 12; Missoula: Scholars, 1977) 178–179.

20. See R. Horsley, "Spiritual Marriage and Asceticism," *VigChr* 33 (1979) 30–54.

21. Musonius Rufus XIIIA; C. Lutz, *Musonius Rufus* (New Haven: Yale, 1947) 89.

22. Musonius Rufus, XII; Lutz, 85–89.

23. Musonius Rufus XIV; Lutz, 91–97.

24. See Fitzmyer, "Divorce Texts," 79–85; W. Scrage, *Ethik des Neuens Testaments* (Grundrisse zum NT, NTD 4; Gottingen: Vandenhoeck & Ruprecht, 1982) 92–99; J. Murphy-O'Connor, "The Divorced Woman in 1 Cor 7:10–11," *JBL* 100 (1981) 601–602; R.A. Guelich, *The Sermon on the Mount* (Waco: Word, 1982) 197–211; J. Lambrecht, *The Sermon on the Mount* (Wilmington: Glazier, 1985) 99–103.

25. So Guelich, *Sermon,* 200–202.

26. Guelich, *Sermon,* 197–98.

27. Fitzmyer, "Divorce Texts," 98.

28. In addition to the authors already cited, see B.N. Wambacq, "Matthieu 5,31–32. Possibilité de divorce ou obligation de rompre une union illegitime," *NRT* 114 (1982) 34–39.

29. Guelich, *Sermon,* 207–210.

30. Paul, in fact, has just the opposite problem. He must invoke community sanctions against an "incestuous" marriage between a man and his stepmother in 1 Corinthians 5:1–5.

31. See D.O. Via, *The Ethics of Mark's Gospel* (Philadelphia: Fortress, 1985) 103–116.

32. Cf. W. Meeks, *The First Urban Christians* (New Haven: Yale, 1983) 100–101; Collins, *Athens and Jerusalem* 149–51; cf. 1 Thess 4:3–8; Acts 15:20,29; Gal 5:19; Eph 5:3; Col 3:5.

33. See K. Niederwimmer, "Zur Analyse der asketischen Motivation in 1 Kor 7," *TLZ* 99 (1974) 241–48; W. Wolbert, *Ethische Argumentation und Paranese in 1 Kor 7* (Munchener theologishe Studien 8; Dusseldorf: Patmos, 1981).

34. Schrage (*Grundrisse,* 218) speaks of it as a special manifestation of the obligation of love. B. Brendan ("Sinning Against One's Own Body: Paul's Understanding of the Sexual Relationship in 1 Corinthians 6:18," *CBQ* 45 [1983] 613–15) argues that the sexual act for Paul is a self-communication of persons unlike any other. Consequently, Paul is concerned that self-surrender to the power of the other never be at odds with the union of the Christian and Christ. Paul's primarily negative counsel, marry rather than become involved in *porneia,* is grounded in the larger argument against fornication.

35. Falk, "Jewish Private Law," 516–517.

36. "Divorced Woman," 603–604.

37. So Fitzmyer, "Divorce Texts," 81; Murphy-O'Connor, "Divorced Woman," 601f.

38. See Murphy-O'Connor, "Divorced Woman," 602–603.

39. "Divorced Woman," 605–606.

40. It is impossible to gauge the extent to which Paul's advice may also have been shaped by the common Jewish prohibition against remarriage to a spouse who had been married to another person after the divorce.

41. Yet Paul later acknowledges that Peter and most of the other apostles were married (1 Cor 9:5). There, marriage is an apostolic "right" which Paul chose not to exercise—not an obligation for apostleship or service to the Lord.

42. See Schrage, *Grundrisse,* 219–220.

43. A classic example of this procedure is 1 Cor 11:2–16 (see H. Conzelmann, *1 Corinthians* [Philadelphia: Fortress, 1975] 182–91).

44. Since women were married to older men at a young age, remarriage after the death of a spouse was extremely common. Tombstones express admiration for the woman who is the wife of only one spouse (cf. Meeks, *Urban Christians,* 101).

45. See D. MacDonald, *The Legend and the Apostle* (Philadelphia: Westminster, 1983) 17–53.

46. PG 50:747; MacDonald, *Legend,* 52–53.

47. See MacDonald, *Legend,* 90–96.

48. MacDonald, *Legend,* 95–96.

49. See M. Dibelius and H. Conzelmann, *The Pastoral Epistles* (Philadelphia: Fortress, 1972) 39–41, 48–51; D. Verner, *The Household of God. The Social World of the Pastoral Epistles* (SBLDS 71; Chico: Scholars, 1983) 1f, 13–25, 91–111, 129–147, 161–171, 177–180.

50. So MacDonald, *Legend,* 54–59, 65–77; Verner, *Household,* 166–171, 176–178.

51. See Verner, *Household,* 161–166; J. Bassler, "The Widows' Tale: A Fresh Look at 1 Tim 5:3–16," *JBL* 103 (1984) 23–41.

52. "Widows' Tale," 35.

53. Bassler, "Widows' Tale," 38–39. Bassler hypothesizes that the pressures which led the Church to retreat from a *communitas* form of association to the patriarchal household might have had an effect other than they intended. Women left with no "place" in the household church of the late first century may have been even more vulnerable to gnosticizing heresies than those mentioned in 1 Tim (ibid, 40–41).

54. See E. Schweizer, *The Letter to the Colossians* (Minneapolis: Augsburg, 1982) 127–163.

55. Schweizer, *Colossians,* 213–228.

56. See J. Gnilka, *Der Epheserbrief* (HTKNT X/2; Freiburg: Herder, 1971) 290–294; R. Schnackenburg, *Der Brief an die Epheser* (EKK 10; Zurich: Benziger/Neukirchen-Vluyn: Neukirchener, 1982) 241–259.

57. See Schnackenburg, *An die Epheser,* 260.

58. Schnackenburg, *An die Epheser,* 261–262.

59. See J.J. Buckley, "A Cult-Mystery in the Gospel of Philip," *JBL* 99 (1980) 569–581.

RESPONSES

LISA SOWLE CAHILL

I have two questions. The first has to do with our contemporary under-standing, as derived from the New Testament, of the relationship between authoritative teaching and application. I want to make that question specific by referring to the divorce texts. As Pheme indicated, some scholars in the past few years have looked at the exceptions allowed to Jesus' prohibition of divorce in the New Testament as a way of saying that divorce is really permissible in some kinds of circumstances. So they have seen those exceptions as a liberalization of Jesus' divorce sayings. Pheme has pointed out, however, that there are other possible interpretations of those exceptions, and that they are not best understood as a liberalization of Jesus' statements. I would like to ask whether we might in any way understand those exceptions as an adaptive influence, perhaps, or as a witness to the fact that authoritative teaching always has to be applied in the circumstances of concrete communities and reformulated so that it meets the needs of those communities.

My second question has to do with the household codes that have been a great subject of debate especially in feminist literature. The household codes are those passages which say wives should be submissive to their husbands, children to their fathers, slaves to their masters. Some scholars, such as Elisabeth Schüssler Fiorenza, have said that these codes are a sellout to the larger pagan culture. The early Christian communities didn't want to be subversive to that culture, they didn't want to be annihilated basically, and so they accommodated themselves to the patterns of hierarchy that already existed in the larger society. Pheme has called our attention back to the fact that these patterns are very much transformed by the early Christian reformulation of these codes. My question is: Can we see in the household codes some sort of larger model for the way that Christianity relates to existing social institutions, by accepting them on the one hand and critiquing them on the other, and, if so, what kind of model would that be?

PHEME PERKINS

In regard to the first question: when Jesus talks about divorce and no divorce he almost makes fun of the way in which the Pharisees want to deal with it. The Pharisees in Matthew 19 want to deal with it legally. They want to get legal definitions. Jesus, on the other hand, keeps calling for an obedience to God which breaks with that. So I think that the real route to go is to say that if we transform authoritative teaching into a new legalism then we've lost what we're being asked to consider. We're being asked to consider not a new legalism, which is going to catch people in traps of laws and courts, but we are being asked to consider how we can best be faithful to the created intention of marriage and sexuality. And I think that would sponsor a kind of divergence. I think that Matthew and Paul, had they talked about it, would have been in real disagreement about the question of a Christian married to a pagan. Paul says those marriages continue; some Jewish Christians would have thought no. I think there would have been some real tension if you got the two Christian communities together to try to talk about what happens when one spouse converts and the other one doesn't. We see in the New Testament a lot of these concrete wrestlings with authoritative teaching. This gives us some guidance on how we have to wrestle with it.

The second question deals with the household codes. They are not going to tell us everything about Christianity in the larger culture, but I do think that they serve as a kind of model. Christians live in cultures, and Christianity doesn't create a complete counterculture. At the same time, Christianity is critical of the culture and raises questions about it. This means you affirm some things in the culture and you question others. If you find a model for marriage in Christ's action and his relationship with the Church, then you're both affirming the cultural expression of marriage and questioning some of the standards in it. I think that the dynamic that goes on in the New Testament is an example of a dynamic process that doesn't stop. It didn't come to an end.

PETER HUIZING

You have been speaking of Jesus' divorce sayings. Jesus' original statements are not in the exact form as they appear in the Gospels, but they are absolutely against divorce. These sayings are used in the magisterial teaching on the indissolubility of marriage as an argument—and a preemptive one— that divorce is not only forbidden, but it is not possible. Marriage, especially between Christians, is objectively indissoluble. Do you think that the real meaning of the sayings of Jesus implies the objective institutional indissolubility of marriage?

PHEME PERKINS

No, I don't think so, because I think that there's another kind of thing that comes into the conviction that marriage is indissoluble—that's the sacramentalizing trend which then says it's a heavenly reality. You can't dissolve Christ and the Church, and when you move marriage into that level and start to describe what sacrament is, using that kind of imagery, then it becomes indissoluble. But, of course, since Jesus has the biggest stick, you go back to his anti-divorce sayings and claim that they prove that marriage is indissoluble; but that really comes out of a way of handling sacramental symbolism. What

Jesus says is obviously in a context in which Jesus is criticizing persons for whom divorce is a kind of merely secular contractual phenomenon, as long as you do it according to the legal forms. What you have in Matthew 19 and in the parallel texts are Jewish Pharisees coming up and saying: "Tell us the conditions; give us the laws," and you get Jesus saying: "We're not looking for that; we're looking for what God intended, and what God intended in creation is a permanent union of husband and wife." That doesn't address the concrete phenomenon that marriage can never be dissolved. There you've made a whole second jump. And I really think that the kind of sacramentalizing tendency is what underlies that second jump. One can hardly imagine Jesus making a preemptive legal pronouncement. It's not the way he operates.

2.

How To Understand the Sacrament of Marriage

Theodore Mackin, S.J.

Prenote

From the beginning of the political secularizing of Europe and its colonies the Catholic authorities used the theology of marriage as a weapon for fighting off the secularist demands. Once this secularization was accomplished the fight ended. The theology was left to work out its own intelligibility. But it has done so sluggishly.

There have been two main reasons for this sluggishness, although they may be reduced to a single reason of method. First, the examination and use of the marriage passages in the New Testament became critical only at about the middle of the present century. Until then the passages were rarely permitted to speak for themselves. More seriously, as a second reason, the theologians had no anthropology of marriage that could be trusted. What they had was a tour-de-force produced by canon law.

But now Gaudium et spes *has presented an anthropology of marriage, and critical interpretation of the Scriptures has matured. So now the task is this: how to use these two sources in consort—and both of them in consort and in counter-poise with established doctrine—to develop the theology of the sacrament.*

A sub-question here is especially demanding. The marriage sacrament, like all sacraments, has as its matrix a complex human experience. And there is no understanding the sacrament unless we first understand its matrix-experience. From whom shall we get this understanding, and how shall we get it? And do normative magisterial statements illumine and modify the experience? Or does the experience illumine and modify the magisterial statements? Or, finally, does each modify and illumine the other, and in what ways?

My intent in this essay is to recommend a path we ought to take in seeking to understand Christian marriages as sacraments. (For a reason that will emerge later I do not formulate the project as ". . . to understand Christian marriage as a sacrament.") To state this intent colloquially, I urge that the sacrament in Christian marriages be approached from its human underside; less colloquially, that it be approached from its anthropological matrix.

Every one of the Christian sacraments begins as an action. It expresses itself in an action, and in actual Christian life as a ritualized action. As such it is made up of two components, God's action and human action. The latter is joined and used by the divine action which uses it as its instrument in working the effect it intends.

The human action is by definition sensate—visible, tangible, audible. God's action is the converse of these, supra-sensate—invisible, intangible, inaudible. But it uses the human action to work the more effectively in the sensateness where our human needs are felt most and our desires are most urgent.

When one sets about studying a sacrament one can begin with either of these two elements. One could begin by clarifying the character of either, by discussing what intentionality it gives to the conjoined actions, what it intends to produce as its portion of the effect. I say that this first step in examining the sacrament can be taken at either of the two levels just mentioned. But I believe that to date the study of Christian marriages as sacraments has worked from above downward. It has examined the divine action and intent first, but only afterward searched the human matrix. I recommend that the examination begin instead with the human matrix and work upward because of certain advantages that I hope to show in the course of this essay.

It is true that knowledge of Christian marriages' sacramentality comes in one sense from the divine source first. This is knowledge gained from *doctrina,* knowledge that is verification of the fact of sacramentality. But in another sense it comes from the human matrix first. This is the knowledge gained *per experientiam.* We find this also in the examination of the Eucharist. The fact that the risen Christ acts in this sacrament to nourish and strengthen we can know only from God's revelation. But unless we knew first from experience what it is to be hungry and to need nourishing and strength, God's revelation would be wasted on us.

So too with marriage. We may have revealed to us that through spouses' specifically marital conduct the same Christ acts in them to draw them into union with himself. But unless we first understand which conduct of the spouses is specifically marital, and especially unless we understand which among the many kinds of marital conduct are most vulnerable to Christ's intervention, this revelation too is wasted on us.

I make my recommendation for a second reason involving method. The conventional Catholic study of the sacrament of marriage begins with certain

classic passages from the Bible interpreted within the theological definition-
axiom, *sacramentum est sacrae rei signum*—a sacrament is a sign of a sacred
[invisible] reality. These passages, in the books of prophecy of Hosea, Jeremiah, Isaiah and Ezekiel and from the Epistle to the Ephesians, picture God
as husband to the people Israel. Both roles are transposed in the Epistle to the
Ephesians, where Christ is husband to his bride, the Church.

I believe these analogies have been misused in the theology of the sacrament. But before detailing the misuse itself I would point out that the metaphors making up the facets of the analogies are by no means culture-
transcending. Inspect the details of the two metaphoric marriages in the divine
facet of each analogy and one finds them to be thoroughly semitic. For one
thing, each husband figure *takes* the girl to be his bride. There is little evidence
that she has a choice about being taken. This raises questions about the applicability of the analogies to real-life marriages. Thus, even if the husband
figure takes his bride in love, one must wonder what kind of marital love takes.
And which kind of love is appropriate as the reaction to being taken? (The
methodological moral here is clear enough: the metaphors in which virtually
all points of divine revelation are communicated are drawn from culturally
conditioned human experiences. To get to the core of the truths revealed in
them one must reduce the metaphors; one must interpret them in terms of existence and relationships in existence—which is the work of the regrettably
neglected science, metaphysics.)

The most evident misuse of the analogies has consisted of forcing the one
in Ephesians as evidence to prove two interlocked points of Catholic teaching.
The first of these is that Christian marriage is a sacrament; the second, that any
marriage of two Christians is a sacrament.

The attempted proof of the first doctrinal assertion is in structure a sub-
sumption of the analogy under the defining axiom recorded above, *sacramentum est sacrae rei signum*. The axiom dates from the neo-Platonic era in
Catholic theology and was produced by a Platonic vision of the universe, that
the things of our sensate world are shadows, or images, or signs, of invisible
divine realities. Sensate things are the more true the more faithfully they image
the invisible divine realities. This fidelity is the more possible the more that
sensate things are, in understanding, abstracted from their material concrete-
ness and uniqueness. This is what sets the doctrinal statement in the formulation "Christian *marriage* is a sacrament" instead of "Christian *marriages*
are sacraments." According to this theology it is Christian marriage taken in
the abstract that is deemed a sacrament. It is so taken because, taken as an
abstraction drawn from the sensate reality of marriage—and withdrawn from
it—it *must* be an image of the invisible and divine marriage of Christ and the
Church.

Whether this or that pair of Christian spouses is in fact united with Christ by their faith, hope and charity is irrelevant to this way of thinking. The objection that the formulation "Christian marriage is a sacrament" cannot be accurate, because not universally predictable due to the failure of some real-life Christian marriages to image the Christ-Church relationship, would draw the reply that the objection misses the point. The doctrinal formulation is not about real-life marriages; it is about "marriage."

The second point of teaching holds, in interlocked fashion, that any and every marriage of two Christians is a sacrament. What makes it so is the fact of the spouses' having been baptized, and the function in their souls of the perduring baptismal character. Again, whether the spouses are united with Christ by their faith, hope and charity is irrelevant. They may as adults be religiously dead, even agnostic, after having been baptized in infancy. But provided they do not expressly reject sacramentality in their marriage, it is spontaneously a sacrament.

The juridical dispute that needed this point of doctrine and forced its installation is well enough known. It was a dispute that extended through the eighteenth and nineteenth centuries between Catholic ecclesiastical authorities and Catholic civil authorities in Europe over the marriage contracts of Catholics. The civil authorities insisted on the separability as well as the distinction of contract from sacrament in these marriages. This would leave the contract within their jurisdiction, since contracts are the concern of the state. The ecclesiastical authorities insisted on the inseparability of the two despite their distinctness, insisted that for Christians the contract is the sacrament, that conversely the sacrament is nothing other than the contract itself elevated to the status of a grace-giving instrument. This would keep the contract within ecclesiastical jurisdiction, since sacraments are the concern of the Church.

The need for insisting that any marriage of two Christians is a sacrament is obvious here. If some marriages were not, civil authorities' claim over them would be strengthened. And the Church's claim of juridical competence over the marriages of all Christians would be in principle undermined.

The exceeding difficulty of explaining how the marriages of even religiously inert and agnostic Christians can be sacraments by being images, or signs, of Christ's love relationship with the Church has driven theologians who maintain this teaching to search elsewhere for an explanation than in the theology wrung from Ephesians 5:21–33. Some have turned to a theology of incorporation in the mystical body of Christ. According to this theology baptism incorporates a person in the body of Christ taken in the Pauline sense, sets him or her in the life-stream of the Spirit of Christ and the Father. As a consequence when they later enter and enact any life-changing moment that the Church has acknowledged and adopted as sacramental, their enacting of this moment is made a sacrament by Christ through his Spirit working in them. That they are unaware of this, and if told of it may care nothing about it, does not block the divine work—any more than an infant's unawareness blocks the Spirit's sanctifying work in baptism.

It is not my intent to dig seriously into this debate. Here I would only suggest that the Christian sacraments are sacraments each in a different way. Much of the difference is determined by the human matrix in each case. An infant may, by being bathed, be born into the new life of God's intimacy without being aware of what is done to it. Birth is not a product of, nor is it conditioned by, one's awareness and choice. But one does not marry unconsciously and indeliberately. Nor does one love in marriage unconsciously and indeliberately. And where a marriage is a Christian sacrament, it is in the character of the love that its sacramentality is found.

I believe the summary doctrinal formulation would be more true to life if it read not "Christian marriage is a sacrament," but "All Christian spouses can, provided they co-work with the Holy Spirit, make their marriages to be sacraments."

The Life of the Church
as the Context of the Sacrament

I have suggested that we can more readily understand the sacramentality available in marriage if we begin the work of understanding it in the human experience of marriage. But on the brink of beginning this work I would establish two definitions and a context.

The first definition is of the term "holiness." I understand this to designate first and fundamentally a person's union with God. It is a union whose substance is love, but a love supported by faith and hope. In our actual world situation, in our given historical context, this love has been given an orientation that takes it outside the person's private union with God. For God's love itself has two orientations to his creatures. The first is creative; he is continually creating them, holding them unceasingly in existence. His love's second orientation, at least toward his human creatures, is paternal. They are strayed and wandering creatures, turned away from him in sin. Therefore his love that creates men and women strives also to call them back to himself—to heal them and rescue them. Therefore too any man or woman who seeks to join with God must join in this striving. Joining thus is not merely a condition for loving God; it is a consequence of doing so. One either takes part somehow in his work of healing and rescuing or one does not love him. Thus holiness cannot be a solipsism for two, God and oneself. It is evangelical or it is not holiness.

The second definition tells the meaning of the term "paschal mystery." This means that God's effort to draw men and women back to himself uses the humanity of Christ to do so. This assumes that Christ's humanity is once again restored and integral despite his having died. More than that, the paschal mystery means that God loves human beings, indeed loves all his creation, by and through Christ's human love. Correlatively the divine love with which men and women join when they seek to love God is Christ's love. This is not an optional way of loving that they can by-pass; it is an essential condition. Fortunately for men and women scattered through the centuries and in remote corners of the world, "Christ plays in ten thousand places/Lovely in limbs, and lovely in eyes not his . . ."

What the Christian Church is, in its essential core and in its best conduct, is a community of men and women carrying on the paschal mystery. It is also accurate to call the Church, this community itself, a sacrament—Christ's sacrament, God's sacrament through Christ. It is a sacrament because, while being the instrument of Christ at work in the world, it carries on this work through the visible, audible, tangible conduct of the men and women making up the community. Thus to sight, hearing and touch enlivened by faith, this conduct is evidence that God is present and at work—it is a sign of his presence and work (*sacrae rei signum*).

Because the Church itself is a sacrament, all its life processes are sacramental. Seven of these are formally established and carried on in set scenarios, or liturgies (or in a selection of the seven in the traditional Protestant churches). Marriage the human relationship has been taken into the Church as one of these liturgies. And the term "liturgy" refers to more than the wedding ceremony. The heart of marital conduct is also a liturgy, since the term designates a sacred service or work.

It is mainly in and by these sacraments that the Church carries on the work given it by Christ. "Do this as a commemoration of me" he could have said, and perhaps did say, of the entire life and work of the Church. "Commemoration" translates the Greek noun *anámnesis*. This signifies more than a memorial. It includes this, but refers more exactly to a reenactment—a reenactment of an original event intended to keep alive the energy and the effects of that event. An anniversary wedding Mass including the renewal of vows is an *anámnesis*. So too is a reprise of the honeymoon.

The Work of the Church in the World

Since marriages in the Christian community are sacraments in that the spouses take part in the work Christ gave this community to do—take part in it by doing married things—it is essential to understand what this work is. This has been stated in many and complex ways. I believe a most succinct yet accurate statement of it says that this is to enable human beings singly, and as a universal family, to enter into the final and unending form of life that God intends for them. It is a form of life that can start up this side of death. But its final, climactic form can be reached only through death. St. Paul in 1 Corinthians 13 said it is a love relationship that climaxes in vision "face to face." The Synoptic tradition pictures it in the metaphor of the great final banquet. St. John's Gospel records Jesus' referring to it by implication in his assuring Martha that she would see her brother again despite his having just died.

It is indispensable, I have said, to examine the sacrament of marriage in its real-life context. This is so because it is first indispensable to examine the work of the Church, the inclusive sacrament, in its real-life context. This context is "the sin of the world," the *hamartía tou kósmou* that John the Baptist assured his hearers Christ had come to take away. This makes the Church's work a history-long effort at rescue, a striving to salvage men and women from this sin.

Finding and identifying the core of this sin in the welter of suspicion, fear, hatred, exploitation and murder in the world has been an elusive task. Yet teachers in both the Old Testament and the New have insisted relentlessly that the sin (whatever it is at its core) is endemic in the human population, and has been so from the beginning.

Christians are used to calling it in a general way a sinfulness inherited from the first parents of the human race. The most common understanding of it in the West has come down from Paul via Augustine and others of the Fathers. It says that the sin is the habitual set of human wills in rebellion against the divine will, with this rebellion's by-product found in the rebellion within men and women of their passions against reason and will.

With critical scholarship's finding that the story of the first man's and woman's disobedience in the garden is not factual history but a Hebrew parable intending to show how misery and evil have come into human experience, the understanding of this sin has shifted ground. Disobedience and willful alienation from God are no longer found at its core. And especially the notion that the sin is passed down from parent to child by a near genetic contagion has vanished. One now thinks more of a sinful condition into which one is born— the condition of the human environment and a condition within the soul.

Whatever this sin is, we can say about it even *a priori* that it is that in human beings that most resists and defeats God's reason for their existence. We do know what this reason is; it is that they be drawn into final union with him, and with one another, a union of vision and love.

It is at this juncture that the theologians, if they are wise, look to the psychologists and to other reflective persons for help. Their question to them asks what they have found in men and women that most effectively defeats their effort to create relationships of trust and love—defeats their efforts to attract one another into such relationships, and defeats their desire to be attracted into them. It is with the same soul that men and women desire God and desire one another. It is most probable that what defeats the latter defeats also the former. If we—theologians, psychologists and whoever else—can find out what this is, we may well find out the core of the sinfulness of the race.

Because of the common religious understanding that sin is an act of the will, a decision to do what contradicts God's will for oneself, a distinction of meanings must be drawn. The term "sin" must be understood analogously. It has a common signification which is a contradiction of God's will. But this contradiction can be found in two forms. One is the consciously rebellious will, as indicated just above. But it can be found also in attitudes, conditions and social structures that contradict God's will just as truly even though they may not be the products of conscious rebellion. Thus pious Christian employers may without a thought pay slave wages. Devout men may take for granted that women are perpetual children. A nation may maintain an economy that by its very nature creates its own destitute. Even if no one in these cases intends consciously to hurt others, the attitudes or conditions are sinful because they contradict God's will.

For almost thirty years as I write this I have as a priest, teacher and counselor talked with young men and women as they hesitated in anxiety on the threshold of marriage. With them I have examined the causes of their anxiety. I have also talked with spouses as they watched their marriages collapsing or looked back on relationships destroyed irretrievably. It is hazardous to search for a single common and dominant cause of their anxiety in the almost but not yet married, and of the failure of marriages that once were. Anyone is familiar with the reasons usually cited to account for the latter: self-centeredness, laziness, inability or unwillingness to bear the ordinary tedium of family life, vagrant passion, unconcern for the spouse's needs and desires, resentment at having one's energy and ambition trapped in domesticity, dreams and plans destroyed by illness or financial failure, exaggerated dependency, collapsed infatuation.

Again, it would be rash to assume that underlying all these is a single cause, one that infiltrates them all and is even the wellspring of all. But even with wariness on the alert against too simple an explanation, I have been drawn by the evidence accumulated in those thirty years' conversations toward the conviction that there is such a single cause. I tend to believe it is fear.

The fear I espy is a primitive kind of fear. It resides ordinarily in the unconscious sector of the soul; in many men and women it stays there undetected and does its damage from there. It is almost but not quite a nameless fear. It is fear of the loss of self. Or not quite so succinctly, it is fear born of the awareness that having but one chance at life and one chance at happiness, one may waste this one chance, or has already wasted it.

If my perception is accurate here, it follows about self-centered persons, for example, that however they got that way, if they stay that way they do so because they fear for what they will lose by becoming self-giving. Or spouses angry at having their expectations denied and their ambitions frustrated are angry because they fear what they will lose by changing their expectations and giving up their ambitions.

And if my perception is accurate on a broader scale, that this fear of the loss of self is the core of sinfulness in the human race, it follows that a saint is first of all a man or woman in whose life fear has no place. But far more significantly for this examination of the sacrament of marriage, it follows that Christ's work in the world, the unfinished work he left his followers to carry on, is to heal men and women of this fear of loss. It follows finally that marriage as a specific sacrament within the inclusive Church-sacrament is a specific strategy for this healing.

The Matrix of the Sacrament

One cannot begin to understand what it means to say that the marriage of Christian spouses can be a sacrament until one first understands the element of any sacrament that is its matrix. For those already acquainted with the hylemorphic interpretation of a sacrament that identifies its two basic elements as the material and the formal, a caution is in order. The matrix of a sacrament and its matter are not identical. The former includes the latter but consists of more. This will be made clear in the paragraphs that follow.

However many one numbers them, none of the Christian sacraments was at its beginning a pure innovation in human experience. In every case the scenario of the sacrament, its patterned conduct, was long established in the customs of the ancient peoples. Washing with water, anointing with oil, the breaking and sharing of bread, the pouring and sharing of wine, the laying on of hands with the calling down of divine power, the pronouncing of forgiveness, the solemn committing of oneself to a lifelong vocation—all these were already in use among the Jews and other peoples.

Because they were religious Jews or Gentiles before becoming followers of Jesus the early Christians were familiar with these mini-dramas and adopted them without hesitation for their religious expression. They did not call them sacraments, and they certainly did not understand them in the exactly defined way that later sacramental theology produced. The name by which they called them most commonly was "the divine mysteries." But they believed without question that in the laying on of hands, in the anointing with oil, and in the others, the Spirit of God acts in and by these small dramas to do good things to the men and women who participate in them with faith.

Two spiritual dynamisms have to work in every execution of the long-familiar ritual if it is to be made a Christian sacrament. A human spiritual dynamism has to work—the faith that God's Spirit can use the sensate ritual to work his effect in the participants, the trust that he will do so, the love that desires he do so. This threefold dynamism animates the ritual, transforms its meaning, gives it an intention, makes it susceptible in turn to God's transforming intention. In short, this human dynamism takes up the ritual and uses it as its instrument.

But in doing so this dynamism cannot tear out and discard the cultural meaning native to the ritual and simply replace it with one of its own. This would create at least ambiguity but more probably deception. For example, what else could the breaking and sharing of bread, the pouring out and drinking of wine mean even in a religious transformation of meaning than the nourishing of men and women who trust one another enough to gather peacefully at table? Or what else could anointing with oil mean than healing and strengthening? There must be homogeneity of meaning from one pole of the transformation to the other. But homogeneity does not prevent transformation. There is more than one kind of family, more than one kind of nourishing, more than one kind of healing and strengthening. (A theologian, if he knows metaphysics, would say that the two kinds at the two poles of the transformation are related analogously.)

The second spiritual dynamism is of a kind transcendently superior because it is God's action in the ritual, the action which is his Spirit. He does to the fusion of ritual and human dynamism what the latter of these does to the former: he animates the fusion with his intention, with his meaning. He uses it as his instrument to do good divine things in the participants. He acts in their wills, in their emotions, in their intellects, in their bodies—which is to say he graces them—in an effort to draw them into union with himself and into union with one another. He uses the entire ritual drama—participants and their actions, their materials (water, oil, bread, wine, bodies)—as instruments of gracing thus understood.

What the matrix of a sacrament is should be evident by now. It is the sensate action, the ritual that God takes up and uses to work his effects in human beings. It is not only the physical components of the action. It is these components animated by the ritual's culturally inherited meaning. It is the action as a drama, as a carrier and revealer of meaning.

The matrix and the divine action that uses it determine one another reciprocally. They must concur in manifesting one same meaning, and they determine together how it will be manifested. For example, if God wills to use a human ritual to manifest his effort to heal human sinfulness, he cannot enlist for this purpose a ritual whose native meaning is final punishment for obduracy. He cannot do otherwise than select a ritual whose own meaning is to heal. (It is obvious that the analogy of expression of meanings from culture to culture raises a problem here.)

This native meaning is determined in turn by God's meaning. He takes up an anointing with oil, or a laying on of hands, whose meaning is to heal physical illness, and elevates and transforms it to mean the healing of the illness of soul that is sinfulness.

It is helpful at this point to clear up something about the causation in the sacraments whose lack of clarification often leads Christians to try to believe the literally unbelievable. Thomas Aquinas suggested the clarification when he pointed out *sacramentum est in genere signi*, "a sacrament belongs to the genus of sign." As a ritual it is a manifestation of meaning, an acting out of intention. Therefore it works to produce its effect by signing, by manifesting, by acting out. Thus, for example, if a modern physician were to object about the sacrament of anointing of the sick that anointing with oil does not send leukemia into remission, he would miss the point of using this ritual in the sacrament. It is not any chemical property of the sacramental oil that does what the sacrament does. It is rather the meaning, the intention manifested in the gesture and used as an instrument of God's intention, that does it.

The same misunderstanding can torment belief in the Eucharist. The transformation in this sacrament is not physical, of a kind to bring the participants to physically break and eat Christ's body. It is a different kind of transformation, but just as real in its own order as the physical. It is a transformation of meaning from that of the Jewish Passover supper reenacting liberation from ancient slavery in Egypt, to the meaning that is a reenactment of Christ's death—in the blessing and *breaking* of bread, in the blessing and *pouring out* of wine—that liberates from the slavery of sin. Because God takes up and uses this transformed meaning through the resurrected humanity of Christ, the participants in the Eucharistic ritual really interact with Christ. In more traditional terms, he is really present to them.

The Contribution to the Sacrament of *Gaudium et Spes*

The most valuable help that the bishops of Vatican II brought to the theology of marriage was to clarify and enrich the understanding of the sacrament's matrix. This they did in their Pastoral Constitution on the Church in the Modern World, *Gaudium et spes,* in Part II, Chapter 1, "Fostering the Nobility of Marriage and the Family." They brought this help despite intending not to address Christians about Christian marriage, but all men and women about marriage the human relationship. Their constitution is a reflection on marriage as it is experienced, or can be experienced, by any persons of theistic mind. The five paragraphs they did devote to the sacrament in No. 48 of the chapter I shall examine presently.

The bishops enriched the matrix of the sacrament by offering a new understanding of marriage that one finds to be an amalgam of two understandings recovered from antiquity. These are the notion of marriage as a covenant taught by the Hebrew prophets' analogy of Israel as the covenanted bride of Yahweh, and the notion of marriage set out in classic Roman law of the third century. Neither of these proposed marriage as a contract. The Hebrew prophets regarded it as a love relationship of personal choice and commitment. Roman law regarded it most generally as a *coniunctio,* a union, of a man and a woman, and specifically as a union that is an undivided sharing in the whole of their lives. One may interpret "the whole" as linear, so that the sharing continues as long as both live. Or one may interpret it as presently cumulative, so that the sharing excludes nothing in their lives that is significant. Or one may combine the two meanings, with obvious rich results.

These two understandings had been kept inert in the official Catholic memory for centuries. It seems evident that the bishops reclaimed them, combined them, expanded them, and offered the combination as their own. The combination includes an element not found in the Roman understanding, one for which there was to be no place in the traditional canonical understanding of marriage as a contract. But the element is all but explicit in the Hebrew prophetic understanding. It is marital love. Whether the bishops drew it from its Hebrew source and appropriated it because they thought men's and women's experience of marriage demands the inclusion, or because it is there in the prophetic understanding, we would have to guess. A combination of both these motives is probable.

The following are the most revealing of the bishops' statements about marriage in *Gaudium et spes.*

A marriage is a community or partnership of love (*communitas amoris*). It is an intimate partnership, or sharing, or community of marital life and love (*intima communitas vitae et amoris coniugalis*). The bishops called it an institution (*institutum matrimonii*), a marital vocation (*vocatio maritalis*), a marital covenant (*foedus coniugale*). (These are the predicates found in Nos. 47, 48 and 49 of this chapter.)

In No. 50 they expanded the notion of marriage the covenant, calling it unbreakable (*foedus indissolubile*). They added there that it is a partnership, or sharing, in the whole of life, a communion of life, that is indissoluble (*totius vitae consuetudo et communio perseverat, suumque valorem et indissolubilitatem servat*).

More revealing than even this list of substantives the bishops used to describe marriage are their statements about the kind of act that creates a marriage. It is there that they develop the notion of marriage as covenant.

They said first (in No. 48) that marriage, which they had already called an intimate partnership of marital life and love, is formed by "a marital covenant of irrevocable personal consent'' (*foedere coniugali seu irrevocabili consensu personali instauratur*). Here it is the reciprocal personal commitment creating the marriage that is the covenant, whereas it was earlier the marriage itself. But the two affirmations do not contradict one another.

The passage goes on immediately to say that this covenanting is a human act in which the spouses ''mutually bestow and accept one another'' (*actu humano quo coniuges sese mutuo tradunt et accipiunt*). The effect of the term *actu humano* is to make clear that the covenanting act must be an informed decision. The bishops come back a second time to this notion of calculated self-giving. Referring again to marriage as an intimate union, they call it a mutual gifting of the spouses' persons to one another (*mutua personarum donatio*). This notion of the reciprocal gifting of persons is a charged one. It is biblical; it is pre-juridical and pre-contractual. Indeed it excludes contractuality because precisely what an act of contracting is not is an exchange of gifts. What is given under contract, or given initially to create a contract, is not intended as a gift. It is intended either to create an obligation in commutative justice or to fulfill this obligation.

Marital love has its role in this self-giving, although the bishops do not say expressly what this is. They do say of it (in No. 49) that such love leads a man and a woman to a free and mutual gift of themselves (*talis amor . . . coniuges ad liberum et mutuum sui ipsius donum . . . conducit totamque vitam eorum pervadit*). This can be interpreted to mean not only that marital love leads a couple to the initial self-giving that creates a marriage, but leads them to continue the same giving throughout their lives together. This suggests the answer to the question that asks what is demanded of spouses within their marriage specifically because they have created it by their self-donation. The question is important because it asks about the essential work of marriage, about the content of the gift the spouses make to one another when impelled by marital love, and even about the mode of their giving.

Borrowing the biblical affirmation that their covenant makes the spouses ''two in one flesh,'' the bishops say (in No. 48) that the covenant engages them in the intimate union of their persons and their actions (*intima personarum atque operum coniunctione*), in which they help and serve one another. They say too that in living out this covenant, and as an effect of it, the spouses come to experience the meaning of their oneness and to grow in it day by day (*sensumque suae unitatis experiuntur et plenius in dies adipiscuntur*).

This understanding of marriage the human relationship is far more ready to serve as the matrix of the sacrament than any understanding developed hitherto across the centuries of Catholic teaching. One ought not to ignore that it is the product of culture, indeed of multiple cultures. That it comes from the appointed teachers of the Catholic Church does not make it otherwise. It is not the product of immediate, culture-transcending divine revelation—as if there were such a thing. Anyone who has studied the history of the composition of *Gaudium et Spes* must acknowledge its cultural conception and gestation, a process whose beginning can be verified in the personalist philosophy of German and French thinkers in the 1920's and 1930's.

As a representation of cultures, as a distillation of marital experiences, it is also flawed, and consequently is flawed as a matrix of the sacrament. The most serious flaw I see in it is not an error, but an omission, and probably an inevitable omission. I will explain this allegation presently, but not pessimistically because I think that as a matrix it is open to the supplying of the omission I have in mind.

But because it is the most real-to-life and adaptable matrix of the sacrament in Catholic history, it must have serious consequences in the theology of the sacrament. Keep in mind a principle of philosophy that rules here. The human and the divine agents in the sacrament qualify one another. The human action as matrix and the divine action are reciprocally determining. I offer the following as some of the consequences of this.

First and most simply, a marriage can be created as a sacrament only by a man's and a woman's making a gift of their persons to one another. The gift-giving must create a union of their persons that is a sharing in all of life. If it does not do this, whatever else the relationship that is created, it is not a sacrament.

Spouses act out their sacrament at other times than in the creating of it by their wedding vows. Every moment and kind of conduct that is specifically marital, among the myriad moments and kinds in their life together that are not, is a sacramental moment and experience. It follows that these too must be some kind of self-giving, a self-giving that shares what is specific in their lives, that at least sustains their union but better still enriches it.

Drawing on the ancient theological axiom that a Christian marriage is a sacrament in that, like all sacraments, it images an invisible reality, this matrix demands that the reality marriage images must be itself a self-giving, a creating and a sustaining of union. That divine reality must be a covenantal self-giving, a commitment of one's self and an accepting of the commitment by another.

Limitations of the *Gaudium et Spes* Marital Matrix

Where *Gaudium et Spes* falls short, I believe, is in that territory of the theology of the sacrament that remains most undeveloped. This is the place of sexuality in marriage and therefore in the matrix of the sacrament.

Understandably the bishops in council did not try to explain sexuality's place in the sacrament because they had no intention of explaining the sacrament to begin with. But they did see its centrality in marriage and made one point about it whose significance can be estimated only in the sixteen-century context of Augustinian pessimism about sexuality. They said that sexual expression including intercourse is in itself good.

The pessimism that said it is not, that it is sinful, is well enough known. The reason for the entry of this pessimism into Western Christian thought and feeling is not. The Fathers and other teachers of the first centuries took for granted that the Garden parable in Genesis 2 and 3 is factual narrative. Therefore they assumed that the first man and woman lived, before their sin, in perfect peace with God and perfect peace within themselves. The first couple did have intercourse in that time of peaceful order. But this was motivated only by the desire to produce a child for God's glory, and their wills, guided by this reasonable motive, kept their bodies under perfect control in intercourse.

Their sin, in essence a rebellion against God's will, produced an analogous rebellion within themselves. Their lower powers, their passions and their bodies, rebelled against reason and will. This rebellious condition within them, this uncontrollable urgency of passions and bodies, Augustine identified as concupiscence. It is in itself sinful because it is disorder against the right internal order intended by God.

Augustine also took for granted that this concupiscence thereafter ruled the first man's and woman's every sexual intercourse so as to make it inescapably sinful. But an act sinful because concupiscent cannot fail to infect with concupiscence the fruit of that act. So Adam's and Eve's children were conceived concupiscent. So too were their children's children; and this will be the inheritance of all their descendants until the end of history.

Augustine believed that Christ merited grace, to be dispensed by baptism, in the strength of which Christian spouses could control their inherited concupiscence. If they cooperate with grace they can at least keep their concupiscence within marriage and thus avoid the deadly sins of fornication and adultery. But even if they confine it within marriage Christian spouses can at best only control concupiscence. With the exception of a few married saints every century they cannot master it entirely. This is evident in the persistence with which husbands and wives demand intercourse of one another even when conception is impossible because of pregnancy or old age. But because conception is intended by God as the one reason for intercourse, it can be the only legitimizing reason for it. Therefore when spouses cannot claim this reason, their motive can be none other than concupiscence. Hence the sinfulness of their acts. And since intercourse is all but inevitable in every marriage, sinfulness runs inevitably through the heart of every marriage. Thus marriage is the default vocation of the weak. It is not a place of holiness; it is a *remedium*, although not a very effective one. That authentic Augustinian of the early sixteenth century, Martin Luther, said of marriage, "It is a hospital for incurables."

In *Gaudium et spes* the bishops took deliberate aim at this sad interpretation and said no to it. Their denial was all the more incisive because their first reference to sexual intercourse (in No. 48) is in the context of marital love. This is a context within which Augustine and the other Fathers rarely mentioned intercourse, unless one interpret as a context of love their opinion that one spouse may show a kind of love for the other by acceding to the request for intercourse in order to protect the other from adultery by relieving concupiscence, thereby confining his or her potential mortal sin to actual venial sin.

About this love and its expression the bishops said that it is most characteristically (*eminenter*) human because its joining the spouses to one another is done by an act of will. Because it is this act rather than the drive of erotic infatuation that joins them, their marital love can reach for their good as persons, can create a unique friendship, and can therefore make their sexual communication an exercise of caring friendship instead of a satisfying of selfish need.

The bishops went on to say that spouses express this marital love and bring it to completion *singulariter* by love-making with intercourse. The adverb here modifies both functions, the expression and the completion. It means not that intercourse is the only way to realize these two functions. Rather it is the fullest way of doing so, the way most characteristic of marital love. Since the bishops had already said that this love has its origin in God, the conclusion is obvious: sexual intercourse for the married is a way of expressing and completing a love designed and awakened by God. The bishops do not hint that because of the first parents' sin even Christian spouses' intercourse is inescapably sinful because inescapably infected by concupiscence. They do not hint it is sinful even if they do not intend to conceive.

Their most express claim to sexual expression's goodness in marriage is this: "Hence the acts by which spouses join to one another intimately and chastely are good and honorable." More than being essentially good and honorable when carried on in a truly human way, they act out and strengthen the giving over of their persons as gifts to one another, and they enrich one another as persons.

Very quickly (in No. 50) the bishops went on to point out a second and derived goodness of sexual intercourse. Precisely because it is the fullest expression of a love that is marital, intercourse tends by nature to be fruitful in children. This tendency goes beyond the obvious biological orientation of reproductive anatomies. It is a tendency of marital love itself. This love is inherently a love of life. Therefore it wants to communicate life, to contribute to the human family and keep it in existence. The bishops did not say, although they could have said, that marital love seeks to defeat death, and works best at this by the sexual expression of itself. In doing so it co-works with God's love, which is in essence the giving of life.

I have already noted that the bishops' explicit consideration of marriage the Christian sacrament (in No. 48) is quite brief. Like their consideration of marriage itself and of sexual intercourse, this too is set in the context of marital love. This suggests that they were aware that the nature and demands of this love must condition the sacrament. They said again that it is God who has designed marital love, and he it is who awakens it in men and women. They reached without explanation into the Epistle to the Ephesians (5:21–33) to say that marital love is modeled on the love relationship of Christ and the Church, even though at this point they had in mind the love relationships of all spouses, not only of Christians. They added that Christ's abiding presence in the spouses' lives through the sacrament strengthens them to do what marital love itself already urges, that they give themselves unreservedly to one another—as Christ gave himself to the Church. The Holy Spirit enters their lives through the sacrament. Therefore they can mature in faith, trust and love by the living out of their sacrament.

How far the bishops of Vatican II moved beyond Augustine's pessimism about sexual expression in marriage becomes clear when we join their words about the sacrament with those about marital love. The exercise of this love is for Christian spouses simultaneously the living of their sacrament, and vice versa. Since the fullest expression of this love is in sexual love-making, their sacrament is lived most fully there. Since Christ comes to them in their sacrament, he comes to them most fully in their love-making. And since the Holy Spirit works in them through the sacrament to bring them to maturity in faith, trust and love, he does so through their love-making.

The Unmet Need for an
Understanding of Sexuality

In light of these richly human statements, and assuming that the equally rich conclusions just above can be drawn from what the bishops of Vatican II actually said, where does their understanding of marriage and marital love fall short by omission, and fall short precisely as an understanding of the matrix of the sacrament?

I think it does so within the inclusive understanding of sexuality, and within this understanding in three sectors that overlap in varying degrees.

Within the inclusive understanding, what the bishops understand sexuality to be is not quite clear. Certainly their implicit understanding of it is far more accurate than the Augustinian and Scholastic near-Freudian perception of it as lust, as raw genital urgency, and male genital urgency at that.

(Augustine's moral judgment followed necessarily from this perception. If he were right, the only permissible use of sexuality would be for conception. The only way husbands and wives could express their love sexually would be to try to conceive a child. And sexuality's only sanctifying capacity as an exercise of the sacrament would be that of conceiving. Among other consequences of this, specifically marital holiness would be impossible for wives past menopause and for their husbands, as also for spouses sterile for any other reason.)

But the case is very different if one understands sexuality more accurately because more inclusively. Suppose one includes in it ingredients acknowledged by Jungian psychology, such as the impulse of a masculine or a feminine archetype developed in the unconscious dimension of the soul, and the seeking for a real-life incarnation of and union with the archetype. Or suppose one includes in sexuality the urge to constellate anima and animus in one's soul, to have these masculine and feminine elements come together, energize and mature one another by external physical union with a partner of the opposite sex. If one includes this, it follows that to love sexually is to help one's spouse gain this interior maturity through the joining of imaginative, sensitive passivity with assertive physical reality. It follows too that growing in the holiness available in the exercise of the sacrament consists in part of gaining this maturity and helping one's spouse to gain it.

Or suppose one includes in sexuality the desire for emotional participation, for interpenetration with a partner—the longing to "live inside" the love-partner and to have him or her do the same with oneself; the desire to know totally and to be known totally, the desire that is probably the most powerful impulse to physical interpenetration as well in sexual love-making among partners who truly love one another.

If one includes this desire, it follows that to love sexually demands the ability and the willingness to take down the barriers to this emotional interpenetration. It points too at what sinfulness may be where it takes root in men's and women's sexuality. It may be their unwillingness and even their inability to take down these barriers, and conversely the need and the will to hold the supposed love-partner at an emotional distance in order to guard privacy and independence. It points finally at the healing that the sacrament of marriage can bring—about which more presently.

Of course this limitation in the bishops' ability to interpret sexuality's place in the sacrament, to verify inclusively the elements and the dynamics of sexuality, besets anyone who attempts the same interpretation. But the inevitability of the limitation points at an urgently needed element of method here. Understanding sexuality's place in the sacrament waits on information that can be supplied only by Christian spouses—by such spouses who command reasonably the theology of the sacrament, and who have reflected intelligently on their own experience of sexuality in marriage.

I suggested above that in addition to lacking an adequate understanding of sexuality the bishops' statement falls short also in three overlapping sectors within this understanding.

First, they do not venture to explain the role of passion in sexuality and marriage. Consequently they say nothing about its function in the sacrament.

Second, they leave almost entirely out of consideration the one most valid part of Augustine's reflection, that marriage can carry on a healing of human sinfulness. Perhaps they omitted it because this is the work of the sacrament, and they intended no thorough consideration of the sacrament. But even there they hint at it gently in saying that the model of Christian marital love, Christ's love for the Church, brought him to deliver himself up for it.

Finally, the bishops reckon not at all with sexual pleasure. Consequently they ignore its place in the sacrament, in the sacrament's work of healing sinfulness, and they ignore its relationship with passion. In light of this pleasure's place as a universal and commanding motive for marrying at least in the West since the romantic age—as a motive just as compelling among devout Christians as among others—the omission is not inconsequential.

When I refer to passion I have in mind not one of the *passiones animae* about which Scholastic philosophy speculates. And I certainly do not have in mind passion taken currently as lust. I mean rather passion in the classical Greek sense of eros. This is the desire for the perfection of goodness and beauty, for complete and lasting happiness in the experience of this goodness and beauty. It is the emotional energy that drives men and women to search for them, to produce them in great art and in ardent love. As such an energy it can be channeled through different avenues of the soul and the body. When it is channeled through sexuality, passion's assertion and release may be powerful and dramatic. When it is denied, its disappointment may show itself with equal power and drama, as Othello demonstrated, and Romeo and Juliet, and Dido. In our own day in the English-speaking world thinkers as diverse as Norman O. Brown, Daniel Day Williams, C.S. Lewis, Rollo May, Martin d'Arcy and Erich Fromm have written about it. But also in our own day the Catholic authorities have either ignored passion as eros or distrusted it silently because of its consecration by the Greeks to homosexual love and by the medieval romantics to adulterous love.

One Christian interpretation of passion says that it is an implicit desire for union with God, a desire implanted by him in every human soul as a kind of magnetic opposite pole by which he may draw men and women to himself. Assuming the truth of this, and given the fact that many men and women channel their passion into their sexuality, this raises serious questions. And it is evident again that only the married can begin to answer them.

For one, since partners in the sexual expression of passion must be both physically and emotionally penetrable if they are to fulfill this desire in any measure, how do they accede to an attraction to God himself by following the lure of a man's or woman's goodness and beauty and locking their passion there? Where is God to be found and communed with in physical and emotional communion with a human being? This is a consideration neither exotic nor over-fine. We recall that the bishops of Vatican II themselves said that Christian spouses find Christ in loving one another. What they did not say is how the spouses can do this by putting their passion, their desire for union with God, into sexual love-making. Nor could one expect them to have said it. Again, the answer to this can come only from spouses who experience both the passionate desire for union with God and passionate sexual love-making.

The Role of Sexual Marital Love
in the Paschal Mystery

About the bishops' neglect to consider the healing function of the sacrament of marriage, again information is needed from the married, but here from Christian spouses who are reasonably learned in psychology. What must be found out from them is the territory of married love that is most vulnerable to damage by sinfulness. I do not mean damage by sins, by deliberately destructive conduct, but by the underlying attitude, the profound condition of soul about which I wrote much earlier.

Assume that this sinfulness is at heart the fear of the loss of self, the fear of being drawn out of one's protective defenses into the risk of the self-giving and the accepting that make up married love. One must first of all acknowledge the vulnerability, must admit that the effort to give and accept sexually can damage as well as it can heal. Making oneself naked emotionally as well as physically can put oneself at great risk. It seems the damage here can be finally ruinous if it destroys irreparably a man's or woman's ability to trust. For how can a person love if he or she cannot trust?

But if we can find in sexual love-making something that can redeem the risk, that can heal the fear and distrust, we can find perhaps the most justifying of all reasons for calling a marriage a sacrament. Here again it must be the married who have experienced this healing who must inform us. I have asked a few married friends who are willing to tell of their experience. They have said that finding someone willing to remove all barriers to intimacy, willing to trust without reserve, to be naked in soul with oneself as well as in body— this is healing. One is willing to trust that an intimate partner who makes himself or herself so vulnerable has no intention to harm, especially not by the harm of someday taking flight.

In the same vein, a love partner's bringing his or her passion out of protective hiding and loosing it on oneself tends to evoke the same in oneself. It awakens desire and intensifies it. In doing so it makes one vulnerable simultaneously to great happiness and to great sorrow. One knows even in the moment of happiness that someday death will end this. But this is what makes a man or woman vulnerable to God's calling because it is in great happiness or great sorrow that he can most effectively call a human being.

Spouses report too that the happiness they experience in their sexual loving is in direct proportion to their unreserved abandoning of privacy and self-protection. But they find this is possible in love-making only if it goes on in a married life dominated by the same unafraid self-giving in all other quarters, as reciprocally that self-giving is made the more possible by repeated surrender without reserve in love-making. Because trust knows no bounds in them, love has unlimited possibility, and has it everywhere in their marriage.

Sexual Pleasure and the Sacrament

The two most insistent questions about sexual pleasure are simple ones. First, what is this pleasure? Then, if its character can be identified, can this pleasure be incorporated in the work of bringing spouses into union with God and intensifying this union? Can this pleasure take a place in the paschal mystery? Can it save from death of the soul?

But the questions, even if simple, are difficult in the answering. About the character of sexual pleasure, if everyone agreed that it is found in orgasmic release and nothing more, the difficulty of identifying it would vanish, but the difficulty of finding place for it in joining with God would soar.

Because Augustine and the Scholastics apparently identified this pleasure almost exclusively as release, they found condemning it as sinful easy enough. They acknowledged only one other possible pleasure in sexual intercourse, that found in anticipating the conception of a child for the kingdom of God. It was because of either their experience or their assumption that the first of these pleasures almost inevitably swamps the second, with bodily excitement sealing an irrational triumph over reasoned motivation, that they judged the sexual pleasure common to the human race since the first man and woman to be sinful.

And if one were to agree with their narrow understanding of sexuality as a premise, one would have to agree with two conclusions arrived at in sequence by the early and the later medieval theologians. The first was that because of orgasmic pleasure's sinful ever-presence even in the marriages of Christians, these marriages cannot be sacraments. For a sacrament is by definition grace-giving. But it is contradictory to say that a sinful action can be such.

The later and slightly more benign conclusion was that the marriages of Christians are sacraments because they can in fact be grace-giving, but giving of a unique grace. This is remedial grace, which—as noted earlier—enables spouses to exercise self-control in two domains: outside their marriage to resist temptation to adultery; within their marriage to resist temptation to the pleasure proper to adulterers and fornicators, which is any pleasure other than that found in anticipating conception of a child for the kingdom of God.

But suppose one takes as a premise the far more inclusive understanding of sexuality outlined earlier in this essay. What then would one find to be the ingredients of sexual pleasure? Here again I report conversations with dear married friends. Among spouses who love one another deeply, and in addition have remained in love, the pleasure beyond compare is that of intensifying happiness in one's mate, and doing so in a most complete way. This does include helping to the physical pleasure of orgasmic release. But it puts this pleasure in a more inclusive context. This context includes the pleasure of having all one's defenses willingly obliterated, of being trusted, of being desired, and desired at a quite primitive, unguarded and spontaneous level. Add to these the elements identified by Jungian psychology: the sense of participation, of emotional and physical interpenetration; the constellating of anima and animus within each soul; the joining with the other-sex archetype with its sense of completion.

The spouses report an essential reciprocity here. A great part of the pleasure one can give sexually to a spouse is that of allowing and even helping him or her to give back pleasure, of accepting this effort at pleasure-giving. It involves making oneself vulnerable to the other's loving invasion of one's privacy of body and soul; it is a convincing because tangible and primitive act of trust.

There is an element of sexual pleasure that is elusive because the presence of many children already born into the family, or the spouses' advancing years, can mask it or block it all together. About it the bishops of Vatican II said (in *Gaudium et Spes* at the beginning of No. 50) that marriage and marital love are by nature oriented to the conceiving, bearing and nurturing of children. Their *a priori* determination aside, is it true that one of the pleasures of sexual love-making is in the anticipation that the act of love may conceive a child? If love-making is freed from all anxiety, is conceiving a child in order to put an image of the spouses' love and a product of it into existence a consistently present source of pleasure? Again only the married can say.

It should be obvious how this giving and receiving of sexual pleasure can be a healing. It can heal feelings of isolation and of worthlessness. (How can one be alone and worthless if one can give great pleasure?) It can heal the fear of being untrusted and unable to trust. It can heal the fear of being sterile in life. The total surrender of defenses that is the proportioned condition for greatest pleasure can be itself a commitment to fidelity and permanence, and thus a healer of the fear of eventually having risked foolishly and lost all in the effort to love.

Put this under a new metaphor, one that may contain too much of life itself to be merely a metaphor. Assuming that the most fundamental work of life is to defeat death; that Christians, because of their belief in bodily resurrection, are the only human beings who believe in the ultimate victory of life over death; that at heart sinfulness is the incipient victory in men and women of the feat that death gets the last word—then there is a place in sexual pleasure for pleasure in life's victory over death. There is place for this pleasure not only in the obvious victory gained through life prolonged into another generation by the birth of a child, but in the victory over death of the soul in the spouses— the death that comes in loneliness, in abandonment and worthlessness, in final despair.

If we understand sexual pleasure in this way, we understand how spouses can grow in holiness by this pleasure. Recall that in essence holiness is union with God, and that in the context of a human population crippled by sinfulness, it is also the willingness, empowered by that union, to work at healing this sinfulness. The lure and the experience of a pleasure that intensifies desire, that takes down barriers to intimacy, that sets firmly the ground of trust, that takes one out of oneself to do all these for a partner in love—all these open the way to God's entering and working in the soul.

Christian Marriage as Sacramental Ministry

What I have said thus far about the healing and sanctifying work of a marriage that makes it a sacrament justifies accepting it as a form of Christian ministry. But accepting it for this depends first on expanding one's understanding of ministry beyond the narrow notion of appointment by authority to a Church office. In a more inclusive sense Christian ministry consists of doing Christ's work in the world, doing it as the fruit of commitment, of a commitment made publicly (whether juridically authorized or not), of a commitment worked at consistently and in verifiable form.

When Christians celebrate their sacrament of confirmation properly they volunteer for ministry in the Church and commit themselves to it. By their baptism they were born into childhood there. They became recipients of God's gifts given in the Church, but they were not expected to share these gifts with others.

Then in their confirmation they step willingly into adulthood of Christian life. In this sacrament they receive the empowering of God's Spirit to share the gifts of faith, hope and love. This empowering is to enable them to keep their commitment. But thus far the commitment is to sharing these gifts in only a generic way. When they go beyond this and create their marriage, and create it as a sacrament, they extend their commitment made in confirmation, focus it, make it specific. They commit themselves to co-work with God specifically by their sexuality, by its uses in the ways we have already seen.

Surely this is to carry on ministry in the Church. This is all the more evident if we recall that the Church itself is a sacrament in that, as a community of men and women animated by the Spirit of Christ and the Father, it works with this Spirit to carry on Christ's work in the world—to carry it on visibly and tangibly in such a way as to show that it is indeed still Christ of the paschal mystery who is at work. Christian spouses using their sexually expressed love to defeat bodily death by bringing children into the world, and to defeat the death of the soul by keeping passionate desire for God alive along with belief and hope that he will fulfill this desire—surely this is to carry on not only Christian ministry but ministry that is sacramental.

The Use of Scripture in the Theology of the Sacrament

The use of Scripture in the theology of marriage has been hampered, I believe, by the abduction of key passages into a kind of Platonic discourse. The traditional demonstration intending to verify that Christ "raised the marital covenant between baptized persons to the dignity of a sacrament" (to use the formulation of the Code of Canon Law, Canon 1055.1) assumes the definition of a sacrament as we have seen it, *sacrae rei signum*. The demonstration goes then to Christ's dispute with a group of Pharisee interrogators recorded in the Synoptic tradition (in Mark 10 and in Matthew 19). There Christ appropriates the Yahwist teaching (in Genesis 2) that it is God who created marriage—created it as the most valuable human relationship ("That is why a man leaves his father and mother and cleaves to his wife"), a relationship so lasting and so intimate that husband and wife become as one person before the law (". . . and the two become one body")—and this after having the first husband claim his wife as his intimate companion in every facet of his life ("This one at last is bone of my bones and flesh of my flesh"). Because of such a husband-wife union created by God himself, Christ commanded, "Therefore what God has joined no man must separate."

The husband-wife union thus understood, the demonstration continues, is indeed a sign of a sacred reality. This reality is the relationship of God with his people. (A patristic and medieval variant interpretation said it is a sign of the union of the two persons in Christ.) The Platonic character of the demonstration becomes clear when one notices that by now "sign" means "image."

This part of the demonstration is then reinforced by drawing on the metaphor used so richly by the prophets Hosea, Jeremiah, Isaiah and Ezekiel, the metaphor that pictures the people Israel as the bride of Yahweh.

But now the people Israel has been supplanted by the Christian people, the Church, and God's husband relationship has been incarnated in Christ. At this point Paul's exhortation in Ephesians 5:21–33 is interpolated: "Husbands, love your wives just as Christ loved the Church and gave himself up for her" (verse 25); and ". . . just so husbands should love their wives as their own bodies" (verse 28).

The author's intent in all of Ephesians was to explain how God's *mystérion,* his plan to bring salvation to the human race, to bring peace, to reconcile ancient enemies, began to be realized in the paschal mystery, Christ's dying and rising from death, and to explain how its realization is to be continued through history by the Spirit of Christ who has been given to men and women.

In the later and hortatory part of the epistle (beginning at 4:17) the author explains how Christians, those who have accepted the Spirit, can live and ought to live just because they have accepted him. The passage on marriage is explanation and exhortation on this point to Christian spouses. There the author gives them a model for their love, that of Christ for the Church and of the Church's love for him. Spirit-filled as they are, that is how Christian husbands and wives can love and ought to love one another.

The Platonism of this theological demonstration emerges still more clearly when it turns the instruction and exhortation into ontological declaration. It has the author go beyond saying that Spirit-filled Christian spouses can and ought to imitate the model of Christ and the Church, to make him say that every marriage of two Christian spouses is in fact an image of the divine model—is in this sense a *sacrae rei signum.*

What the author acknowledges as possible though contingent, that Christian spouses can replicate the divine model in their human way, this theology turns into an antecedently given fact, indeed a double fact: that Christian marriage is such an image, and therefore Christian marriages are such images. In the history of Catholic theology the former has become the doctrine; the second has become the conclusion derived from the doctrine.

I have already hinted at the vulnerable links in this catena of reasoning. The hint merits development into somewhat fuller criticism.

When one uses a Biblical author's statements for one's theological demonstration, one must include in one's demonstration his intent in saying what he said. One may reason to conclusions beyond it, but one must at least include it, and include it as decisive for one's demonstration. In Ephesians 5:21–33 the author intended to instruct and exhort about attitudes and conduct in Christian marriages. When he set out the two correlated relationships that make up his analogy—husband-head to wife-body, and Christ-head to Church-body—he did so in the service of his instruction and exhortation. If a theologian goes beyond this intent and says that because of this analogy Christian marriage in the abstract images the Christ-Church relationship, he draws his own conclusion, not the author's. If he ventures further, out of the abstraction into real life, and says that every Christian marriage so images and is thus a sacrament, he collides with the question, "Does every Christian marriage in fact have in it the love that images the Christ-Church relationship?"

Again, when one uses a Biblical author's fabric of reasoning, one ought not to omit from use those parts of the fabric uncongenial to one's own purposes. Present by implication in the reasoning in Ephesians, but transparently present, is the fallibility of the Christian spouses' love. The author exhorts them, and exhortation presumes a possible falling short. Otherwise why exhort? He insists that the spouses have been given the Spirit, but no one was more aware than he (especially if he was Paul) that they could refuse to accept and cooperate with the Spirit. If the letter is immediately Paul's own, surely the majority of the spouses to whom he wrote were married as pagans, before their conversion. Now that they are Christians, he urges, they ought to love as Christ and his Church love, and they can do so in the power of the Spirit. Transposing the exhortation into the language of later theology, we would find him saying to the spouses, "By working with the power of the Spirit you can make your marriages sacraments, signs that God's love for our Church through Christ is at work in you." I believe this is the doctrine that is contained by implication in the passage.

I say the Platonic-minded theologian misunderstands and misuses the passage when he ignores the author's hortatory intent in proposing his model for Christian married love, and skews it instead into an ontological statement about the sacramentality of Christian marriage and the character of this sacramentality. He equivalently has the author say of Christian marriage what Paul said of Christ in Colossians 1:15, "He is the image of the unseen God" (*hós estin eikòn toû theoû toû aorátou*). This interpretation takes a model for a love that the spouses themselves must bring to reality, and turns it falsely into a model of a marital relationship in which they are simply lodged before any effort of their own.

The interpretation also assumes a unique efficacy on the part of the model: it *causes* Christian marriages to be images of itself. (This in fact has been the logic for centuries of the magisterial argument for the radical indissolubility of consummated sacramental marriages: *because* the divine model is an indestructible marital relationship [thus the Christ-Church relationship], it *makes* its image on earth [the Christian marriage] to be indissoluble—but only provided the latter images the divine model perfectly by being "two in one flesh" through consummation in complete sexual intercourse.)

Treating Christian marriages seriously as images of the Christ-Church model could lead to relationships showing nearly bizarre traits. Drawing a scenario from the details of the model, the husband would be the earthly Christ figure. He would sanctify the wife by some kind of cleansing that would do to her what baptism does to a catechumen. She would be assumed to need this cleansing, while he would not, and she would be expected to seek it from her husband. His protecting and cleansing love would demand that he be ready to sacrifice his life for her, but in her passivity she would be presumed incapable of such a love, or perhaps would be excused from it. What this asymmetry of loves would do to the attempt at permanent intimacy in a modern marriage of two educated persons stirs the imagination.

I suggest that if the theology of the sacrament continues to use the terms *sacrae rei signum*, they be understood to mean that a Christian marriage is a sacrament if its conduct is evidence that God's Spirit is present and active in the relationship. What conduct that may be, I have suggested earlier in this essay. Here I would repeat and insist that God's action in the world, whose intentionality is intimate union of the human creature with himself, is a reconciling and healing action because of the sinfulness in the creature that fears intimacy and its demands. Therefore the marital conduct that is sacramental because evidence of God's action must seek and sustain intimacy and in so doing heal and reconcile—both within itself between the spouses, and outwardly from itself in the Christian community and in the human family.

This is done differently in different cultures, differently at different times in the history of the race as well as in the history of a marriage. It is for the married who work at it to tell us how it is done.

RESPONSES

ROSEMARY HAUGHTON

My first comment has to do with the ministry which married couples are charged with toward each other and toward their families. It seems to me that the kind of sacramental experience which Fr. Mackin was describing also tends naturally toward an outreach, and couples who have that kind of experience with one another and with their children reach out to others as well. Consequently, you begin to create a domestic church not just in the sense of the family but also in the sense of a center of faith, a center of charity, a center of loving acceptance, which many people feed into in various degrees. This takes a further step: what often happens is that families with this kind of understanding of marriage come together and assist each other with this kind of ministry. When marriage is a good one, by its nature it reaches out to include others.

I also want to comment on the way in which the passage from Ephesians (5:21–33) has been used actually to demand a model of the husband and wife relationship in which the husband is the Christ-figure, the one who leads, who saves, who nurtures, who heals, while the wife is expected to be passive and to receive this healing and nurturing, this saving from sinfulness. This fits in very well with the age-old assumption that sin probably came mostly from the woman anyway, so that she is the one in need of this healing and saving from sinfulness. This model fed into the whole patriarchal idea of marriage very neatly. Many, many people have tried to live their marriages that way, and it's a terrible distortion. You can get wonderful Christians like C. S. Lewis who tried to justify that kind of theology of marriage. They talked about the theology of headship and said that women shouldn't want to share that headship, for after all that kind of headship means wearing a crown of thorns. In other words the husband was perceived as the suffering redeemer. That passage from Ephesians has really been used to create something which Paul never had in his mind at all when he was writing about marriage.

Finally, it seems to me that Fr. Mackin has proposed a revolutionary re-thinking of the basis of the notion of sacrament and what that means in Christian, indeed, in human life. That is a very important thing and has shattering implications.

THEODORE MACKIN

I think you were pointing obliquely to a terribly flawed way of doing theology, and I'm going to set sail on uncharted seas a bit. If you study the history of theology, I think you will find the neo-Platonic attitude and mind dominant for centuries. It works like this: Go to the Scriptures, and on the assumption that in the Scriptures you have culture-transcending times and space-free revelations from God, from those you design a model in the mind, abstract, detached from reality.

The second step in that neo-Platonic way of theologizing is that once the model is designed abstractly in the mind, then it is applied to real life, generally through juridic devices, and it becomes a kind of Procrustean bed. If the reality doesn't fit the model, too bad for the reality. That's why the real seismic shift I am recommending is that theologizing start from the underside. Start with the human matrix. The reason why the theology of marriage has been literally strangulated for centuries is that the experience of marriage has been neglected; the married have not been asked what marriage is like. How do you in your married conduct heal reluctance, fearfulness, the terrible inclination to protect yourself, lest in risking all you lose all?

BERNARD COOKE

I don't think there is any question that what Fr. Mackin is pointing to is an approach to sacramentality which is quite different from what we might think of as our classic theology of the sacraments. I would like to talk a bit about a complementary way of getting at some of the things that were in Fr. Mackin's treatment.

One of the things we have to look at is what we mean by holiness. I think that is important not only for our theology of grace but also for understanding human marriage and, within that, Christian marriage. I think the tradition is very clear that holiness consists in union with God. But as was already suggested in Fr. Mackin's talk, there has always been a temptation, indeed, a long-standing tradition of placing holiness in a neo-Platonic framework. I think that neo-Platonic framework led us to think of union with God as something that had to be achieved by climbing the ladder. In this hierarchical model, God is perceived to be at the top, while we are down here still mired in bodiliness, which was understood as having overtones of evil. Union with God means a process of ascending to God. In this way we become holier by leaving what is the context of our earthly bodily reality. The effort involves a sort of distancing ourselves from the ordinary life of people.

I suggest that this model of holiness has distorted both our understanding of celibacy and how that is meant to function, as well as our approach to marriage and the role of marriage in the process of sanctification, because if you achieve holiness by distancing yourself from this ordinary bodily existence, then holiness is reserved for those who have removed themselves from sexual activity. By practicing continence, celibates were seen not to have at least dimmed their entry into the area of the holy by ordinary sexual involvement in terms of marriage. Because of this, celibacy for centuries tended to appropriate to itself two very important and absolutely necessary elements of Christian existence—its eschatological orientation and its evangelical guidance. These evangelical counsels were spoken of as belonging to people in that state of life to which most people did not belong. The implication of this is that only celibates really live the Gospel. I don't know what the rest of Christians were supposed to be living.

The *Constitution of the Church,* in its chapter on the universal call to holiness, finally turns that around. It directs us back toward a model of holiness that was prominent in Jesus' own parables. This model of holiness is one of life. It deals with living reality. This model is very biblical, because the Bible is always talking about a living God. God is alive, and is the communicator of life. The Spirit of God is the life-giving or animating Spirit. If you pursue this model, then what you come up with is that holiness means vitality: personal vitality, sensitivity, depth of insight, an ability to relate in concerned and warm mature love to other people.

Applying this to marriage, it seems to me that for the married person holiness means to be involved with the creation of life: the creation of one's own personal life by relating to and discovering another person, and the creation of other persons, particularly the person to whom one is married. Now that means that married life together, and very specifically marital intercourse, is a process of consecration, of sanctification.

Taking it one step more, there is a profoundly sacramental dimension to this. In the process of giving self to another, one becomes more fully oneself, and the other emerges more profoundly as a person. In this experience one has the primary basis for understanding what God's self-giving, and therefore the creative process of sanctification, really means.

I think this is part of the development of sacramental theology which is taking place. If I understand correctly where Fr. Mackin is going, I believe he is asking us to pursue this even further.

3.

Indissolubility: Guiding Ideal or Existential Reality?

Bernard Cooke

Contemporary theological explanation of the indissolubility of Christian marriage consists of as yet inadequate response to fundamental questions that reflect progressive deepening in our understanding of marriage. As we have learned to theologize out of Christian experience as "word of God"—with our hermeneutic shaped by Scripture, liturgy, tradition and interaction with one another—we have been confronted with the existential reality of Christian marriages dissolving. Do we continue to say that these marriages still exist despite appearances?

Responding to this question will require distinctions between marriage as social institution (to regulate the sexual behavior of adults and to provide for begetting and rearing children), as personal/sexual commitment between two persons, as a distinctive form of friendship, as implementation of a societally and ecclesiastically approved and controlled contract. Moreover, we will have to ask what it is that is "indissoluble"—the contractual obligation, the love and friendship, the symbolic reality of these two persons in relation to one another, the unique sexual right/responsibility established by their marital intercourse engaged in as Christian sacrament.

Again, is "indissolubility" rooted in a divine activity, in a societal (ecclesiastical) decision, or in an irreversible ontological/relational characteristic of the two persons as married to one another? Is "indissolubility" an eschatological goal toward which human relations, including marriage, are moving, or is it a modality already existent in these relations? Is "indissolubility" a characteristic of Christian marriage that has been unduly absolutized by the historical use of Greek philosophy and a loss of the eschatological view of human existence?

Obviously connected with "indissolubility" is the notion of "consum-

mation'' of a marriage; and this, too, raises a host of related questions. Perhaps, most basically, we must ask whether a Christian marriage can be "consummated" by a first act of intercourse or whether marital intercourse as a personal (i.e., significant, sacramental) experience comes progressively into existence over the course of years—and if this latter is true, when and to what degree does "indissolubility" occur?

Among the pastoral problems to which Catholic theology should address its attention, few have as widespread impact as the question of the indissolubility of Christian marriages. That we are seriously re-examining this element of Catholic teaching reflects pastoral anxiety for the well-being of the millions of women and men in situations that have separated them from their Catholic roots. But it reflects also the broadened context of doing theology today, and it is to this aspect of reflection on indissolubility that I wish to direct my remarks.

Today's developments in theology constitute a multi-faceted phenomenon; within this complex change, it seems to me that three shifts are of special relevance to the topic of our discussion. (1) Today we are using the life experience of believing Christians, as individuals and as communities, as the starting point for our theological reflection. While other sources of insight— Scripture, traditional teaching, liturgy, etc.—enter in as principles of interpretation, it is the providential action of God in people's lives that provides the immediate "word" of revelation with which we must deal as theologians.[1] (2) We are gradually absorbing into our theological process the historical consciousness, the awareness of *process,* and the general acceptance of evolution that are hallmarks of modern Western thought. In doing so, we have rediscovered the eschatological perspective that characterizes biblical thought.[2] (3) We are beginning to theologize ecumenically, realizing that we cannot ignore other Christian traditions—for that matter, other religious traditions other than Christian—in our attempts to understand more deeply and accurately the workings of the divine with humans. Because of the immensity and diversity of this ecumenical approach, I will not include it in this particular article, but its importance for an adequate treatment of the topic is obvious.

Existential Situation of Christian Marriage

Let us, then, draw upon the first of these methodological shifts, namely the use of Christian experience as a basis for reflection. Here we are faced with the concrete and unavoidable reality that has gathered us together today: large numbers of Catholic marriages do in fact dissolve; according to every ordinary observable measure they cease to exist. Can we in the face of this widespread experience justifiably say that these marriages still continue to exist?

Any response to that question must distinguish among several meanings of "marriage."

1. At the most elemental biological level, where two people mate for continuation of the race, it is undeniable that large numbers of such unions go out of existence; the biological relationship certainly cannot be considered indissoluble, no more so among Catholics than among others.

2. Marriage is also a social institution that has existed to provide stability and order for the process of begetting and raising children, a process upon which societies have been dependent for their well-being. However, in modern societies there is almost total acceptance of and adjustment to persons being involved in a series of marriage, divorce, and remarriage. As elements in this present social structuring of human marriage, countless Catholic marriages cease and the partners go on to other marriage relationships. So, indissolubility clearly does not apply to Catholic marriages simply as social institution.

3. On a more personal level, marriage can be seen as a distinctive personal relationship involving a unique sexual commitment. Here we are definitely approaching some intrinsic aspect of indissolubility, for cultural traditions and present experience both testify to people's belief and hope as they marry that this special self-giving is "forever." However, the incidents of this commitment gradually dissipating as couples move to separation and divorce are now so common that large numbers of people apparently enter marriage—or some roughly comparable situation—with the attitude that they will remain together "as long as things work out." The promise intrinsic to marital sexual self-giving cannot, then, provide adequate grounding for indissolubility.

4. Nor can indissolubility be claimed for Catholic marriages from the viewpoint of their being a paradigm form of human friendship. One can hope that most marriages are friendships, friendships that deepen and mature over the years. Clearly, if such maturation takes place, marriages like any genuine friendship will become an increasingly indissoluble bond between persons. Again, however, experience teaches us the bitter lesson that friendships, even long-standing and treasured friendships, do not always stand the test of time. Persons in a marriage can develop as persons in ways that lead them further and further away from personal communication with one another; with today's increasing longevity and expanded educational opportunities, that has become more of a problem than ever before. While it is true, "eternally true" if you wish, that two persons *were* close friends as a married couple, when the friendship does cease one cannot claim that it still continues to exist.

5. So far, then, we have not found sufficient grounds for universally

attributing indissolubility to marriages, including Catholic marriages. We enter a somewhat different realm, however, when we regard Catholic marriage in the light of the biblical/theological category of covenant.[3] In this context, the contractual aspect of the pledge between woman and man in marriage takes on added dimensions: the couple commit themselves to one another, but they also commit themselves *as a couple* to participate sacramentally and ministerially in the life of the Christian community; they commit themselves to shared discipleship and a life together of working for the establishment of the kingdom of God. Not that all Catholic couples as they begin their married life are conscious of and open to this broader meaning of their marital contract, but this is the intrinsic reality of Christian marriage which we can hope will become understood and appreciated by people.

Certainly, we are closer to a grounding for indissolubility when we regard Catholic marriage as Christian covenant, for the promise involved has clearly eschatological orientation; it reaches in its significance to the divine. But what are we to say when the contract has been broken by one or both parties, when the promise to one another has in actuality been revoked by one or both? We might in some cases say that there has been infidelity that extends beyond the two persons to the Christian community and to God, that there has been sinful negligence or malice, that some responsibilities may still remain from the earlier covenant commitment. But can we say, for example, that an innocent and betrayed person in a marriage, a person who has clearly been irrevocably deserted, is still involved in a one-sided contract? Can a person remain committed to the Christian community to live out a sacramental relationship that is existentially impossible?

One can, of course, give an essentially legal response to this question: we have a law, a law that gives expression to a view of Catholic marriage which we are not free to abandon. Much as it pains us, the overall common good requires that exceptions not be made, so that the indissoluble character of Christian marriage will be safeguarded. But does the preservation of this ideal demand the absolutely universal implementation of this rule? Perhaps this law itself is meant to be the statement of an ideal toward which Catholics should strive with varying degrees of success or failure. Having raised that question, let us bracket it for the moment and come back to it after we have treated some other elements of sacramental theology.

6. A final possibility for grounding the indissolubility of Christian marriage lies in the sacramentality of the two Christian persons as they live in relationship to one another. They are the sacrament, not simply because they are recognizable in the community as the two who publicly bound themselves by marital contract, but because and *to the extent* that they can be recognized as translating Christian faith into their married and family life. For Christians the parameters of personal destiny, of personal responsibility and commitment, of

personal development and achievement, in brief of human life, are broadened by the revelation contained in the life and death and resurrection of Jesus of Nazareth. This is true of individual human existence; it is true of the shared existence that is marriage.

When two Christians are married they commit not only their growth as persons to one another; they commit their faith, their relation to God in Christ to one another—obviously, not totally, but to a very considerable degree. The concrete interaction with one another in their daily life will unavoidably serve as "word of God" in the light of which they will develop their self-image, their freedom, their values, their faith and hope and love.

But God's word, no matter what the medium of its transmission, has always been a promise of unconditioned divine fidelity. No characteristic of the God of Israelitic faith is more emphasized in the biblical literature; Israel's God is a faithful God. When we come to the New Testament, the raising of Jesus from the dead is seen as the culminating fulfillment of God's promises, the supreme proof of divine fidelity. And the question comes then: Can a Christian marriage truly sacramentalize, i.e., both speak of and make present, this divine fidelity unless it itself bears the mark of unfailing, irrevocable endurance? Can a marriage speak experientially about a divine love that never fails, unless it itself is lived as a relationship that is indissoluble? Or—to change the question slightly, but perhaps importantly—if it is not lived this way can one speak of it as sacramental?

In this context, we can return to the question raised earlier about the commitment implicit in marital intercourse. That there is some special personal commitment signified by this action is hard to deny, but it is also hard to deny that it is signified only to the extent that this act is one of genuine personal love, expressive of each person's selfhood and honest respect of the other's selfhood. The extent to which an actual situation of sexual interchange symbolizes an irrevocable, i.e., indissoluble, commitment of each to the other seems, then, to be commensurate with the attitudes, understandings, etc., of the two people engaged in marital intercourse. Apparently we must ask, in a somewhat more restricted form, the question we just raised about the broader reality of Catholic marriage: When are we justified in applying the term "sacramental"?

Without suggesting any final answer to these questions, it does seem that we can associate the indissolubility of Christian marriage more satisfactorily with the sacramentality of marriage than with any other aspect—which perhaps is not saying anything we have not said for a long time, for, as you have no doubt noticed, we have been very quickly reviewing the various attempts in past history to ground the indissolubility of human and Christian marriage. But perhaps we can state the case with a bit more understanding.

I believe that we can speak with more insight and more accurate under-standing because of modern historical study of Christian sacraments and be-cause of a resultant reconsideration of the nature of Christian sacramentality.[4] Historical studies have, for instance, pointed out how the meaning of "sac-rament" as applied to marriage has shifted from the emphasis on "binding promise" which it had in Augustine's explanation of Christian marriage to greater stress in medieval and subsequent centuries on the meaning of "Chris-tian symbol." Thus the care that must be taken in appealing to Augustine's thought when explaining today the sacramentality of marriage.[5] On the other hand, contemporary sacramental theology has increasingly broadened the scope of sacrament beyond simply the liturgical ritual; and it has moved away from the "automatic effect" mentality that characterized so much post-Tri-dentine explanation of sacraments and has instead re-emphasized the extent to which the sanctifying effectiveness of sacraments depends on the awareness and decisions of the Christian people involved in one or other sacramental con-text.

We have, then, a much richer and fuller understanding of "sacrament" upon which to draw in speaking of Christian marriages as sacrament and con-sequently indissoluble. So far, we have only begun to exploit this potential.

Inadequate as our understanding of the sacramentality of Christian mar-riage is, it does seem to provide some focus for the practical pastoral judgments about indissolubility that we face at this moment in Christian history. Perhaps we can sharpen the focus a bit by raising the question: If indissolubility is in some way and to some degree "intrinsic" to Christian marriage, what is the source of this indissolubility *in a particular case?*

Is God the source—or, to put it more bluntly, is God doing something extra to make a particular Christian marriage indissoluble? Given our present inchoative attempts to understand more accurately the reality we have sym-bolized by the term "divine providence," Catholic theology would be hard pressed to identify any such special divine activity. Unless I misread present theological developments, it seems that we are presently moving toward a rein-terpretation of "providence" in terms of the divine *presence* in the lives of humans. But if this is so, and if we then apply this to marriage, it would ac-centuate the importance of awareness and free decision in the sacramentality of any given marriage, for God's presence to humans is conditioned by their conscious and free acceptance of the divine saving love.

Is the Church the source? Does the Christian community, more specif-ically do the bearers of authority in the Church, have the power to make Catholic marriages indissoluble? And if they do have such power, is their exercise of this power the cause of Catholic marriages being indissoluble? I know of no theological voice that would clearly respond "yes," that would go beyond claiming for the Church the power to proclaim and defend and socially implement (within the Church's own internal life) an indissolubility that already exists in Christian marriage prior to any Church action or regulation.

But has not the official Church, at least as far back as the "Tametsi" of Trent, claimed the power to govern the *existence* of Catholic marriages by its legal activity. Despite the most Christian self-giving on the part of two devoted Catholics, the absence of the legally-established form or of proper delegation on the part of the witnessing cleric rendered their marriage invalid, i.e., non-existent. Let me approach a reconsideration of this claim by an example.

Years ago, when I was studying the canon law of marriage, the teacher highlighted the importance of "proper form" by repeating a canonical "horror story"—whether factual or not, the story quite clearly made its point. According to the account, a socially prominent young couple, wishing to avoid all the fuss of a big public wedding celebration, went for advice to the chancellor of a large U.S. diocese, since he was a close friend of the woman's family. Sympathetic to the young people's desire, he offered to marry them privately in his office; so, he requested his secretary to join them as witness to the marriage, the marriage was performed, and the young couple on their honeymoon informed their respective families of the fait accompli. However, the next day the chancellor—obviously with great embarrassment—realized the lack of due form because there had been only the one witness to the marriage. Clearly, it would have been catastrophic to contact the newly married in the midst of their honeymoon and ask them to return so that they could be married. Legalism was able, however, to triumph: the chancellor obtained a "sanatio in radice" and the young couple never had to know that they began their married life in a state of material sin.

Common sense seems to say that there is something wrong here. To make clear the artificial unreality of this scenario, and to question the underlying presuppositions, let us suppose that the diocesan chancellor had never realized his error, and that without any legal "sanation" the two people had lived a life together that reflected to their children and to all who knew them the transforming presence of God's love. Could one truly say that there did not exist a deeply sacramental Christian marriage? My purpose in citing this example is not to ridicule canonical arrangements in the Church; rather, it is to raise some basic questions about ecclesiastical claims to make things be or not be. More precisely, it is to question ecclesiastical power to condition the indissolubility of marriages.

We seem to be left, then, with no other clear alternative than the one we have already discovered: the source of whatever indissolubility attaches to a particular marriage must be the character of the marriage itself, more specifically its symbolic import as a Christian sacrament.

Christian Marriage as Process

Up to this point our reflection together could quite justifiably be faulted for the static way in which it has treated marriage, and more generally Christian sacrament. So, drawing from today's theological shift toward recognition of process, toward an eschatological viewpoint, let us examine the indissolubility of Christian marriage from the perspective of *marriage as process*.

In actual reality any given marriage, and marriage as a social institution in any culture, exists only in process. Marriages come into existence over a considerable length of time, conditioned by any number of occurrences and experiences and choices, progressing—if they do progress—through stages of change that find their Christian explanation in terms of the mystery of death and resurrection. Men and women are gradually initiated into marriage as a human relationship and a Christian sacrament; the initiation is never completed in this life—no more than is a person's lifelong initiation into Christianity, for becoming married is for most Christians a major element in the broader initiation into Christ.

It would seem, then, that one should not talk about a marriage as being completely or absolutely indissoluble but as becoming increasingly indissoluble as it becomes increasingly Christian—which is to say quite simply that the more profoundly Christian a marriage relationship becomes, the more inseparable are the two persons as loving human beings, and the more does their relationship sacramentalize the absolute indissolubility of the divine-human relationship as it finds expression in the crucified and risen Christ. Exactly how all this will occur in a given instance is as diverse and distinctive as are the people involved and the overall social situation of a given culture or historical period.

To put it in biblical terms, a Christian marriage, like any other created realities, does not exist absolutely; like anything in creation, particularly anything in human history, a marriage exists eschatologically; it is tending toward its fulfillment beyond this world. However, the fact that it does not yet have in full fashion the modalities—such as indissolubility—that should characterize it does not mean that it is devoid of them. A Christian marriage is indissoluble, but short of the eschaton it is incompletely indissoluble. Perhaps we could profitably borrow a notion from recent New Testament scholarship, namely "realized eschatology"[6]—Christian marriage already realizes to some degree the indissolubility which can mirror the divine fidelity to humans, but it cannot yet lay claim to the absoluteness which will come with the fullness of the kingdom. Similarly, two Christians can be very genuinely and sacramentally married, but they are still being married to one another; their union can become yet richer and stronger.

One wonders if the understanding of Christian marriage, as of everything else in Christianity, has not for centuries suffered the fate of being overly struc-

tured and frozen by the use of Greek categories of thought with their pre-
sumptions of universality and absoluteness. Since "absolute" is a
characteristic reserved to divinity, one cannot strictly speaking apply it to any
created reality or to any bit of human knowledge. On the other hand, the view
of all creation as eschatological accords with the first of all biblical commands,
"I alone am the Lord, your God."

Indissolubility is an aspect of the intrinsic finality of any marriage, more
so of a Christian marriage because of its amplified significance. As such, it
shares in the responsibility to fulfill that finality which a woman and a man
undertake when they enter upon a marriage. Indissolubility is something they
should strive to intensify in their shared life. But that does not say that it is
impossible for them to fail at this task, impossible for the actual indissolubility
of a marriage to gradually weaken and ultimately disappear.

Perhaps we can and must say that the *promise* not to engage in marital
intimacy with any other person, the promise that each party made at the time
of beginning their marriage, remains in force no matter what happens. Perhaps
we can and must say that *responsibility* for the other which each undertook
upon becoming married rests permanently on each of them. But how can we
say that a relationship that in its human and existential aspects, and therefore
in its sacramentality, has dissolved is indissoluble.

The contemporary Church is rapidly regaining its sense of Christian existence as a process, a lifelong initiation into relationship with the Christian
community and with the risen Lord. This is the clear import of the post-Vatican
II revision of the rite for the initiation of adults. As in the past, liturgical action
points the way for our theological reflection and our doctrinal clarification: *lex
orandi, lex credendi.* "Being Christian" is something a person only gradually
and incompletely achieves.

For Christians, married life is meant to share in this initiation into Christ.
The clear conclusion is that an individual Christian marriage does not from its
first moments completely reflect the Christ-mystery, completely reflect the indissoluble bond of saving love that links Christ with his spouse, the Church,
any more than a person is completely Christian with baptism. One *becomes*
Christian; one *becomes* married.

By way of corollary, it might be well to extend these remarks to the notion
of marital consummation. There is a long history of the role of first sexual
intercourse between a couple as establishing a societal bond, and along with
this a long history of Christianity considering first marital intercourse as somehow intrinsic to the marriage contract and therefore to the very existence of the
marriage. I have no intention of summarizing, even briefly, that history.[7] Suf-
fice it to recall the operative Church law that regards a marriage soluble if it
is only *ratum* and not *consummatum*.

What I do wish to do is suggest the impropriety of such an abstract understanding of sexual intercourse, especially of marital intercourse. Only if one is regarding nothing more than the biological aspect of the action, or perhaps if one is regarding the act as one of establishing claim to and dominion over another person, can one possibly talk about the first act of intercourse as "consummation." It is true that for two people deeply in love, there is often profound meaning in their first full sexual intimacy, but theirs will be a sad married life if they do not progress in their self-giving far beyond this first experience.

Too much of the discussion of sexual intercourse among moral theologians and canonists has forgotten that it is a *human* activity, even though they have verbally nodded in that direction. Precisely because it is so human, distinctive with each couple, fragilely linked with all the other elements of a couple's relationship to one another, symbolically expressive of so much that cannot find explicit verbalization yet is itself in need of communication between persons to make its meaning clear, truly human sexual intercourse needs to be learned over a long period of time. And when one introduces Christian significance into this action so that it can become the heart of the marriage's sacramentality, the need for lifelong learning becomes only too apparent. Sexual intercourse does consummate Christian marriage, but only in this context of ongoing personal intimacy, for it can only authentically say what the two Christians honestly are for one another.

Tragically, very many marriages are scarcely consummated as personal relationships; they do not grow. Among these are many that begin in a Catholic wedding ceremony. If consummation is intrinsic to the establishment of a Christian marriage, one can only wonder how many marriages qualify as "Christian," and therefore how much claim they can lay to indissolubility.

Conclusions

Finally, what can one say by way of conclusion? Actually, the conclusions to my foregoing remarks are more a listing of questions.

1. To what extent does modern process view of reality affect the way in which we consider a particular Christian marriage as indissoluble?

2. If Christian couples themselves are the sacrament of Christian marriage, and couples obviously differ greatly in the extent to which they are genuinely Christian, to what extent is a particular marriage truly sacramental, to what extent does it actually symbolize the love between Christ and the Church?

3. And if the special indissolubility of *Christian* marriage is tied to sacramentality, in what way does indissolubility pertain to marriages that seem to have lost all operative sacramentality?

4. Or are we to say that the covenant pledge, with one's partner and with the Christian community, which one took at the wedding ceremony remains a

promise to the community even if the actual human marriage relationship dissolves? In this case the indissolubility attaches to the overall ecclesial sacramentality of the institution of Christian marriage rather than to the sacramentality of this or that particular marriage union.

5. But, to return to our emphasis on doing theology out of experience, is not the experience of "getting married" and the significance (sacramentality) attached to it one of promise to the other person rather than to the community?

6. Finally, it seems that we need a somewhat new though tradition-respecting look at indissolubility, to discover whether we are justified in applying it as absolutely as we Catholics have done in more recent centuries. It strikes me that a more flexible and individualized approach will still continue to honor the teaching that Christian marriage is of its nature indissoluble.

Notes

1. Cf. the volume *Consensus in Theology* (ed. L. Swidler, Philadelphia, 1980) in which the short descriptions of this shift by H. Küng and E. Schillebeeckx are followed by reactions of several present-day theologians.

2. While attention has focused on "process theology," i.e., the technical application of Whiteheadian philosophy to theological issues, the movement toward a process mentality is earlier and much broader. One can find clear traces of the shift in Catholic discussions of the nature of theology, such as Congar's article "Theologie" in the *Dictionnaire de theologie catholique* or G. Van Ackeren's 1949 study of "sacra doctrina" in Thomas Aquinas' *Summa theologica*. Perhaps the most telling documentation of the shift is contained in chapter seven of Vatican II's *Constitution on the Church* which deals with the eschatological character of the Church in history.

3. Vatican II, in its *Church and the Modern World* (n. 48) employed the category of "covenant" rather than "contract" to describe Catholic marriage, and this usage has carried over into the revised Code of Canon Law. Cf. M. Lawler, *Secular Marriage, Christian Sacrament*, 1985, pp. 50–54.

4. The past three or four decades have seen considerable scholarly research into the nature and function of Christian symbolism, especially liturgical symbols. For suggested descriptions of this shift toward deepened understanding, cf. section five (pp. 525–656) of my *Ministry to Word and Sacraments* and the more recent *Sacraments and Sacramentality*.

5. Cf. E. Schillebeeckx, *Marriage,* pp. 281–286, 302–343.

6. The term is specially associated with C. H. Dodd, but has been widely used by others.

7. It is treated at length and in detail by the works of Schillebeeckx and Mackin already cited.

RESPONSES

JACK DOMINIAN

For the past twenty-five years I have been dealing with broken marriages and have been a participant in the pain and the suffering that broken marriages produce and the adverse affect that they have on the children. I wonder if we can dismiss this pain and the adversity on children as easily as Dr. Cooke seems to have done. I wonder whether there is not something innately to be preserved as indissoluble in the continuation of the relationship. I know that suffering can go on in unsatisfactory marriages. But what we have learned in the last five years about the desires of children, for example, is that they want their parents to stay together even if they are unhappy. And so I'm wondering whether there isn't a human element of indissolubility in the very distress, the very pain that solubility solves.

The second point I would make about indissolubility is not from the covenant and eschatological point of view, but from the more direct point of view: the point of view that if you are aware that your marriage comes under God's umbrella, under God's protection, whether in fact in psychological terms this does not give you a motivation to try harder, to love more deeply, to respect more widely the other person. In looking at both Catholic and non-Catholic marriages daily in my work, I wonder whether we have a little example on our TV screens in England, trying to promote one type of battery. They show the battery that is promoted as struggling a bit further than all of the other batteries put together. I wonder if there isn't a Christian battery in this sacrament which motivates us, gives us the energy to try much harder to use the Christian language of forgiveness instead of the language of suppressed anger.

Finally, there is a question that I really want to put to Dr. Cooke and all theologians. Can we speak of indissolubility, whether in terms of the intrinsic nature of the marriage or in terms of eschatology, if we do not take account of the responsibility of the community for making that indissolubility possible? How can you talk of indissolubility if we have only woken up in the last ten or fifteen years about preparing people for marriage and supporting people for marriage? Is not an essential part of the indissolubility issue the question: what does the community do to support marriages and enable them to be indissoluble?

BERNARD COOKE

I am very glad that Dr. Dominian raised the points he did. I may very well have given the impression that Christian marriages are easily soluble. I certainly did not have that intention. It seems to me that what we are wrestling with are the situations that occur from time to time in which, after very responsible, valiant efforts, a marriage simply does not work out. Or the cases where one of the persons walks out of the marriage and the other person is simply left there. The question that emerges then is: Are they for the rest of their lives somehow in the situation of a one-sided contractual arrangement? I think I would agree entirely with the fact that indissolubility is, in one way or another, intrinsic to the human marriage situation. I think, as Dr. Dominian points out, what happens to children and the responsibility to children is a key issue, which I think reflects something about indissolubility.

One of the things that Dr. Dominian's last suggestion, I think, fits in with beautifully is the shift that takes place at the Second Vatican Council where the notion of contract is moved into the biblical category of covenant. Covenant, even if it is between two people, takes place within the context of a community. I agree with Dr. Dominian that there is a whole aspect of the covenanting that goes on between a man and a woman in a Christian community, that includes their commitment to the community to be sacrament in their midst, as well as the correlative obligation of the community which pledges itself to accepting these two, and to be a support to them.

THEODORE MACKIN

In your presentation you spoke of degrees of indissolubility. You talked about a union that is "increasingly indissoluble," which of course points to its correlate, a union which is less indissoluble. You also spoke of a marriage being "incompletely indissoluble." I have always thought that indissolubility is all or nothing. The canonical language of the Church which calls marriage indissoluble and then proceeds to dissolve it has bred that sarcasm which talks about two species of indissolubility: dissoluble indissolubility and indissoluble indissolubility.

What I wanted to ask you, Dr. Cooke, is whether it would not be a good idea to just avoid the whole vocabulary of indissolubility. I modestly suggest a replacement, a replacement that does admit of degrees: imperishability. In doing so I run the risk of perishable imperishability and imperishable imperishability. I realize that.

BERNARD COOKE

I have to think over whether perishability would be a better category. I rather suspect that we have something here that we are going to have to struggle with no matter what name we give it. For the good of the two people, for the good of the community as a whole, and for the good of the children of the couple, we do not want simply to dismiss the element of indissolubility or permanence. That would be a tragic mistake. On the other hand, I think there are situations where there has been great injustice done to the damaged or innocent party and where, through no fault of their own, the human situation of a marriage has simply evaporated. Is it justice to lay on such people the claim that they have to be faithful to a contract or a covenant when it is impossible for them to relate to the other person as a sign within the community, because that person has vanished or remarried? I think somehow we have to deal with this.

Part Two
Ethical and Canonical Issues

4.

Community and Couple: Parameters of Marital Commitment in Catholic Tradition

Lisa Sowle Cahill

To develop an effective contemporary theology and ethics of Christian marriage, it is important to revitalize the dialogue between the experience of married people and theological interpretations of it. The experience of marriage can be understood both as a personal relationship and as a social institution. While earlier in Judaeo-Christian history, the social, institutional contributions of marriage were stressed, there is a much greater tendency today to see marriage primarily as the relation of two personally committed spouses. It is important to recognize that these aspects are integrally related. For instance, the institutionalization of the roles of women and of men in marriage, family, and society helps determine the sorts of personal relationships which are possible between spouses.

A point of departure for the discussion of the relation between these two aspects will be the "personalism" of John Paul II in some of his addresses on marriage. Other examples will be provided from the writings of Catholic philosophers, theologians, and social scientists.

The theses of the presentation will be: (1) we need to give special attention to the ways in which the experience of marriage in the twentieth century West is similar to or different from that experience in other cultures and times; (2) these similarities and differences should have implications for normative Catholic teaching; (3) we need a critical integration of our views of the marital relation of husband and wife with the social context of marriage in family and in society.

It is clear to many in the Church today that a new beginning point in the experience of married persons is needed in the Catholic theology and ethics of marriage. This is not because the celibate clergy who have in the tradition made the most extensive contributions to a normative understanding of marriage are incapable of insights into an experience they do not share directly. A degree of distance from an experience can in fact assist appropriate analysis.[1] But since interpretation given by those outside a particular experience must rely on analogy to similar but different experiences, it seems difficult to deny that the testimony of married persons should have a prerogative in normative evalua-tions which it has not been granted thus far. Before we can give the experience of marriage its due weight, it will be important to consider more exactly what is meant by saying that this move is important, and why beginning with ex-perience is not as simple a task as it might at first appear.

First of all, experience is an important resource for Christian ethics in all areas but it is not the only source in any area. A Christian perspective on any moral issue derives from the interaction of a number of insights, which orig-inate in at least four basic reference points or sources. These are Scripture, tradition, philosophy, and descriptive or empirical information about human persons and communities. These sources are not separate, though they are somewhat distinct from one another. Any one is understood, implicitly or ex-plicitly, in relation to the others. For instance, the collection of biblical liter-ature already represents within itself several different strands of religious tradition, which evolved within faith communities over hundreds of years. In addition, when we read the words of Scripture today, we bring to them our own religious concepts and images, which will be in some ways the same as and in some ways different from those of the communities who originally pro-duced the biblical witness. Tradition, as another source, includes not only au-thoritative Church teachings, but also the faith and practice of the whole believing community more broadly understood. Philosophies of course can vary, and Christianity has borrowed from many over the centuries. The phi-losophy most central in Catholicism has been the ''natural law'' method which Thomas Aquinas developed from Aristotle. To speak of the natural law is to presuppose that there are some basic human moral values which are shared by all persons, no matter what their cultural or religious heritage. Last, but in a sense most fundamentally, is experience. It is important to grasp the reality of any act, situation, or relation which we intend to evaluate. This reality can be described in many ways, such as the personal story, or, in a more scientific manner, through biology, sociology, anthropology, and psychology. Although ideally all four major sources should be influential in Christian ethics, it is usually the case that our attention is focused explicitly on one or two, while the influence of the others becomes for a time less direct. Eventually, it will become necessary to shift the focus of attention so as to take into account the influence of sources and insights which may have been neglected. Today, this is the case with experience. In the past, Catholic teachings about sexuality and marriage have been based mostly on the natural law. In turn, what the natural law is said to require is determined in a context of great reliance on past teachings of the Church. Scripture and experience (including social-scientific studies) have been understood largely as supports for the natural law tradition. The task for Catholic Christian ethics today is to bring its interpretation of the human and Christian values which marriage represents back into fruitful contact with the actual lives of married persons.

To achieve this new beginning may be a complicated project. In the first place, "experience" is never "pure" and unmediated. For experience to have meaning and significance at all, it must be interpreted; that is, it must be received and appropriated in categories of value that provide intelligibility both to those who participate in the experience and to those to whom the experience is communicated. In the case of marriage, there is already a strong normative tradition in Catholicism which provides such categories: monogamy, indissolubility, inseparability of procreation and sexual acts, the dangerous quality of sexual pleasure, to name a few. For experience to serve as a beginning point will require not that all categories be set aside, for that is impossible (without categories there is no understanding), but that categories be truly exposed to a *critical* movement between the theological traditions they represent and the *de facto* relationships which they supposedly explain. This means that honest reflection on the experience of marriage cannot begin with an a priori commitment to render the traditional categories in more or less the traditional ways, when all is said and done. To do this would be to short-circuit the mutually revelatory dialectic between theology and experience. Also required is a recognition of the extent to which Catholic married people tend to mediate their experience (even to themselves) in received categories, without allowing the real texture of their relationships to pose serious questions to their religious and moral vocabularies.

On the other side, the fact that intelligible experience never is unmediated also supplies grounds for relying upon the *prima facie* authority of those categories which have been most central in a religious or moral tradition to whose essential truth we are committed. Examples from the Catholic tradition of marriage are the importance of commitment and fidelity, the link between being a spouse and being a parent, the coherence of the "Christian" and the "natural" meanings of important human relationships such as marriage and parenthood, and the reciprocity of the personal and social dimensions of such relationships. The challenge of experience is to examine whether some of these categories can be articulated in new and better ways, and whether there are layers or aspects of experience which would emerge more fully to consciousness if our descriptive and evaluative concepts could more flexibly elucidate them.

Even after the critical dialectic between experience and categories is recognized, difficulties remain. The fact that the experience of everyone is not the same seems true in a special way for marriage. Perhaps even more prominently than it is a personal and sexual relationship, marriage is a social institution. It is undergirded by and opens out to family and society in ways which can vary drastically with culture and era, and which impinge radically on the nature of the relations between wife and husband, parents and children, and sisters and brothers. It might not be going too far to say that the institutionalization of marriage determines these relationships. An intimate interpersonal relation of equal affection and responsibility between spouses *is not possible* in a culture in which both men and women see the husband as the superior, controlling partner. Conversely, the integration of spouses and their children into a network of familial investment in and social support for the success of a marital relationship *is not possible* in a culture in which romantic involvement and reciprocal self-fulfillment are viewed as the purposes of marriage and the responsibilities solely of two autonomous agents, freely contracting to realize them. Thus the "experience" of marriage never can be severed from the particular social, religious, and moral milieu in which it arises and out of which particular interpreters express it. This is not to say there are no "constants" in the experience of marriage. It is rather to call for another continual, mutually critical dialogue, this time among cultures past and present. Only on the basis of the dialogues between theology and experience, and among the complex, varied experiences of individuals and of groups, can we understand the reality of Christian marriage and rearticulate that reality in categories which are at once more descriptively accurate and more helpful in evaluating marriage's successes and failures.[2]

Marriage as Couple or Marriage as Family?

Two aspects of marriage can be contrasted: the interpersonal and the social. The importance of each can be substantiated by any one of the four sources of ethics, and is certainly reinforced when we view the experience of the married and their families. Although both aspects are essential to marriage, the aspects which a thinker, group or culture takes to be primary can color the analysis of marriage in decisive ways. In more traditional soceieties both secular and religious, marriages tend to be seen as links within a larger family structure, in whose framework they have meaning and which they perpetuate.

The social, economic, and especially procreative contributions of the spouses to this larger, encompassing order are paramount. In turn, the family sustains marital relationships, with economic, psychological, and even procreative support. The practice of levirate marriage in ancient Israel (Gen 38:8; Dt 25:5–10) is an example of this interdependence, as are marriage customs in some twentieth century "pre-industrial" societies. At the 1980 Synod on the Family, the bishops from Zaire reported: "The importance which is attached to the marital bond by the family is evident from the care with which the family group prepares for and progressively works out its institution."[3] To cement or dissolve the marriage is not the decision of the couple alone, but a decision in which both families have considerable economic and social stakes. Since family structures in pre-modern societies are distinctively patriarchal, family-oriented marriages typically are patriarchal also, even allowing for quite variable influence of women within those structures (cf. Prov 31:3–31).

The most influential author in post-Reformation Catholic thought, Thomas Aquinas, takes a solidly communal view of marriage. Even while he follows tradition and his culture in subordinating the wife to the husband, he does achieve some original insights into the quality of their relation as "friendship." This friendship is intensified by sexual expression and has a highly personal quality. Nonetheless, the primary purpose of sex is to serve the human community through procreation, and the primary definition of marriage is as domestic and social partnership, rather than interpersonal fulfillment.[4]

An alternative approach to marriage is to take as its paramount meaning the relation between the two spouses, especially its sexual expression. While the social implications of this relation hardly go unrecognized, it is the union of the two partners which forms the basis or "bottom line" of the theological and moral evaluation of marriage. Examples are Augustine's preoccupation with the problematic nature of sexual acts and their justification within marriage, Roman Catholic Canon Law with its stress on consent and consummation (almost conflated in the 1917 Code's emphasis on the *jus in corpus* as that to which consent is given[5]), the predilection of modern papal teaching to focus on the ostensibly "natural" meanings of sexual intercourse and to identify these with the purposes of marriage, and some recent Roman Catholic writings about marriage which elaborate its "sacramentality" in terms of the love union of the couple, culminating in sexual intercourse.[6]

Most Western Christians today take it for granted that the individuality of neither wife nor husband, nor their intimate relationship, ought to be subordinated almost entirely to the interests of family, tribe, or nation. What is not so clearly a part of the Western consciousness is the degree to which a "marriage" is a nexus of interdependent relations among couple, family, and larger social arrangements. We tend to idealize and isolate the couple in their love,

their freedom, and their responsibility, and so to arrive at an unrealistic or sim-
plistic view of the many elements which constitute a marriage, contributing to
its success or failure.

Recent Papal Teaching

As a focus for my discussion of contemporary Catholic views of marriage, I will take the thought of the present Pope as expressed especially in his
"Apostolic Exhortation on the Family" (*Familiaris Consortio,* 1981) and in
some of his Wednesday general audience talks on "The Theology of the
Body" (1979–81).[7] This will not be a comprehensive study, but will briefly
illustrate the direction of the thought of John Paul II by means of his phrase
"the nuptial meaning of the body." This phrase occurs during the Pope's
"Catechesis on the Book of Genesis" (the first part of the "Theology of the
Body" series) and is a commentary on the exclamation of Adam, "This at last
is bone of my bone and flesh of my flesh" (Gen 2:23). John Paul's thesis is
that the statement expresses the man's recognition of the woman's human identity, manifested bodily not only as "femininity" but also as "the reciprocity
and communion of persons" which sexual difference makes possible. This is
said to be substantiated by the fact that the following verse "establishes their
conjugal unity" (Gen 2:24, "Therefore a man leaves his father and his mother
and cleaves to his wife, and they become one flesh"), and that it is testified
that they are naked before one another without shame (Gen 2:25). The "nuptial
meaning of the body" so disclosed is "the fundamental element of human existence in the world," and consists in the fact that "a creature God willed for
its own sake . . . can fully discover its true self only in a sincere giving of
self."[8] The Pope, conflating the creation stories in the first two chapters of
Genesis, tells his audience that, moreover,

> Genesis 2:24 speaks of the finality of man's masculinity and femi-
> ninity, in the life of the spouses-parents. Uniting with each other so
> closely as to become "one flesh," they will subject, in a way, their
> humanity to the blessing of fertility, namely, "procreation," of
> which the first narrative speaks (Gen 1:28).[9]

There are several undoubtedly positive things to be said about John Paul's
exposition of these texts. The first is that he attempts to engage the Roman
Catholic view of marriage with relevant biblical accounts, and to recover elements which are more distinctively "Christian" than the standard "natural
law" analysis of the "ends" of marriage and of sexual acts. Second, he por-
trays the sexuality of the man and the woman as enabling a mutual relation of

self-donation. The affirmative and egalitarian tone of the portrayal sets it apart from virtually all official Catholic statements before the Second Vatican Council. Third, the influence of "personalist" philosophy on the Pope's approach allows him to introduce into the ethics of sex and marriage the importance of the intersubjective relation of the spouses, and also to portray this relation in terms of high interpersonal ideals, which open onto the Christian ideal of self-offering love. Finally, the Pope transforms the traditional Roman Catholic reading of the "nature" of sexuality so that it not only includes both physical and psychological aspects, but also integrally relates the two aspects in the "nuptial" meaning of sexual acts. The person is embodied as a sexual being in whom physical and spiritual aspects coalesce in interaction with another.

Now for the problems. Most Catholics, including John Paul II, have not worked out adequately the relation of biblical evidence to traditional theological and moral commitments. The fact that Catholic thinkers are not always well informed regarding critical historical studies of the texts they desire to use has not assisted the process. I will mention just three of the things such studies may indicate about the texts in question. First of all, the personalist language of "mutual self-gift" and "total surrender" of spouses through sexual union does not fit comfortably into Israelite views of marriage, nor even into the Genesis creation stories, though the latter are quite exceptional in the originally equal status given to the woman, and in the importance given to the couple as distinct from the family. It might be better, though, to speak of the "unity" of the couple, or even the "equality" of spouses, than of the intersubjective "gift" which John Paul II wants to associate with the body's "nuptial" meaning. It is easier to get intersubjectivity out of personalist philosophy than out of the biblical accounts he is using this philosophy to interpret. Secondly, neither the first nor the second creation story speaks of the institution of "marriage" as such, and certainly not of any "sacramental" marriage. Finally, the "one flesh" unity of Genesis 2 is proposed in the context more of social partnership than of a procreative one. The "blessing of increase" in Genesis 1:28—"Be fruitful . . ."—is not directly associated with the "one flesh" unity (Gen 2:23–24) of two equal partners who are interpersonally commited to one another, but with the responsibility of each species to perpetuate its own kind.[10] I do not mean to suggest that any theological interpretation is wrong if it goes beyond demonstrably "biblical" views, but rather to call for more explicit and nuanced development of the method or means by which one moves from biblical "evidence" to a contemporary interpretation, and for the justification of such means.

Another difficulty is whether the biblical ideals, or even the Pope's extrapolation of a "nuptial" significance of the body, really yields the norm that every authentically loving sexual union also will be procreative. In *Familiaris Consortio,* referring to the teaching of Paul VI (*Humanae Vitae*) that the "conjugal act'' has a ''unitive'' meaning and a ''procreative'' one which are ''inseparable,'' John Paul II expands in language which recalls the personalist approach of his ''Theology of the Body'':

> When couples, by means of recourse to contraception, separate these two meanings that God the Creator has inscribed in the being of man and woman and in the dynamism of their sexual communion, they act as ''arbiters'' of the divine plan and they ''manipulate'' and degrade human sexuality and with it themselves and their married partner by altering its value of ''total'' self-giving. Thus the innate language that expresses the total reciprocal self-giving of husband and wife is overlaid, through contraception, by an objectively contradictory language, namely, that of not giving oneself totally to the other. This leads not only to a positive refusal to be open to life, but also to a falsification of the inner truth of conjugal love, which is called upon to give itself in personal reality (n. 32).[11]

Denise Lardner Carmody remarks on a ''questionable—even unseemly— tendency''[12] of the Pope to interpret the experience of married women (and men) rather than letting them speak for themselves. In this interpretation the temptation to read the experience so as to fit the already standard categories is not entirely withstood. More serious dialogue with married persons about the relation of having children to their conjugal commitment and to their sex lives (especially ''each and every act''!) is in order. We shall return to this dialogue below.

Last but not least—indeed the thing that most strikes me about the Pope's development of ''the nuptial meaning of the body''—is its isolation from the social conditions necessary for its realization, especially the structure and social location of the family, and the roles of women within the family.

What view of family would seem to be suggested when one understands sexuality in terms of a ''nuptial meaning of the body''? The stress on the mutual self-gift of the couple really places attention on their free, interpersonal relationship rather than on their extended families, or the social, economic, or religious communities within which first the man and the woman, and then the conjugal couple, take on an identity. But certainly these other realms of meaning help determine whether a ''mutual self-gift'' is possible and even in what manner ''self'' and ''mutuality'' are defined. The Pope seems to present complete and equal freedom and reciprocity of wife and husband not merely as an ideal to be achieved but as the very *description* of a genuine male-female love relationship. To what extent can this description be accurate if, for instance, there do not exist equal social resources in support of the personal freedom and marital and parental commitment of husband and wife?

A telling point in the papal view is his discussion of "fecundity." The duties and rewards of parenthood today can be shared more or less equally by father and mother. But to what extent are the familial and social *implications* of conjugal equality appreciated? In *Familiaris Consortio,* John Paul II develops further the meanings both of marriage and of parenthood. The decision to marry is described in what seem to me, by virtue of the number of absolutes used, quite ideal terms: it is a decision of the partners "to commit by their irrevocable conjugal consent their whole lives in indissoluble love and unconditional fidelity" (n. 68). As we have seen, "manipulation" of sexual "communion" through contraception is said to be excluded by this love and fidelity (n. 32). The family, paralleling the couple, is also said to be an "intimate community of life and love" (n. 50) which builds up "the kingdom of God" (n. 49) through "generous fruitfulness," "solidarity and faithfulness" and by working together in a "loving way" (n. 50).

What is meant by this concretely? I cannot help but wonder whether the Pope's ideal is not accompanied by rather traditional views of gender roles in marriage and family, in which the woman is in the home ready to welcome new life whenever it might appear, and to nurture both children and husband through whatever hard times the world "outside" the family presents to its "interior" life.

To the Pope's credit, at least in my view, are the portions of his "exhortation" which deal with the roles of women in society and of men in the home as husbands and fathers. He explicitly links "the equal dignity and responsibility of women with men" to "reciprocal self-giving" in marriage and family (n. 22). He also claims that "women's access to public functions" is "fully" justified. Some ambivalence about this claim, though, may be revealed in the qualification which follows it: "On the other hand the true advancement of women requires that clear recognition be given to the value of their maternal and family role, by comparison with all other public roles and all other professions" (n. 23). The role of the father in the family also is said to be "unique" and "irreplaceable." The father seems called on particularly to share with his wife the "development" and "education" of their children but this is not contrasted with the importance of his other roles, nor is it explicitly suggested that the father share in the less elevated duties associated with the daily routines of child care and household maintenance. Jan Grootaers and Joseph A. Selling, Christian husbands as well as theologians, comment with regard to this text:

> As was foreshadowed in his "homily," John Paul is definitely more in favor of married women remaining in the home. Again, no one will dispute the fact that women who do devote themselves full time to child care are performing a task and following a profession on an equal footing with other professions. However, this is not really the

issue. There is a much deeper question of role identification and human classification which has always managed to keep women "in their place" and substantiate genuine discrimination and prejudice against them.[13]

There remains a tension in contemporary Catholic teaching as represented by John Paul II between traditional (patriarchal) views of women, family and marriage, and a budding awareness that these views have had oppressive consequences for both women and men, and that attention to more equal roles is a *sine qua non* of credibility in twentieth century Western theology. At one level, the theoretical, equality is endorsed; but at the *practical* level, the conditions and consequences of true, effective equality are not followed out or perhaps even recognized.

One issue here is the experience or *Sitz im Leben* out of which one speaks. I am fascinated in this regard by an essay by Wanda Poltawska, M.D., who is at present and was under Cardinal Wojtyla the head of the Institute for the Theology of the Family, Pontifical Faculty of Theology of Krakow, Poland. She also is a member of the Pontifical Council for the Family in the Vatican. Discussing the values to be imparted in Catholic sex education, she draws on the personalism of Wojtyla and has this to say about the meaning of human sexuality in relation to the roles of male and female in the family:

> The correct model of a father, responsible for the destiny of his family, causes admiration and high regard; the model of the mother, tenderly loving and caring for all the needs of the child, gives a sense of security. No programs of sexual education will provide what the strong arms of the father and the tender hands of the mother embracing the family transmit to the children. The child learns love at home, and only then is born that deepest reality—the correct interpersonal relationship of the "communion of persons."[14]

The "correct" relation of spouses here described does not explicitly assign the woman a domestic role and the father a public one. But it certainly does assign them psychological and emotional roles which are usually associated with such social divisions. The father is a "strong" and "responsible" leader, while the mother, "tender" and "loving," provides for "all" the requirements of child care. Some theologians in Western Europe and North America find this depiction less than convincing. They often draw on the human and social sciences for improved understandings of the actual situations of married persons and families, and not infrequently provide or rely on feminist critiques of traditional family and marriage.

Next, I will examine a few representative contributions which critically analyze marriage as social institution on the basis of sociology and of feminism and some of which reexamine the psycho-social relation of the couple.

Critiques: The Social Context

In an especially perceptive essay exploring the shifting social context of Christian family life, Lorenz Wachinger highlights seven factors: longer average duration of marriage, calling for more numerous adjustments over the life cycle; rising rates of divorce, especially as initiated by women; sexual liberalization; equal rights and educational and career opportunities for women, making them less dependent; personalization of marriage, involving greater emotional dependence between spouses; marriage and family as a private realm; added emphasis on communication and conflict resolution.[15] Critiques by Catholic feminists such as Rosemary Radford Ruether are even more pointed. Ruether sees the modern Western family to be in a state of crisis created by patriarchy and industrialism, which institutionalize role division and fail to ensure adequate income for all families. In alliance with an "exploitative profit economy" is "a schizophrenic culture that divides home and work into separate spheres, segregates women as primary parents in a privatized domestic culture and alienates the male as worker from co-parenting." Women cannot gain economic independence or even education and cultural development without going outside the home and thus somehow "contradicting" the family roles assigned to them. Ruether calls for a "realignment" of home and work, family and society which would allow both sexes full participation in both public and domestic spheres.[16] Such a restructuring would, however, call for significant cultural shifts such as the serious commitment of resources to parenting by both men and women (including appropriate levels of outside child care). The Church is invoked in support of a "Christian vision of the redeemed society as a new community of equals," and in the creation of "a new understanding of family as committed communities of mutual service."[17]

Critiques: The Marital Relationship

Over and above the question of the appropriate reading of the *social conditions* permitting conjugal equality and commitment in marriage is that of the true reading of the *conjugal relationship* itself, especially in its sexual expression. As we have seen, the psychological dimensions of this relationship are related to contextual factors in family and society. Further, the categories with which this relation may be interpreted theologically are related to these same factors. In her critique and positive recommendations, Ruether is skillful at avoiding an overly *individualized* notion of the equal partnership of spouses within a nuclear family. She sets the relation of spouses within the context of social conditions and responsibilities, suggesting by implication that the success of a marriage or of "marital intimacy" is crucially related to factors beyond the intentional commitment of the partners as such.[18] Sensitivity to these influential factors no doubt can be heightened by participation in a marriage in which intimacy and commitment are not achieved without difficulty deriving at least partially from them.[19]

Yet the contributions of experiential accounts to the theology and ethics of marriage enter not only at the social level, but also at the level of the conjugal relation as a relation between two committed individuals. As I have indicated, recent Roman Catholic teaching tends to portray this relation in idealized, even romanticized terms, to focus disproportionately on sexual intercourse as the epitome of the spousal partnership, to focus on sexual relations in discussions of marital morality, and to delimit the moral boundaries of sexual relations in a manner which is derived directly from past Church teaching, which does not seem seriously open to reevaluation in the light of marital experience, and which seems to presuppose fairly traditional, patriarchal views of women and family. Certainly not all married Catholic theologians would refute this interpretation.[20] At this point we enter into the critical dialectic between categories and experience. In my judgment, at this time in the history of the Catholic tradition of sexuality and marriage, it is important to avoid using experience simply to "exemplify" categories already assumed inflexible, and instead to concentrate on the discernment of areas of experience to which these categories have not drawn our attention or from which they even have distracted us.

One example of an attempt to do this is the work of Mary Durkin, who is committed both to working critically within the recent papal tradition as expressive of important religious values and to "a better understanding of the lived experience of marital intimacy" accomplished through "the ongoing experience of various individuals and groups."[21] An important effort in the development of such an understanding was Durkin's participation in a two year (four meetings) colloquium, among social scientists and theologians. The colloquium attempted to let the "life wisdom of the participants and the perspectives of the social sciences" speak before theological categories and evaluations "moved in."[22] The result was a cyclical interpretation of marital intimacy, a view of marital intimacy as paradigmatic for other intimacy relationships, and a commitment to a sacramental understanding of marriage as revealing the mystery of the divine presence. The cycles named may not fit the experience of every married couple but they are tied in concrete, commonsense ways to the role of sexual attraction in evoking opportunities for intimacy, to the many barriers great and small which deter all married persons at least some of the time from total intimacy, to the reality and even probability of marital discord, dissatisfaction, or boredom, and to the possibility of making a difficult relationship better if the partners use imagination and try to maximize any positive experiences still remaining in their relationship. The cycles are described as "the falling in love of courtship and early marriage," "the settling down of the early years," "the painful bottoming out due to surface harmony," and "the beginning again of recapturing the beginnings and moving upward, reborn and renewed."[23] The authors do not deny that it is in fact possible for some marriages to fail, or that some marriages may be so destructive for one or both partners that to end is better than to continue. They do resist the tendency to dissolve a relationship because it has come upon hard times, or because it becomes apparent that it does not measure up to the ideal for which the couple may have hoped. They urge spouses to build on the commitment they have made, and to seek actively opportunities for making their relation a more satisfying one. The morality of particular sexual acts deliberately was not a focus for the group. The theme throughout was "a vision of healthy marital sexual intimacy" which allowed a "sexual scenario" individual to the love of each couple, and not prescribed by the equally rigid codes of the "old" or of the "new" morality.[24]

Durkin herself has developed this vision in more specific ways in the form of a response to John Paul's "Theology of the Body." In *Feast of Love,* she ties the papal ideals more closely to experience. For one thing, though endorsing the Pope's affirmation of marriage and sexuality, she is much more attentive to the difficulties couples must surmount to realize these relations positively. In regard to the "nuptial meaning of the body" she observes that many persons do not have a sense of self-worth about their bodies or their sexual identities, are ignorant about their own bodily responses and needs or cannot communicate them to their partners, are physically and emotionally lazy about the effort required to maintain intimacy, or at least sometimes want to retain "control" through solitude more than they want to share in a "communion of persons."[25]

Durkin does see parenthood as an important part of marriage but sets it in the larger context of a "generativity" which extends beyond the parenting role.[26] Although she thinks that "a bodily act that leads to reproduction is part of an ongoing commitment to form a union that will reflect the glory of God,"[27] she warns nevertheless that because of the historical need for reproduction, "we have tended to overemphasize the reproductive aspects of sexuality and, consequently, we have subjected our sexuality to criteria that judge how it influences reproduction."[28] She also has stated that the assertion of a moral difference between artificial and natural methods of regulating birth and "the claim that contraception contradicts the total reciprocal self-giving of husband and wife" "do not seem to relate to the actual experiences of many people.'' Indeed, more needed in the marital experience of many is encouragement to *nurture* their sexual attraction, rather than to control and restrain it.[29]

To be noted also and commended is the contribution of David M. Thomas in his recent book, *Christian Marriage*.[30] Experience-based and committed to the general parameters of the Catholic tradition, it has much in common with Durkin's approach. Taking note as she does of the positive and negative phases of any marital ''journey,'' Thomas places perhaps more emphasis on distinctively Christian values. He notes the importance of humility in defining marriage, and of cross, forgiveness and even will power in living it out successfully. He too sees marital sex as integrally related to having children, but relates it more basically to the commitment of wife and husband to each other, and I think avoids the temptation to overinterpret the significance of sexual acts as the occasions on which the relationship as a whole is at its peak moments.[31] This is consistent with recent suggestions of moral theologians and canonists that *love* is the basic meaning and ''end'' of marriage, even though marital love has sex as its expression and children as its outcome. Authors differ still on how necessary this outcome is to a ''complete'' or ''Christian'' marriage, and on what means legitimately may be taken to avoid or space children.[32]

The social dimensions of the love which is fruitful in children are not to be forgotten. As feminists and social scientists have pointed out, the successful and satisfying nurturance of children within a cohesive family is not contingent simply on the ''commitment'' and ''generosity'' of parents but requires certain forms of social support for the family as a unit and for all its members. On the other side the purpose of having children is not merely the fulfillment of their parents, nor even the expression and perfection of the parents' love. Through the birth and education of children, married persons may make a contribution to the larger human communities, particularly of the next generation. To bring up children well is to exercise a responsibility to others and to teach children that social responsibilities belong also to them.

Conclusions

In pursuit of better understanding of the essential character of Christian marriage, I would like to venture a definition of marital ''love,'' which is undisputedly the quality by which it should above all be characterized. The love which belongs in marriage is a *commitment to partnership,* that is a *commitment to achieve* social and domestic cooperation, mutual and equal respect, understanding and support, permanent fidelity, and the forgiveness which will be necessary to go beyond the inevitable failures in the realization of these ideals.

I think this definition would withstand the institutionalization of marriage in both traditional and modern cultures, even though I do not think all cultures have institutionalized marriage in ways which are of equal value. For example, the definition does not exclude love from polygamous marriages though I believe monogamy is a far superior setting for equality and mutual respect. (I would also stress that what I have defined is marital "love," not *marriage* in the legal or institutional senses, which may not require "love" at all.) This commitment is expressed in and intensified by sexual union, but does not consist preeminently in it. Both the sexual union and the intentional commitment can express or even help create the affective, emotional dimension of marital love, but the good faith commitment is more definitive of marital love than the emotional response. I hesitate to say that the desire or attempt to have children is definitive of "marital love," though I am willing to venture that having children expresses the love of spouses more fully and enhances it. This statement, like others about marriage and sexuality, should be taken at the rather abstract level of an ideal or generalization, not as a specific or inflexible moral norm. In all areas of marital commitment—marital friendship or "intimacy," marital sexuality, and the fulfillment of the social roles of spouses, parents, and family—experiential situations are always diverse, and are often compromises with or adjustments to preexisting factors which are less than ideal. These situations usually manage to challenge our attempts to capture their reality with categories induced from other, albeit similar, experiences. We need not capitulate to the sort of relativism which throws up its hands in the face of complexity and abandons any further search for common ground. After all, a key commitment of the Catholic tradition of theology and ethics has been to seek out objectivity and shared values. However, it is important to insist that in the discussion of marriage, as in other realms of Christian ethics, the critical dialogues must go on, for "objectivity," "values," and "common ground" are disclosed and given substance only in and through the lives of many individuals, relations, and communities.

Notes

1. For a historical study of marriage in Catholic tradition, see Theodore Mackin, S.J., *Marriage in the Catholic Church: What Is Marriage?* (New York/Ramsey: Paulist Press, 1982). Also relevant are John T. Noonan, Jr., *Contraception: A History of Its Treatment by Catholic Theologians and Canonists* (Cambridge MA: Harvard University Press, 1965), and Anthony Kos-

nick, *et al., Human Sexuality: New Directions in American Catholic Thought* (New York/Paramus/Toronto: Paulist Press, 1977).

2. See a special issue of the *Journal of Ecumenical Studies* on "Marriage in the World Religions," edited by Arlene Swidler (22/1; Winter 1985). Traditions included are Judaism, Orthodoxy, Catholicism, Protestantism, Islam, Hinduism, and Buddhism. Also see summaries of episcopal position papers from Black Africa, Southeast Asia, Latin America, and North America in *The 1980 Synod of Bishops "On the Role of the Family": An Exposition of the Event and an Analysis of Its Texts,* by Jan Grootaers and Joseph A. Selling (Leuven: Leuven University Press, 1983), pp. 29–65. In the preface to this volume, Louis Janssens writes,

> I find it impressive that this study of a Synod which dealt with the role of the family has been written by two married Christians. They write in a realistic way, informed by their own daily experience. They are also rather hesitant to accept a deductive method of reasoning which too easily results in abstract conceptions having little to do with reality. Both contributions demonstrate the enriching character of their reflections which are grounded in the personally experienced givens of marriage and family life (p. i).

3. Grootaers and Selling, p. 31.

4. See the *Summa theologiae* II-II. Q 153; *ST Suppl.* Q 49, 65, 67; *Summa Contra Gentiles* 3/III. 123, 126.

5. On this, see Geoffrey Robinson, "Unresolved Questions in the Theology of Marriage," *Jurist* 43 (1983), pp. 69–102.

6. An example of this latter interpretation is Charles A. Gallagher, George A. Maloney, Mary F. Rousseau and Paul F. Wilczak, *Embodied in Love: Sacramental Spirituality and Sexual Intimacy; A New Catholic Guide to Marriage* (New York: Crossroad, 1983). See also n. 30 below.

7. The "Theology of the Body" series by John Paul II is published in three volumes by the Daughters of St. Paul (Boston). They are *Original Unity of Man and Woman: Catechesis on the Book of Genesis* (1981); *Blessed are the Pure of Heart: Catechesis on the Sermon on the Mount and Writings of St. Paul* (1983); *Reflections on Humanae Vitae: Conjugal Morality and Spirituality* (1984). *Familiaris Consortio* (Apostolic Exhortation "On the Family") is available from the United States Catholic Conference, 1312 Massachusetts Ave., N.W., Washington, D.C. This document and commentaries are collected in Reverend Michael J. Wrenn, ed., *Pope John Paul II and the Family* (Chicago: Franciscan Herald Press, 1983). Rev. Richard M. Hogan and Rev. John M. LeVoir offer commentaries on many of the Pope's writings in *Covenant of Love: Pope John Paul II on Sexuality, Marriage, and Family in the*

Modern World (Garden City, NY: Doubleday and Co., Inc., 1985). They introduce the Pope's thought as "the priceless gift of the truth in the teaching of the present successor to Saint Peter" (p. xi). Appreciative but somewhat more critical approaches are adopted by Grootaers and Selling, and by Mary G. Durkin, *Feast of Love: Pope John Paul II on Human Intimacy* (Chicago: Loyola University Press, 1983). An apology for the tradition which the Pope represents is Rev. Ronald Lawler, O.F.M. Cap., Joseph Boyle, Jr. and William E. May, *Catholic Sexual Ethics: A Summary, Explanation, & Defense* (Huntington, IN: Our Sunday Visitor, Inc., 1985).

8. Quotations taken from John Paul II, *Original Unity*, pp. 109–10, 119.

9. *Ibid.*, p. 111.

10. See Phyllis A. Bird, " 'Male and Female He Created Them': Gen 1:27b in the Context of the Priestly Account of Creation," *Harvard Theological Review* 74/2 (1981), pp. 129–59.

11. Compare the language of John Paul II with that of Paul VI in Humanae Vitae, n. 13: to use contraception is to act "in contradiction with the design constitutive of marriage. . . ."

12. Denise Lardner Carmody, "Marriage in Roman Catholicism," *Journal of Ecumenical Studies* 22/1 (Winter, 1985), p. 38.

13. Grootaers and Selling, p. 314. Mary G. Durkin remarks of *Familiaris Consortio* that

> though there are some references to an anthropological understanding of the family, the implications of an evolutionary perspective on human sexuality and marital intimacy are not specifically addressed. The interplay between the sexual, psychological, and social dimensions of marital intimacy is not acknowledged. Indeed, much of the attention to sexual intimacy is linked to its reproductive possibilities, leading us to wonder if the agenda of previous cultures and their interests are not active here (p. 56 in "Love and Intimacy: Revealing God in Family Relationships," in Stanley L. Saxton, Patricia Voydanoff, Angela Ann Zukowski, eds., *The Changing Family: Views from Theology and the Social Sciences in the Light of the Apostolic Exhortation Familiaris Consortio* [Chicago: Loyola University Press, 1982]).

14. Wanda Poltawska, M.D., "The Church and Human Sexuality," *Catholic Medical Quarterly* 36/2 (1985), p. 98; also reprinted in *Linacre Quarterly* 52 (1985), pp. 349–360. For a similar view by another Polish author, see W.B. Skrzydlewski, O.P., "Conflict and Schism in Moral Theology and Sexual Ethics," *Homiletic and Pastoral Review* 85/8 (May 1985), pp. 23–32.

15. Lorenz Wachinger, "Die christliche Ehe and Familie: Ihre Chancen und Probleme heute," *Stimmen der Zeit* 203 (1984), pp. 170–180. See also Elisabeth van der Lieth, "Pädagogische Aspekte kirchlicher Lehrschreiben zur Sexualität," *Stimmen der Zeit* 202 (1984), pp. 743–754. Van der Lieth comments on *Familiaris Consortio,* and maintains that the anthropology behind official Church teaching does not ring true to the experience of those whom it addresses. A rigid handing on of past formulations is likely to cause the very confusion it is supposed to avoid.

16. Rosemary Radford Ruether, "Church and Family V: Feminism, Church and Family in the 1980s," *New Blackfriars* 65/767 (May 1985), especially 209–211. Related social-scientific analyses are given by Dana V. Hiller, "Sex Equality, Women's Employment, and the Family," and Patricia Voydanoff, "Changing Roles of Men and Women: The Emergence of Symmetrical Families," in Saxton *et al.,* eds. *The Changing Family* (citation in n. 13 above), pp. 109–124 and 125–137, respectively.

17. Ruether, pp. 210–211.

18. See Theo J. Majka, "The Family in Social-Historical Perspective," on the socially egalitarian base required for a "companionate affective family," and Voydanoff on the relation of "symmetrical role allocation" to marital and family "solidarity," both in Saxton *et al.,* eds., pp. 171–188 and 125–137, respectively.

19. Eileen Zieget Silberman details many of these in *The Savage Sacrament: A Theology of Marriage after American Feminism* (Mystic CN: Twenty-Third Publication, 1983). She focuses on unjust role expectations for women. She is also sensitive to the positive aspects of Christian marriage and family, and suggests a reorganization of these institutions rather than abandonment of them.

20. See William E. May, "The Vatican Declaration on Sexual Ethics and the Moral Methodology of Vatican Council II," *Linacre Quarterly* 52 (1985), pp., 116–129; and Lawler, Boyle, and May, *Catholic Sexual Ethics.*

21. Durkin, "Love and Intimacy," p. 61.

22. Joan Meyer Anzia, M.D. and Mary G. Durkin, D.Mn., *Marital Intimacy: A Catholic Perspective* (Chicago: Loyola University Press, 1980), p. 3.

23. *Ibid.,* p. 10.

24. *Ibid.,* p. 11.

25. Durkin, *Feast of Love,* pp. 59–61.

26. *Ibid.,* pp. 91–92. Another important experience-based contribution is William Johnson Everett's *Blessed Be the Bond: Christian Perspectives on Marriage and Family* (Philadelphia: Fortress, 1985). Everett carefully distinguishes the often interdependent but distinct relations of marriage and parenthood.

27. *Ibid.*, p. 219.

28. *Ibid.*, p. 218.

29. *Ibid.*, pp. 58–59.

30. David M. Thomas, *Christian Marriage: A Journey Together* (Wilmington: Michael Glazier, Inc., 1983).

31. A well-intentioned study which, to my eye, goes too far in this direction is Gallagher *et al.*, *Embodied in Love*. Is it really true that "the divine life" is revealed in marriage most of all in orgasm (p. 32)? Or is it in the faithful partnership, the journey through good times and bad, which is the ensemble of all marital acts and not just sexual ones? Is it true to experience to say that "sexual passion . . . must be the total aura and context of the life of the spouses" (p. 41)? Can it possibly be true that "every encounter between (any) two persons, even a simple 'Good Morning,' . . . must be sexual and passionate" (p. 119)?

32. See Carmody, "Marriage in Roman Catholicism;" John R. Connery, "The Role of Love in Marriage: A Historical Overview," *International Catholic Review: Communio* 11 (1984), pp. 244–257; Dennis J. Burns, "The Sacrament of Marriage," *Chicago Studies* 23 (1984), pp. 63–76; and Walter Kasper, *Theology of Christian Marriage* (New York: Crossroad, 1981), especially pp. 17–21, on procreative responsibility.

RESPONSES

PHEME PERKINS

First of all I appreciate Lisa's attempt to try to move us out of a kind of narrow focus on marriage, and to call our attention to the cultural context, as well as to the real questions about parenting. Up to now these questions were pretty much constrained within the definition of what it meant to be married and were based on a presumption of two-parent families.

That leads me to this reflection: What is the cultural context of personhood and family and parenting? Even though Lisa keeps struggling to get us out of it, we always keep coming back and talking about the nuclear marriage—the husband and the wife. Obviously that has created strain for persons who are single parents. It also creates a kind of strain on the presumption that the husband and wife have to be everything to each other all the time. Affective relationships, friendships outside of the marriage with other people both of the same and of the opposite sex, are obviously very important to personhood, yet sometimes they get cut off. Somehow a nuclear family cannot bear that. In antiquity we were not talking about nuclear families. We were talking about large extended units that included married partners.

Obviously, this also raises some questions about who is responsible for parenting, who is responsible for the next generation? I submit that it is not rational or reasonable as a community to hold simply the biological mother and father as the only responsible parents for the next generation. If you have children left with a mother, you simply cannot manage on that small a unit. As we look toward the twenty-first century we must find ways in which the community can provide support mechanisms for parents.

JACK DOMINIAN

I enjoyed very much your presentation and in particular I think you brought focus to the point which is being made again and again in this symposium that the post-Vatican II period has been a period in which celibate theologians have gone from one extreme of pessimism about sexuality in marriage to the other extreme of idealizing marriage. This idealization is in contrast to the social reality. There are several studies now both in America and in Britain that show that marital satisfaction drops from the first day of marriage. It dips into its worst when the children are adolescents, and doesn't recover until they leave the home. You can fill in those findings with as many individual stories as you want, but they contrast wildly with some of the optimism, including the

100

Holy Father's, about marriage. I am not saying that these ideals are impossible, but I think in your paper you have really drawn us into the heart of reality.

The second thing I want to say is that when you express the importance in your categories of the experience in marriage, I would like to really point out that this experience has to be very carefully balanced between the experience of men and women within marriage, because sexually, emotionally and socially these experiences are different. So, when in talking about marriage we coalesce male and female, we are doing an injustice to reality. I think that the two experiences are different. Hence, in drawing out these experiences from marriage, the two have to be shaded in different ways.

Finally, I would like to ask you this question. In your methodology you said that to reach an ethical decision we must pay attention to the Scriptures, to the tradition of the Church, to philosophy, and to experience. My trouble is that the Church is very selective in what it chooses in order to prove its point, and that it doesn't enter into a really fair interaction between these categories. Particularly in sexual ethics, one moment it is quoting St. Paul on homosexuality, and the next moment it is quoting natural law, and in a third instance it is quoting some previous papal statement. I think that the way the Church presents ethical teaching is really not at all an expression of serious interaction between these categories. They really like to choose one that best suits their purposes. I think this is not really doing justice to what you described. I would like you to comment on that.

LISA SOWLE CAHILL

I really agree with the point of Dr. Dominian that experience needs to be balanced between men's and women's experience. However, we need to try to sort out to what degree is men's and women's experience intrinsically different, and to what degree is the difference created by the social and cultural context within which men and women form their identities and try to fulfill their roles. We are never going to get an answer to that question, because we never will have a specimen of pure masculinity and pure femininity apart from the culture. But one of the things that I try to develop in my paper is the fact that men and women do see marriage and the marital relationship differently because their role definitions are quite different. These definitions have very diverse implications for men and women.

What Dr. Dominian said about the various categories being used selectively by the Church is absolutely correct. We need to avoid this kind of selectivity and to bring these categories more into contact with the experience of married persons.

5.

Canonical Implications of the Conception of Marriage in the Conciliar Constitution *Gaudium Et Spes*

Peter J. Huizing, S.J.

The Code of Canon Law of 1917 stated that marriage is a contract defined by its object: a reciprocal, exclusive, perpetual right to each other's body with regard to acts directed by nature to procreation (c. 1081 §2). The existing marriage is the existence of that right. The central concern of the Church's law is the validity of the contract, hence of the marriage. It is practically the only right in the Church controlled by Church tribunals.

Vatican II describes marriage as "an intimate partnership of life and love"; the notion "contract" is replaced by "covenant," i.e., "a human act by which the spouses mutually give and accept each other" (Gaudium et Spes 46), but it does not deny the juridical notions of the Code of Canon Law. Both doctrine and jurisprudence give different answers to the questions: did the Council change the notion of marriage of the Code, and, if so, what are the consequences for the Church's marriage law?

The 1983 Code of Canon Law adopts some words from the Council— "covenant"; "partnership of the whole of life" (c. 1055 §1); "irrevocable covenant"; "mutually give and accept each other" (c. 1057 §2)—but it maintains the essentially juridical treatment of marriage, without, however, giving a new juridical definition of marriage or its "essential obligations" (c. 1095 §3) or its "essential elements" (c. 1101 §2).

The questions this chapter presents for discussion are these: are the contractual conception of marriage of the Code of 1983 and the personal conception of Vatican II essentially different, and, if so, what would be the effect on Church law?

One aspect of the issue of this Symposium on "Marriage in the Catholic Church: A Contemporary Evaluation" is its juridical or canonical aspect, and a crucial one at that. Also on this aspect the Second Vatican Council has had and still has a considerable bearing. To be sure its pastoral constitution *Gaudium et Spes* does not contain any explicit teaching about marriage law; indeed, the conciliar preparatory commission was explicitly prohibited from going into canonical matters. However, its conception of marriage has had and has a decisive influence, first, on the judicial treatment of marriage cases and, then, on the marriage law of the 1983 Code of Canon Law. To make that clear this paper will give a survey of the conception of marriage in the 1917 Code of Canon Law and in the constitution *Gaudium et Spes,* and of its effect on the jurisprudence of the Roman Rota and the 1983 Code of Canon Law; finally, in conclusion, it will attempt a contemporary evaluation of this process.

The Concept of Marriage in the 1917 Code of Canon Law: The Contractualist or Institutionalist Concept[1]

The authors of canon 1081 left no doubt on how they conceived the substance of marriage. The act by which marriage is brought into existence is a contract, that is the matrimonial consent, lawfully exchanged by a man and a woman as legally capable persons (c. 1081 §1). This matrimonial consent is an act of the will, whereby a man and a woman give and accept the mutual, lifelong and exclusive right to one another's bodies in regard to the acts, ordered by their nature to procreation (c. 1081 §2). The existing marriage, the *matrimonium in facto esse,* resulting from this contract consists in the relationship between a man and a woman, determined by its object, viz. the mutual, lifelong and exclusive right and correlative obligation to conjugal intercourse. Some canonists thought it useful to note that this right was not a *ius in re,* that is to say, that the spouses were not owners or proprietors of each other, but a *ius ad rem,* which means that they had a mutual right and obligation to the performance of determinate acts. For those canonists St. Paul, declaring that "a wife does not belong to herself but to her husband; equally a husband does not belong to himself but to his wife" (1 Cor 7:4) did not use a quite correct language.

It must be noted that the Code, as well as the doctrine on which it was based, did not intend to give only a definition of the juridical *aspect* of marriage, but a real, ontological definition of what marriage essentially *is.* This conception was closely linked with the conception of marriage as primarily a social institution, whose primary and, one may say, even essential end was the procreation of the human race, in which the personal aspects of the conjugal relationship were viewed as secondary and functional in regard to the primary end (c. 1013 §1). The human quality of the conjugal union was not looked at as essential to marriage, but only as belonging to its perfection or integrity.

It was this concept that determined the attitude of the Church toward marriage, and it also ruled the Church's consideration of marriage *qua* sacrament. For the first canon *De Matrimonio* says it bluntly: "Christ the Lord has elevated the contract itself of marriage between baptized persons to the dignity of a sacrament. Therefore, it is impossible for a valid contract of marriage between baptized persons to exist without being by that very fact a sacrament" (c. 1012 §1-2). Consequently the contractualist or institutionalist concept was not intended to be only juridical and ontological, but also theological. Between baptized persons it is the contract, simply as such, that is, at least presumably, the sacrament. The canon does not say "between persons baptized in faith" or "between baptized believing faithful persons," but "between baptized persons," clearly intending that it is enough if the marrying persons had gone through a valid baptism rite, even unknowingly. This marriage was presumed to be a sacrament, because it was also presumed that spouses, celebrating their marriage in the Catholic Church, had had at least some implicit intention "to do what the Church does," what was deemed to be a sufficient intention to administer and to receive a sacrament, or, better, to establish together the one sacrament.

This conception of marriage was the result of a long evolution. In the medieval tradition marriage was still considered to be essentially a community of life, but this concept was hardly elaborated. In the medieval society—and long after it—the procreative finality of marriage was by far its highest estimated social value. This view was backed by Augustine's authoritative doctrine on the three goods of marriage, first of all the good of offspring, protected by the goods of fidelity and indissolubility—the "sacrament"—as justifying the in itself sinful sexual intercourse. In the public estimation the social value of the conjugal union in itself was so much secondary to its procreative function that finally this value faded away and the substance of marriage was more and more identified as the lifelong and exclusive mutual right to sexual intercourse. The community of life became part of its accidental perfection or integrity. This extremely institutional concept, predominant from the middle of the nineteenth century, and strongly upheld by Cardinal Gasparri in his canonical treatise on marriage, was sanctioned by the 1917 Code, redacted under his influential direction. It is noteworthy that this institutional notion of marriage corresponds to the equally extreme institutional conception in the 1917 Code of the Church itself, the universal Church and the local churches in ecclesiastical provinces, dioceses and parishes, of religious "institutes" and ecclesiastical associations, all considered as super-personal institutions, not as unions of persons. The underlying policy of this juridical construction of

Church law was the social or juridical controllability of those institutes in the supposedly general interest of the universal institution, an institutional construction to which all personal interests were subordinated. As for the institute of marriage, the central concern of Church law is obviously its juridically controlled social existence. This is understandable because the law was formed during the centuries, in which the Church was held responsible for the integral social protection of marriage as an institution.

From this conception of marriage as an institution were derived its characteristic features of unity and indissolubility that were joined to it by the Creator in the creation of marriage. The spouses, contracting marriage, entered into this institution, which became concretely realized in their union as a superhuman, ontological reality and which concrete existence could only come to an end through the death of either spouse. Also the moral doctrine on conjugal life, especially concerning conjugal sexual behavior, was ruled by the conception that the specific nature of marriage was substantially determined by its procreative function—a conception reaffirmed by Pius XI in his encyclical *Casti Connubii* December 31, 1930; on numerous occasions by Pius XII, relying on his trusted advisor in moral issues, Fr. Franz Hürth, S.J.; by the rotal jurisprudence, notably by the decision *coram* Wynen, January 22, 1944; and by the famous decree of the Holy Office, April 1, 1944, rejecting the doctrine which either denies that the primary end of marriage is the procreation and the education of children, or teaches that the secondary ends are not essentially subordinate to the primary end, but equally principal and independent. As a result this conception was also most commonly held by theologians and canonists.

The Constitution "Gaudium et Spes": The Personalist Conception

In the personalist conception marriage is viewed as consisting in the relationship between a man and a woman, which has its first raison d'être and its first value in itself as being a human relationship of two human persons who cannot be a means to anybody or anything else. This relationship has been signified by several expressions: community of (conjugal) life; community of love; marital society, etc. Since the medieval reception of Roman law, from about the year 1000, the most frequently used in the canonical and theological tradition were expressions borrowed from the descriptions of marriage in Justinian's *Institutes* 1,9,1: "Matrimony, or marriage, is a union of a man and a woman, involving an undivided living together,"[2] and his *Digest* 23,2,1: "Marriage is a union of a man and a woman and a community of the whole of life, a participation in divine and human law."[3] It was almost unanimously

admitted that the object of marriage consent and marriage itself was this conjugal society, to be sure, ordered to its natural potential human fertility, but
not identical with it, as especially clearly appeared in the marriage of Mary
and Joseph. We already mentioned why this conception of the conjugal society
in itself was hardly elaborated, though by some scholastics this personal character was stressed in their description of marriage.[4]

While from the mid-nineteenth century the predominance of the procreative end of marriage was stressed in such a way that even marriage itself was
defined as mutual right to conjugal intercourse, at the same time a reaction
became noticeable in writings of theologians and canonists who began to pay
more attention to the "secondary end" of marriage, the good of the spouses
themselves. But the first to challenge openly the monarchy of procreation was
the so-called "personalist school," inaugurated by Herbert Doms with his
study "Vom Sinn und Zweck der Ehe" (Breslau, 1935), maintaining that the
first purpose or end—Zweck—of marriage is the realization of what marriage
is, namely a community of life of man and woman, which is the meaning—
Sinn—of marriage, and that this same realization tends also to the procreation
and education of children, as a natural part of their own fulfillment.

It must be noted, however, that the tendency to a higher appreciation of
the personal dimension of marriage was already noticeable in the public estimation. Pius XI's encyclical *Casti Connubii* itself, though firmly maintaining
the absolute priority of procreation, at the same time attaches such a high value
to the mutual formation of the spouses that he even qualifies this as follows:
"The mutual inward molding of a husband and wife, this determined effort to
perfect each other, can, in a very real sense, be said to be the chief reason and
purpose of marriage, provided marriage be looked at not in the restricted sense
as instituted for the proper conception and education of the child, but more
widely as the blending of life as a whole and the mutual interchange and sharing thereof."[5]

The constitution *Gaudium et Spes,* Part II, Chapter I, "Fostering the Dignity of Marriage and the Family,"[6] sees as its purpose "to offer guidance and
support by presenting certain key points of Church doctrine in a clearer light"
(47,3). The constitution, though being pastoral, does not at all intend to give
merely moral and pastoral exhortations or advice, but rather sound principles
of Church doctrine, as safe guidelines for moral and pastoral behavior. The
assertion aired by some canonists that the constitution has to be classified as
"merely pastoral," and of therefore diminished doctrinal value, was a contradiction not only to the expressed intention of the constitution itself, but also to
the teaching of John XXIII at the beginning of the council that the Church's
doctrinal teaching *is* pastoral and that its magisterium is predominantly pastoral
in character.

There is no doubt possible about the constitution's definitely personalist conception of marriage, without denying, however, that at the same time it is an "institution" rooted in the creation itself of human persons as man and woman and in their own nature.

The act whereby the spouses bring their marriage into being, their "conjugal covenant" and "irrevocable personal consent," is "a human act by which they each mutually give themselves and accept each other" (48,1). The expression "covenant"—*foedus*—is a biblical and theological expression, inspired by the Old Testament image of God's covenant with his people. The first and immediate "object" of their covenant is not a determinate right or obligation, but the spouses themselves, the union of their own persons and lives.

Consequently, the terminology employed by the constitution to signify the reality of marriage, resulting from this covenant, is by itself an expression of the council's conception of marriage as being essentially and first of all a personal union of man and woman. It is called a "community of conjugal love" (47,1); an "intimate community of conjugal life and love"; a "sacred bond"; an "intimate union of their persons and actions"; a "mutual self-giving of two persons"; an "intimate union" (48,1); an "unbreakable bond between two persons"; a "community and sharing of life" (50,3). Where the constitution speaks of conjugal love, this love is described as eminently human because, given from one person to the other through an affect of the will, it embraces the good of their entire persons; their bodily union, as the expression and fulfillment of their love, both manifests and nourishes their mutual self-giving (49). Wherever the constitution intends to describe the reality of marriage, this is identified not as an institute for procreation, but as a personal union which has its raison d'être in itself.

Treating of conjugal love and procreation, the constitution gives priority to the first. After the doctrinal exposition in n. 48, n. 49 is devoted entirely to a discussion on conjugal love and only then, in a separate section, is the topic of fruitfulness brought forth in n. 50. The doctrinal part intentionally intertwines the two aspects so closely as to make it impossible to separate them or establish a hierarchy. Hence it is impossible to interpret the constitution as having no impact upon the doctrine of the hierarchy of ends. On the other hand, it is equally impossible to interpret the constitution as reversing the traditional hierarchical order by teaching the primacy of conjugal love. Both these extremes should be avoided. But, indeed, conjugal love does not depend on fruitfulness. This love exists before children are born and is not extinguished if they don't come. Evidently this love, "involving the good of the whole person" and "pervading the whole of their lives" (49), is understood as a total human experience, to be sure, including its physical sexual expression, but by no means equivalent to it. It is called a "Christian vocation," which means a project involving the whole of life and demanding "notable virtue." It is into this project that the physical sexuality is integrated and finds its only full meaning. That is why real sexual life is only humanly possible within the totality of conjugal life.

The so-called essential properties and ends of marriage are also seen in a new light. Full fidelity and unbreakable unity are not, as in the old canon 1013 §1, attached to the institute of marriage, but presented as arising from the intimate union of the spouses as being a mutual self-giving of two persons to one another, and also required for the well-being of the children (48,1). Not an "institute" but the inner nature of marriage and conjugal love itself is ordered to the procreation and education of children (50,1). In this context the "various goods and ends" with which marriage is bestowed (48,1) cannot be identified with the Augustinian "three goods of marriage" needed to justify the otherwise sinful conjugal intercourse; the constitution declares that this conjugal act, instead of being sinful, is the full expression of conjugal love. Likewise the expression "mutual assistance"—*mutuum adiutorium*—(48,1) in this context cannot be meant as a "secondary end" as in the old canon 1013 §1; the constitution emphasizes the high value of the growing oneness in conjugal love and the mutual inner formation of the spouses (49).

This personalist vision of marriage of the council was made even clearer by the vigorous resistance put up to it by a strong minority. According to Bernhard Häring's commentary, this minority apparently numbered about two hundred of the council fathers. He reports that the council kept the explicit affirmation that love is an element essential to marriage against the *modi* which objected that the preeminent role given to love is in contradiction to earlier magisterial documents and seems to suggest that marriage can be dissolved once this love is dead. The request to confirm the "traditional" hierarchy of ends of marriage, confirmed by the magisterium and by Church law—in fact the 1917 canon 1013 §1 was the first magisterial formulation of this hierarchy!—was rejected by the conciliar commission with the laconic reply that this hierarchy could be viewed from various angles. The effort to replace the word *foedus*—covenant—by *contractus*—contract—was rejected against numerous and repeated petitions for the substitution. Thirty-four of the fathers sought to return to a more juridical concept, either by defining the content of the contract as the mutual giving over of specific rights and duties, or by the insertion of the definition of the right to each other's body as in c 1081 §2. One hundred and sixty-one wished to replace the mutual gift of two persons by the exchange of specific rights and duties. Against the concept of the sacrament as a blessing of love, one father wished to designate it as a contractual blessing, and one hundred and forty-eight fathers sought to say that the blessing is given for the sake of a fecund union.

The second section of *Gaudium et Spes* n. 48 treats of the sacramentality of marriage between spouses who believe in Christ—*Christifideles coniuges*.

Häring's commentary tells us that here the sacramentality too is expressed in a fully personalist way. It is an encounter with Christ, who abides with both of them, the spouses who in his name have become an inseparable unity. It is a dynamic presence by which he seeks to assimilate their love for one another more and more to his love for the community of his faithful, so that finally it becomes a reciprocal gift given in a totally faithful love. Natural conjugal love itself, in its totality, becomes richer and more authentic through the sacrament because more intimately linked with the source of all love. To this Selling's commentary adds that when here the constitution teaches that "Christ the Lord abundantly blessed this many-faceted love, welling up as it does from the fountain of divine love and structured as it is on the model of his union with the Church," this love of Christ reveals a model of the fidelity of all Christian love, specified in its strongest human expression of conjugal love. This is why for this love the special assistance of Christ to his married faithful is signified by the sacramental character of the marriage celebration. Ephesians 5:22-23, often quoted in this context, is certainly misunderstood as an ideology of the man as Christ and the woman as the Church. The sacrament of marriage is a gift, sign and reality of Christ's special assistance, and at the same time a call, a vocation to realize the fidelity of his love, a love "of perpetual fidelity through mutual self-bestowing."

From all this the conclusion emerges most clearly that the council refused to accept the juridical and contractualist concept of marriage of the 1917 Code as expression of the ontological and theological reality of marriage. It adopted the personalist concept, both for marriage in general and for marriage specifically as a sacrament. In composing this document the conciliar commission was obliged by a formal command of higher authority to concern itself exclusively with the pastoral aspects of marriage and to leave its canonical aspects to the Commission for the Revision of the Code of Canon Law. However, though abstaining from any interference in legislative matters, the commission had to explain its own conception of marriage, which was different from the conception underlying the regulations of the 1917 Code. From this one ought not to conclude that the council intended to deny the existence of relationships in justice between the spouses, relationships in justice specific to marriage. Spouses certainly have a right to conjugal life, to cohabitation, to physical marital union, to fidelity, to the taking up of fatherhood and motherhood, to each other's material assistance, etc. But for the question how these relationships in justice have to be conceived, the council itself provided no answer. My own thinking is that these relationships, insofar as they are typically marital rights and obligations, cannot exist outside the personal conjugal relationship itself, and that they belong to a category of right which supposes the existence of a personal relationship between the subjects of these rights, and which I therefore would call the category of personalist rights, which, as such, cannot be the object of any positive law, imposed from the outside. They have to be exercised in freedom, or they are not exercised at all.

Post-Conciliar Jurisprudence[7]

In his survey of the rotal jurisprudence from 1966 till 1977 Fellhauer distinguishes three periods.

In the *early post-conciliar jurisprudence*—1966–1968—the teaching of Vatican II had no bearing on the rotal jurisprudence. The community of life continues to be viewed as not belonging to the substance of marriage, and the first and principal objective end of marriage as well as its only specifying element remains procreation. From this primary right arise the rights to community of life and mutual aid (*coram* Beja, March 1, 1967). Notwithstanding the opinion of many, the intimate community of life and love does not belong to the essence of marriage, but only to its perfection (*c.* Fiore, November 30, 1968). Some references to *Gaudium et Spes,* however, seem to suggest that the constitution has some juridical value, and it is affirmed that the essence of marriage does not depend only on its procreative finality, which is not its only finality (*c.* Fagiolo, May 18, 1968, and July 2, 1968).

The *second period of the beginnings of a jurisprudence according to Vatican II*—1969–1972—was inaugurated February 25, 1969, by a famous decision *coram* Anné: the right to the body of canon 1081 §2 views only what is most specific to marriage, but not its entirety. The intimate community of life, as declared in *Gaudium et Spes,* has juridical significance, looking not to the mere fact of inaugurating a community of life, but to the obligation regarding this community, the most specific element of which is the union by which the spouses become one flesh. This points out that marriage is a most personal relationship and that matrimonial consent is an act whereby the spouses hand over themselves and receive each other. In evaluating this community three aspects always have to be kept in mind: the natural law, the cultural aspect, and the existential or personal dimension. This position was maintained and elaborated in several other sentences *coram* Anné. Others state that the right to the body is a consequence of the intimate community, spiritual as well as corporal, intended by the spouses when giving their consent (*c.* Pompedda, December 22, 1969); conjugal love has juridical value as in some way necessary for the eliciting of a valid consent; matrimonial consent looks not only to conjugal intercourse, but to the total object of marriage, unity, indissolubility, intimate community of life, etc. (*c.* Fagiolo, October 30, 1970 and November 27, 1970).

On the contrary, other decisions argued that love is not a juridical element of marriage (*c.* Pinto, July 30, 1969; *c.* Palazzini, June 2, 1971); that *Gaudium et Spes* did nothing to change the hierarchy of ends of marriage (*c.* Lefèbvre, December 16, 1972); that no substantial change in the juridical structure of marriage had been brought about by *Gaudium et Spes:* it had not attempted a juridical treatment of the object of consent; the juridical value of the community of life as a distinct element in marriage had not yet been demonstrated (*c.* Staffa, December 5, 1972).

In the *third period*—1973–1977—the jurisprudential controversy in the Roman Rota continued. Decisions *coram* Serrano affirm the juridical value of the community of life, of which the most specific feature is its interpersonal nature. Marriage cannot be conceived as a contract with an impersonal object. In this covenant rights and obligations are viewed which in a real sense have to be identified with the subjects themselves. These decisions insist on the community of life as a juridical entity, its intra- and interpersonal nature and the mutual capacity required for establishing such a relationship (April 5, 1973; April 30, 1974; July 9, 1976). Anné sustains the right to the community of life as an essential matrimonial right, distinct from all other rights of marriage and separate from the three goods, distinct likewise from the sum of the other essential matrimonial rights (February 6, 1973; March 11, 1975; December 4, 1975). In this last decision Anné mentions that the judges considered the question of the juridical value of love in the act of matrimonial consent to be principally one of terminology, viz., what exactly is meant by love, and feels it advisable to avoid using the word in a juridical context. Besides these, several other decisions uphold the juridical value of the community of life as a distinct essential element of marriage.

But still a minority of the rotal judges (like Pinto, Massala and Staffa) continued denying any juridical relevance of the community of life, practically reducing the conciliar conception of marriage and marital consent to the conception that prevailed from the mid-nineteenth century and was encapsulated in the 1917 Code of Canon Law and in the pre-conciliar jurisprudence and doctrine based on that Code.

Fellhauer formulates his conclusion as follows:

> The *consortium omnis vitae* has also been given juridical significance within the Roman Rota. The two most visible exponents of the *consortium* in that tribunal to date have been the Auditors Lucien Anné and J.M. Serrano; and they have been joined by others, particularly Fagiolo, Raad, Di Felice, Lefèbvre, and Ewers. But only Anné and Serrano appear to have developed the concept to a significant degree, primarily by their analysis of the interpersonal relationships of the conjugal union.
>
> While there is evidence of a current "wait-and-see" attitude within

the Roman Rota, only two Rotal judges, Pinto and Massala, seem to have taken a definite stand against attributing juridical value to the *consortium*. A sentence written by the late Cardinal D. Staffa of the Apostolic Signatura has also denied the relevance of the notion (p. 155).

What this in practice means can best be illustrated with a concrete case. On February 13, 1963, an Italian citizen married a Dutch woman. Three months after the wedding a daughter was born, and one month later the man deserted his wife. Civil divorce was obtained, but at that time the Italian law did not recognize divorce. Hence, the cause of nullity was brought before Dutch Church courts. The final sentence of nullity, dated August 12, 1971, was based on the lack of the intention to establish a real community of life. This sentence was communicated to the Supreme Tribunal of the Apostolic Signatura for transmission to the Italian authorities for the civil effects. Dino Cardinal Staffa, at the time prefect of the Signatura, obtained from Paul VI a decision that the case had to be judged in the third instance by a commission of five cardinals. Their sentence, written by Staffa and dated November 29, 1975, decided that there was no evidence this marriage was null. They argued that the Dutch tribunals took the principle "marriage is made by the consent of the parties" in a sense entirely different from the common doctrine and jurisprudence, and that the Dutch tribunals stated, without foundation and erroneously, that the Second Vatican Council changed this doctrine. This marriage, then, which had been definitely declared invalid, was, for all practical purposes, more than four years later, again declared valid, in contradiction with the then already prevailing jurisprudence of the Roman Rota.

Some Notes on Recent Rotal Jurisprudence[8]

According to Serrano—"Le droit . . ." 272ff—matrimonial consent has no "object," i.e., no material reality existing outside the subjects. Only by reflecting on oneself can the subject perceive herself or himself under the formality of an object, without however being in reality an object. Today the interpersonal and intrapersonal nature of matrimonial consent—i.e., of a consent existing between persons and concerning themselves—is admitted by the Church magisterium—*Gaudium et Spes* 47-52 and *Humanae Vitae*—and by jurisprudence of auditors of the Roman Rota like Lefèbvre, Anné and Serrano. Instead of the expression "object of consent" should be used "terme du consentement," perhaps "content of the consent." There are two subjects striving after nothing else than themselves, giving themselves and accepting each other in a perfectly immanent covenant. The community of common life and love is not the immediate content of the consent, but the commitment to it. As was already exposed by Anné in his famous decision of February 25, 1969, the nature of the community of life which is called marriage depends closely on the human culture in the existential order, according to the variety of forms this culture represents in different historical and local conditions. Serrano regrets that the most recent Rota decisions unanimously reject love as an essential element of matrimonial consent and marriage, notwithstanding the excellent scientific and jurisprudential work of Fagiolo.[9]

In his study "Recherches . . ." Serrano underlines the importance of considering the peculiar features of the existing cohabitation in the evaluation of the consent. The jurisprudence, however, is still far from being unanimous on this point, as appears from the sentences *coram* Fiore August 26, 1977 and *c.* Agustoni February 20, 1979. The first reason to insist on this principle is the almost exclusive attention to the moment of consent, which is not very representative of the cultural and existential factors which determine the real image of the concrete conjugal relationship. Another reason is that spouses do not ask a declaration of nullity because they discovered a canonical ground existing at the moment of consent, but because they want to be freed from a common life that has become an intolerable reality. This by itself is not a ground of nullity, but it is always an indication of an initial weakness of the relationship, as explained *coram* Serrano May 9, 1980.

The notion of consent as "act of the will" should be developed to the existentially more correct and more appropriate notion of interpersonal conjugal engagement or commitment. There is no abstract act of the will referring to equally abstract qualities or properties like indissolubility, exclusivity or procreation, but an authentic attitude of persons giving themselves and accepting the other self into the most intimate community of life. That would be an indispensable attitude for a Christian marriage. The notions of aptitude-capacity-attitude, as well as the notions of immaturity-incapacity-exclusion of real marriage, would come nearer to each other. Sometimes—as *c.* Fagiolo Feb. 29, 1971 and Serrano March 7, 1977—there appear signs of the importance of authentic sincerity, human dignity and nobility, inseparable from marriage as a natural bond. These signs could lead to an urgent revision of the overall physiognomy of marriage which has to be considered in nullity cases and is so often blocked by indiscreet use of so-called principles like protection of the right to marry or the minimal requirements for a valid celebration or the predominant, if not exclusive, attention to the usual, stereotyped list of properties of marriage. Consideration given to marriage in itself and its overall entity is not less but more important than that given to any of its aspects.

The personalist conception of marriage provoked also an evolution of the traditional jurisprudence concerning the error about the person of the other party. A marriage, declared null by two French tribunals in two instances, on the ground of error concerning not the physical identity of the partner but the partner's moral and social qualities, was simply confirmed by the Rota. A decision *c.* Canals, April 21, 1970, declares that today attention must be given to those qualities which are commonly estimated to shape the image of a person—not to physical identity, or identity as civil state, but identity as moral and social reality. Decisions *c.* Ewers, Feb. 10, 1973, *c.* Di Felice, March 26, 1977 and Jan. 14, 1978, and *c.* Pompedda, Nov. 25, 1978, were favorable to Canal's sentence. His sentence, however, was rejected by various auditors as being impossible in Canon Law or not intended in canon 1083. Indeed, Serrano feels it is more correct to rely on c. 1081, interpreted in the light of Vatican II: the unique personality is criterion of the validity of the partner's consent, due to the importance given to the person's qualities in relation to the community of life: *c.* Serrano, July 14, 1978. A first instance decision, stating the nullity of a marriage contracted because the man had concealed his sterility from his spouse, who was anxious for a family, on the ground of error about the identity of the partner, was ratified by a sentence *c.* Serrano May 28, 1982, because in the light of Vatican II there is more to marriage than the *ius in corpus* and there is more to personal identity than simple physical means of identification may reveal; and in this case the error was serious, and likely to interfere seriously with conjugal harmony.

Some auditors of the Rota, however, still continue deciding nullity cases on the basis of their principle that the only object, given and accepted in contracting marriage, is the exclusive and perpetual *ius in corpus,* and that only in a rhetorical sense the partners can be said to give themselves to one another, and certainly they cannot do so totally. Likewise, the only "interpersonal relationship" essential to the existence of marriage is the mutual, exclusive and perpetual right to the conjugal acts. Love and good personal relationship can be necessary for success, but they are not required for valid consent and valid marriage.[10]

The 1983 Code of Canon Law

Regarding the present issue, viz., the influence of the conciliar conception of marriage on the 1983 Code of Canon Law, three points have to be noted.

The fundamental general rule of interpretation of the Code, embodied in the apostolic constitution *Sacrae Disciplinae Leges,* by which the Code was promulgated, states that the first source of interpretation is the Second Vatican Council:

> The instrument which the Code is fully corresponds to the nature of
> the Church, especially as it is proposed by the teaching of the Second

Vatican Council in general and in a particular way by its ecclesiological teaching. Indeed, in a certain sense this new Code could be understood as a great effort to translate this same conciliar doctrine and ecclesiology into *canonical* language. If, however, it is impossible to translate perfectly into *canonical* language the conciliar image of the Church, nevertheless the Code must always be referred to this image as the primary pattern whose outline the Code ought to express insofar as it can by its very nature.[11]

The meaning of this rule seems to be clear. The contrary opinion, sustained by some canonists, that the council of itself had only moral and pastoral value but no bearing on the juridical Church order, and that we had to wait for the new Code as the authentic source of interpretation of the canonical principles of the council, has been inverted. The council has its magisterial authority in and by itself, not depending on any other superior source, other than Scripture and tradition, including the Code of Canon Law, so that this code must be understood and interpreted in light of Vatican II. Likewise the committee of consultors of the commission of cardinals for the revision of the Code of Canon Law, who had to prepare the bill of the section on marriage law, continuing the line initiated by Lucien Anné February 25, 1969, and followed by the *senior pars* of the judges of the Roman Rota as well as by many others in various regions of the Church, expressed their conviction that also this law had to be formulated according to the teaching of the constitution *Gaudium et Spes* regarding the nature of marriage and the ends of marriage, omitting, as the constitution did, any indication referring to an order of priority of these ends.[12]

Secondly, the Code sanctioned the personalist conception of marriage found in *Gaudium et Spes*. This personalist conception had already been accepted by the majority of judges of the Roman Rota and other ecclesiastical tribunals, who had abandoned the over-institutional conception of Gasparri and the 1917 Code. The act by which marriage comes into being is called, as in the constitution *Gaudium et Spes*, a ''covenant''—*foedus*—a biblical and theological expression signifying the bond between Yahweh and his people, which bond was often symbolized with the image of marriage (c. 1055 §1). This act is described as an irrevocable, mutual giving and accepting on the part of a man and a woman of each other, in order to establish marriage (c. 1057 §2). Yet the principle is maintained that the covenant, the *matrimonium in fieri*, cannot be performed by a man and a woman who have not the potency to have intercourse together, whereas the existing marriage, the *matrimonium in facto esse*, can exist without this potency. The potency for procreation is not required either for the performing of the matrimonial covenant or for the existence of conjugal partnership (c. 1084 §1-3). The nature of marriage is described as a partnership of the whole of life, and, as such, is first ordered to the good of the spouses themselves; because marriage is by nature the source of new human life, it is also ordered to the procreation and education of offspring (c. 1055 §1). Whereas the "essential properties" of marriage, its unity and indissolubility, in *Gaudium et Spes* are viewed as natural characteristics of the mutual self-gift of the spouses to one another and their human fertility, in c. 1056 they remain attributes of the institution of marriage. Canon 1097 §1-2 rules about the effect that an error concerning the identity of the partner has on matrimonial consent. In doing so it neither excludes nor explicitly includes the above mentioned personalist conception of this identity as it was interpreted by some of the judges of the Roman Rota. Canon 1084 §3, stating that sterility neither prohibits nor invalidates marriage, explicitly refers to canon 1098, thus indicating that fraud concerning the partner's sterility indeed is a fraud concerning a quality which of its very nature can seriously disturb the partnership of conjugal life. This paragraph is a confirmation of the above-mentioned jurisprudence.

In the over-institutionalist conception of marriage as a mutual right to intercourse, where indissolubility and unity were attributed to the institution of marriage, regardless of the personal constitution of the partners, the only constitutional incapacity for marriage was the physical incapacity for intercourse. A rotal decision *coram* Alberto Canestri, February 21, 1948, seems to have used for the first time the concept "moral impotence" as incapacity to commit oneself effectively to an unbreakable and especially exclusive community of life.[13] Canon 1095,3°, declares incapable of contracting marriage those who are not able to assume the essential obligations of matrimony due to causes of a psychic nature. It does not consider causes external to the marrying partners, which eventually could prevent them from realizing their partnership, but only causes which regard their personal relationship and which make them incapable of carrying out the obligations which, according to the normal, natural and human standards of their social and cultural environment, are deemed essential to a conjugal partnership, to the extent that the incapacity to fulfill these obligations turns this partnership into a humanly unbearable reality. As has been clearly explained by José Serrano, a judgment on this incapacity can only be given when taking into account not only the moment of the celebration of the marriage, but the whole history and course of the cohabitation, during which this incapacity has revealed itself, whereas Lucien Anné has underlined the indispensable consideration of the existential setting of the breakdown of the relationship. This incapacity, once its existence has been proved, must lead to a declaration of nullity, even when both parties in contracting their marriage had the positive intention to assume and to fulfill these obligations. In case they are, indeed, capable to do so, but either or both through a positive act of the will should exclude marriage itself, i.e., the partnership of the whole of life, or some essential element thereof, or an essential property, viz., its unity or indissolubility (c. 1056), their marriage would be invalid (c. 1101 §2). If or how far the positive exclusion of the sacramental character of a Christian marriage invalidates the consent, either as an essential element or as an essential property, is not determined in the law.

A third point and perhaps the most important to note is the explicit and detailed attention paid to the pastoral care of marriage in the first canons of the first chapter under the title "Marriage" (1063-1064). The introduction of these canons and the place given to them in the very first special canons indicate that the juridical order of the Church is no longer exclusively interested in the juridical, social control of the validity and indissolubility, c.q. the legal invalidity and dissolubility of marriage, but also and, as it seems, first in the pastoral service that the Christian community itself has to offer to their marrying and married members. This is a service due to them in justice, as a part of the very mission of this community.

It may seem significant that the most "pastoral" and final paragraph of the constitution *Gaudium et Spes,* Part II, Chapter I, "Fostering the Dignity of Marriage and the Family," recommending the care of all for the well-being of marriage and family (n. 54), has been "translated" into the canonical order and even given the first place. This indicates the primary purpose of the Church's marriage order, viz., to support the realization of an efficient pastoral care for its marrying and married members.

Contemporary Evaluation

When the group of consultors charged with the redaction of the title on marriage started the examination of the reactions to the first draft, the president of the commission for the revision of the Code, Pericle Cardinal Felici, told them not to rethink the theological implications, but to formulate the new law. For all practical purposes his order was, indeed, the only one possible. However, the underlying theological and pastoral implications remain, and they are many and serious. This paper can only indicate some bottlenecks and some of the proposed solutions.

The identity of a valid marriage of two baptized partners as a sacrament (c. 1055 §2).

The problem does not regard the many Christian spouses who really believe and really intend to marry "in the Lord," regardless of how they conceive or how far they are able to express this reality. The problem regards the equally many, though baptized, spouses who have neither this belief nor this intention.

In the first place this intention is required as a condition for the marriage to be a sacrament. The International Theological Commission stated: ". . . where there is no trace of faith (in the sense of 'belief'—being disposed to belief), and no desire for grace or salvation is found, then a doubt arises as to whether there is the above-mentioned general and truly sacramental intention and whether the contracted marriage is validly contracted or not. . . . The absence of faith compromises the validity of the sacrament."[14] Also the 1980 Synod of Bishops reflected that in the contemporary world the simple request for a church wedding could no longer be deemed to be sufficient to admit an "implicit belief" or an "intention to do what the Church does." The present law places the parish priests in a dilemma: either they refuse the sacrament, thus excluding the only way for Catholics to a valid marriage, or they admit marginal or non-believers to the sacrament, compromising its validity as well. They have no right solution.[15]

The theory of the "implicit will," current in the contractualist conception of marriage, is criticized for accrediting to marginal or non-believers, requesting a church wedding, an interpretative non-existing will. To admit that it is not required that the parties be conscious of the indissolubility or unity of marriage, because they have an "implicit will," is irreconcilable with two fundamental principles of moral theology: namely, that nobody is bound who does not know the precept, and that nothing is wanted that is unknown. A knowledge proportionate to the seriousness of marriage is required. While the Roman Rota often underscores the fact that marriage requires more consciousness than other contracts, at the same time it minimalizes the requirements of reflection and prudence.[16]

The related presumption that the internal consent of the mind is presumed to conform to the words or the signs used in the celebration of marriage (c. 1101 §s), while juridically correct, should not be as rigorously applied as it used to be in the rotal jurisprudence. In light of the contemporary mentality, such a rigorous application of this presumption is highly questionable.[17]

An even more urgent question is whether baptized non-believers, who cannot receive and administer a valid sacramental marriage as long as they don't want it, retain the right to a natural valid marriage and the ability to establish it. This is denied by the International Theological Commission. The Church cannot in any way recognize that two baptized persons are living in a marital state equal to their dignity and their life as "new creatures in Christ" if they are not united by the sacrament of matrimony. For the Church, no natural marriage separated from the sacrament exists for baptized persons, but only natural marriage elevated to the dignity of a sacrament.[18] Therefore it is deemed to be dangerous to introduce the practice of permitting the couple to celebrate diverse wedding ceremonies on various levels, or to allow a priest or deacon to assist at or to read prayers on the occasion of a non-sacramental marriage which baptized persons wish to celebrate.[19] However, the Commission admitted a certain psychological relationship in these cases, which has a completely different meaning than simple concubinage, thus progressing beyond the hitherto dominant view of the matter.

The 1980 Synod's proposition 12, dealing with the problem of marginal believers who request a church wedding, asks that a fundamental study be initiated to investigate whether the rule that a valid marriage of baptized couples is always a sacrament applies to those who lose the faith, and to determine the pastoral and juridical consequences of the result of such an investigation. Moreover, it is suggested that a study be undertaken to determine the pastoral criteria for discerning the faith of the engaged couple and to examine to what degree the intention "to do what the Church does" must imply a minimal intention also to believe with the Church.[20] Yves Congar holds the opinion that baptized non-believers do not lose their natural right and their ability to establish a valid natural marriage.[21]

According to the Code of Canon Law, Catholics who have defected by a formal act from the Catholic Church are not bound by the canonical form of celebration of marriage (c. 1117) nor by the diriment impediment of disparity of cult (c. 1086 §1). This exemption does not seem to make much sense if it is not its intention to allow also formally defected Catholics to remain capable to contract valid marriages, which, however, presumably cannot be sacraments. The questions arising from this exemption and its presumed intention are not considered by the preparatory commission and probably neither by the legislator.[22]

The Juridical Indissolubility of the Sacramental Consummated Marriage

The International Theological Commission stated that the Council of Trent, because of doctrinal doubts (opinions of Ambrosiaster, Catharinus and Cajetan) and for some more or less ecumenical reasons, limited itself in the formulation of the much discussed *canon 7 de matrimonio* to pronouncing an anathema against those who deny the Church's authority on the issue. While the I.T.C. goes on to point out that consequently it cannot be said that the Council had the intention of solemnly defining marriage's indissolubility as a truth of faith, it nevertheless subjoins that account must be taken of the stricter interpretation of this canon given by Pius XI in his encyclical *Casti Connubii*.[23] Obviously the Pope followed the contemporary common understanding of the canon, which subsequently was proven to be historically incorrect.[24] The 1980 Synod of Bishops, though not treating directly the issue of indissolubility, called for a new and extensive study in the area of pastoral care for divorced remarried Catholics, explicitly asking that this study should take into account the practices of the early Eastern Church, so that pastoral charity may appear more clearly.[25] It was even accepted to add that a commission be set up to study the authority of the Pope with respect to marriage.[26]

Johannes G. Gerhartz, actually secretary general of the Jesuit order, in a study dealing with the foundation of this juridical indissolubility, first distinguishes this clearly from the theological-moral indissolubility.[27] Every marriage is by its very nature a lifelong faithful union. Proclaiming its dissolubility certainly would be against Jesus' commandment. The Church's magisterium upholds this theological-moral indissolubility of all marriages. Nevertheless the Church's law admits the canonical, extrinsic dissolubility of all but sacramental consummated marriages. What is the foundation of this exception?

Considering the various sources where an answer to this question could be found, the author comes to the following conclusions. As to the Church's magisterium, the prevailing opinion of theologians today is that there is no unchangeable, obligatory doctrinal pronouncement that sacramental consummated marriages, and these only, are by divine law *juridically* absolutely indissoluble. Regarding Jesus' commandment, "What therefore God has joined together, let no man put asunder,"[28] it is an absolute pronouncement, not admitting exceptions. Modern exegetes, however, agree that it is an absolute moral commandment, or rather an absolute call to live marriage as it was intended in God's creation, not a juridical regulation of juridical capacity or incapacity to marry. Moreover Jesus' words and the teaching of the New Testament cannot be separated from their reception in the Church. In the Church's tradition it is clearly confirmed that Jesus' word is the unconditional rule for every Christian marriage, but not itself another law in the juridical sense.[29] The tradition of the Eastern churches has understood Jesus' logion, in Matthew's version: "But I say to you that everyone who divorces his wife, except on the ground of 'impurity,' makes her an adulteress" (5:32) in the sense that adultery is a ground for divorce. Likewise the tradition of the Western Church has understood the "Pauline privilege" (1 Cor 7:12-16) as a ground for divorce and remarriage, and even enlarged the conditions allowing it, except in the case of sacramental and consummated marriages. And even for these the Church's law provides, in case of definite breakdown, a legal separation, eventually for life, by which "marriage" in reality is reduced to the canonical incapacity to contract another marriage. Attributing to this incapacity the fulfilment of Jesus' call for irrevocable fidelity, or an "ontological" existence as remaining conjugal bond, or even a "theological" reality as signifying Christ's union with his Church, seems to be short of an ideological mystification, especially in the conception, that the sacrament is the marriage itself and not some independent juridical entity.

The author's final conclusion is, that there is no absolute juridical indissolubility derived from a compelling source of the Christian faith, but that it has been maintained in the interest of the common good or the necessary order of society, especially in the times that the Church was held responsible for the whole social and juridical order of marriage. Whether changing this law would be in the interest of the Church's community, in such a way that it does not harm its social order nor continue to do serious harm to the Church's pastoral mission, is a matter of fact and can only be decided by the hierarchy.

A different approach has been proposed by another German canonist, Matthäus Kaiser.[30] This author starts from the conciliar conception of marriage: not only a juridical relationship, but first a personal and religious reality. A merely juridical relationship can be dissolved by a juridical act. The indissolubility of the personal bond, to which the spouses have engaged themselves and in which they are united by God, is not a juridical effect of a juridical relation, but a proper quality of conjugal life. This personal union however can be disturbed, either by external circumstances, or usually by an often long process of alienation till the definite and complete breakdown. The official civil divorce is the juridical sanction of this fact. Though the personal union is finished, the bond brought into existence by God is not finished. God's action is irrevocable.

Divorce, though not followed by another marriage, is in itself against Jesus' commandment and objectively sinful. Divorced persons, insofar as they are also subjectively guilty, have no right to receive the sacraments. In Kaiser's opinion, in case two persons continue to live as Christians and want to receive the sacraments, it may reasonably be presumed that there is no (more) subjective guilt and they are in good faith. Likewise remarriage after divorce is against Jesus' commandment and also canonically invalid. However, the Church's law itself knows that canonical invalidity is not identical with the morally imputable: "An invalid marriage is called putative if it has been celebrated in good faith by at least one of the parties, until both parties become certain of its nullity" (c. 1061 §3). Marriage, indeed, is not only a juridical, but also and first a personal relationship, and this personal relationship may also exist in a civil second marriage of divorced Catholics, although canonically invalid. In these cases too there may be justifying or mitigating circumstances, either from the beginning or arising in the course of the marriage. Divorced persons, in the reasonable subjective conviction that in such serious personal circumstances they are entitled to marry or to continue in their marriage, cannot be judged to be seriously imputable by reason of malice or culpability (cf. c.1321 §1). Whenever they seriously want to live as faithful Catholics, the presumption that they are in good faith is reasonable. Consequently there would be neither a subjective nor an objective ground to prohibit them from receiving the sacraments. A canonical legitimation, however, of this relationship would remain impossible and senseless, because in this case the Church's action is not and cannot be a sign of God's joining the parties together.

Apart from this the author stresses the urgency of a more developed, preventive pastoral care with regard to Christian marriage.

The issue of an "intrinsic termination" of a marriage has been proposed by Piero Antonio Bonnet as a possible hypothesis.[31] "Intrinsic termination" in this hypothesis means the termination of the conjugal relationship through an essential modification of its terms, consisting in an essential change of the sexuality, either in itself or in its quality of expressing the properties which determine the relationship as a conjugal one, viz., unity, indissolubility, the *ordinatio ad prolem*, the partnership of the whole life. Such a termination would occur, e.g., when the unity of the marriage becomes objectively and definitely unattainable, as in cases of incurable nymphomania or satyriasis. Other cases in point are adduced: transformation of sex; incurable impotence; definite impossibility of a partnership of life, due to sexual pathology, or to traumatic changes of personality brought on by torture, catastrophes, traffic incidents, air crashes, etc. All these are objective, "natural" causes which destroy the conjugal relationship in such a way that it never more can be nor ever become a matrimonial relationship, that man and woman can never more live together as "husband and wife."

Evidently similar situations often cannot be reduced to the moment of the celebration of the marriage. This more integral view of marriage, not only in its origin but also in its existence, allows for jurisprudence not to be obliged to look for grounds of nullity exclusively rooted in the moment of celebration, eventually through presumptive conjectures scientifically scarcely probable—by the author even qualified as "certain jurisprudential acrobatics"—and for the parties and their advocates to avoid the more and more evident divergence between the real reasons why they request the declaration of nullity and the grounds presented to or eventually adduced by the tribunals.[32] In the cases referred to above there is no dissolution or divorce of a marriage, imputable to any human responsibility, and the judgment of the Church, also necessary in these cases, would merely be the juridical acknowledgement of the factual termination of the conjugal relationship, and of its correlative canonical effects.

Otto Hermann Pesch,[33] considering the question whether the Church, in case of an irrecoverable breakdown of a marriage—which is quite different from faithlessness—could admit the possibility of dissolution, feels that, in the traditional ontologic conception of indissolubility, perhaps juridically it would be possible, but not theologically or anthropologically. Practically, however, the anthropological and theological reality of indissolubility neither is juridically ascertainable or controllable nor can it be juridically enforced. As a matter of fact the Church and its tribunals cannot give a judgment on the *real* validity or invalidity of a marriage, but only some moral estimation on the part of (the majority of) the judges regarding the legal evidence of juridical invalidity or the lack of this evidence, which by the law has been declared to be a presumption of the validity. If the Church would limit its juridical norm to a moral commandment regarding the *real* indissolubility, this would not and could not be enforced by any institutional control. Offenses against this commandment would be handled *in foro interno,* in a pastoral and not merely juridical way, with better chances for real justice. The eventual objection that in this way social standards and their institutional protections would get lost overrates the import of a juridical order and underestimates the virtue of a *real* pastoral care.[34] For the time being the present leadership of the Church does not give reason to expect any renewal of the law. Meanwhile the Church should, at least, to be sure, under responsible conditions, tolerate marriages seriously contracted after divorce.

Yet another approach starts from a more personalist conception of consummation of marriage. Under the 1917 Code consummation consisted in the first physical act of conjugal coition. The endless discussions on the physical requirements of the *copula perfecta* and the juridical proofs applied in cases of non-consummation and of annulment on the grounds of impotence were not exactly convincing that this was the right interpretation of the biblical "becoming one flesh." The 1983 Code requires that this act be performed "in a human manner" (c. 1061 §1). The French canonist Jean Bernhard has opened a pleading for a more comprehensive understanding of consummation of a marriage, called "existential consummation," as being a certain degree of mature stability of the conjugal relationship as a whole.[35] In this view non-consummation as a ground for dissolution would have a far broader bearing on the papal power to dissolve. The position of Edward Schillebeeckx seems to rely on the same conception. To the question as to which stage of maturity can be considered as the consummation of marriage, which makes the sacramental marriage indissoluble, his answer is that the weight attributed by canon law to the first sexual intercourse can hardly be made meaningful. Often the first intercourse is a failure and therefore humanly irrelevant or even the first germ of a breakdown. The shorter or longer duration of the cohabitation does not mean a great deal in the consummation of a marriage. Perhaps a sociological inquiry of the backgrounds of divorce could reveal something about the human consummation of marriage. Maybe the result will be that only a definitely successful marriage can be considered as consummated, and that the medieval and canonical distinction between *ratum tantum* and *ratum et consummatum* is irrelevant for this matter.[36]

Deductive and Inductive Conception

This institutional concept of marriage as a determinate juridical relation could be the source of logical juridical inferences, as to validity and invalidity of consent, capacity and incapacity to marry etc.; the personalist conception cannot be encompassed in a juridical definition. The differences of approaches to the questions of marriage in Vatican II and in the 1980 Synod of Bishops came from the tension between the deductive and inductive way of thinking, in other words, between the desire to maintain a clear logical juridical system and the concern to meet the real needs of the faithful. Both council and synod refer to the theology of the *sensus fidei* (*Lumen Gentium* 12, *propositions* 2-4) and to the "signs of the times" (*Gaudium et Spes* 4, *propositions* 5-6). Many bishops insisted that the experience of Christian spouses was one of the sources which belong to theological reflection, and that lay persons, especially married couples, should participate in deliberations about marriage and family.[37] The International Theological Commission expressed the hope that, in accordance with Vatican II and the new wedding liturgy, new liturgical and juridical norms will be developed among peoples who have recently come to the Gospel, to harmonize the reality of Christian marriage with the authentic values of those peoples' own traditions, because the Christian and ecclesial character of the union and of the mutual donation of the spouses can, in fact, be expressed in different ways.[38] In the 1980 synod several bishops, moved by a similar concern, were looking for pastoral solutions to various kinds of marriages which are not in line with the canonical norms: polygamy, divorced remarried persons, neither civilly nor ecclesially recognized marriages, various kinds of mixed marriages.[39]

Already in his famous decision of February 25, 1969, Anné observed that the judges have to take into account not only the cultural setting of the couple but also their personal social situation as one of the determining factors of the conjugal partnership, though it is hardly possible to give a positive definition or description of the "essential elements" of this partnership. Neither the preparatory commission nor the legislator succeeded in more closely defining these "essential elements" (c. 1101 §2). Wrenn[40] mentions some attempts: right to company, affection, help, recognition of each other's personal identity, wishing each other well,[41] or self revelation, understanding, and caring,[42] adding, however, that several other approaches are possible.

A typical aspect of this issue is the discussion whether "conjugal love," which is said in *Gaudium et Spes* to belong to marriage as an "intimate partnership of conjugal life and love" and is characterized as the "soul of the whole life of the spouses,"[43] but is omitted in the Code of Canon Law c. 1055 §1, is one of the essential canonical elements.[44] Likewise it is hardly or maybe not at all possible to give an exact definition of the corresponding "essential obligations'' which the marrying partners must be able to assume for giving a valid consent (c. 1095,3°).

In fact these discussions—with their repercussions in the Roman jurisprudence—reveal a deeper problem. Vatican II indeed did not try to create a new canonical marriage law, but to repeat the evangelical call to the *inner, naturally* human conjugal fidelity and love, which cannot be reduced to juridical categories and is not juridically controllable, but *is* the only realization of this evangelical call. The real testimony of evangelical conjugal life in this world can only be given by the married Christians themselves. Juridical dispositions have no other legitimate purpose than to help people live matrimony "according to the faith" in different human situations and conditions. We may assume that in former times the Church's law effectively has served this purpose. Today the "signs of the times" seem to render highly questionable the tendency to maintain the juridical control over the *external* juridical indissolubility—*and* dissolubility—of marriages or the validity—and invalidity—of marriage consent, for the purpose of helping people live the *inner* validity and the *inner* indissolubility of their marriage. Neither solution, whether interpreting the "essential elements" as the right defined in c. 1081 §2 of the 1917 Code, or as rights to "qualities," which in the *moral* estimation of the judges are deemed to be essential to human conjugal life, can serve this purpose. Tribunals and contentious processes are appropriate in resolving conflicts of rights situations, and when marriage is reduced to such a situation, the judicial judgment alone does not have any effect for this purpose.[45]

Besides, the Church's judicial system is also materially totally inadequate. According to statistics covering the year 1975, there is no tribunal available at all for the vast majority of the world's Catholics: ninety-five percent of all marriage cases terminated in first instance occurred in eleven nations, limited to Australia, Canada, Colombia, Europe, and the United States. The total of cases submitted to the tribunals may be estimated as approximately eleven percent of the total of divorces of Catholics in those countries. For the great majority of Catholics access to a tribunal is physically impossible.[46] The number of divorced US Catholics is estimated to be at least six million. Since 1978, US diocesan tribunals have processed approximately forty thousand annulment petitions each year, and about ten percent of the divorced Catholics have received annulments. It is estimated that seventy-five percent of divorced Catholics have remarried or will eventually remarry, most without a previous annulment and without a Catholic celebration.[47]

It has been observed that tribunals were designed for a society in which the Church's authorities were responsible for the social order of marriage and marriage was primarily a social contract, but have little to offer to the human and religious quality of marriages as they are lived today, as interpersonal commitments. Sociological inquiries reveal that the present system is no longer

taken seriously by lower clergy and laity. Might not the appropriate course for
the Church be to get out of the legal approach to marriage and invest its re-
serves in developing forms of witness-bearing for married couples that would
be pertinent to the situation in which they find themselves?[48]

Also Lawrence Wrenn pleads for a rather radical shift from the tribunal
system—which occasionally could continue to handle nullity cases—to a far
more developed pastoral assistance of the local community, represented by the
parish priest and aided perhaps by a board of lay people. This pastoral system
should be designed to help people to a better understanding of what marriage
means as personal commitment, a covenant and a sacrament, as viewed in
Gaudium et Spes.[49] In France, a similar concern has been formulated by Pierre
Hayot: marriage is a call and a mandate to accomplish, and as such it is exposed
to irreversible failure. Must not the Church accept, beyond the manifest invalidity of marriages, either the "existential non consummation" with respect
to love and the partnership of life, or the "qualitative insufficiency of the initial
consent" as revealed in the process of the subsequent failure? We may ask
whether the highest responsible authorities of the Church discharge themselves
too easily from this pastoral responsibility, leaving to *judicial* institutions conjugal situations, which need far more the pastoral care of the Church than the
jurisdiction of judges.[50]

Some Canonical Desires for Discussion

1. In the process of deliberation of the reform of the Church's marriage law
   qualified Christian married couples should take an adequate part. This
   should be an ecumenical deliberation.
2. There should be a drastic simplification of the law. For the faithful it must
   become an understandable expression of the evangelical message on marriage, in both its substance and its administration.
3. The evangelical principle that marriage by its own nature is a call and a
   mandate to lifelong fidelity should be applied to all marriages. "Pauline"
   and "Petrine" "privileges" should not be presented as "exceptions" to
   this principle, nor should non-consummated marriages.
4. For all marriages the purpose of the Church's ministry should be to help
   people live marriage "according to the faith," "in different situations and
   conditions" (Intern. Theolog. Comm.). This implies the adaptations of this
   ministry to the different cultures and traditions.
5. In cases of irremediable breakdown of marriages this ministry should try to
   help people find a just and livable way to overcome this situation.
6. This ministry should be exercised on a diocesan or even parochial level that
   is known and familiar to the persons concerned. Also nullity cases should

be handled in a pastoral and personal way. In one word: the ministry regarding marriage should become much nearer to and much more understandable for the people concerned, viz., the clergy and other faithful working in direct pastoral services, and their communities of faithful.

Notes

1. In this paper much is borrowed from the excellent study of David E. Fellhauer, "The 'Consortium Omnis Vitae' as a Juridical Element of Marriage," in *Studia Canonica* 13 (1979) 7–171, a comprehensive inquiry into this issue throughout history till its state shortly before the promulgation of the 1983 Code of Canon Law.

2. "Nuptiae autem sive matrimonium est viri et mulieris coniunctio, individuam consuetudinem vitae continens."

3. "Nuptiae sunt coniunctio maris et feminae et consortium omnis vitae, divini et humani iuris communicatio."

4. Hugo of St. Victor (+ 1141), De B. Mariae virginitate, c.1: PL 176, 859: "Marriage is a lawful society between a man and a woman, viz., a society in which both persons by equal consent owe themselves to each other. This owing can be considered in two ways, viz., that they keep themselves for each other and not deny themselves to each other. They keep themselves in that they don't pass over to another society after giving their consent. They don't deny themselves in that they don't separate themselves from that society with each other": Fellhauer p. 43 note 24; Cyno of Pistoia (+ 1336), Super Codice et Digesto, Lib.V, tit.1: ". . . for this reason marriage is called a personal contract, that is, because the object of the contractual obligation is the person. In other contracts it is otherwise. For if I promise you ten of something, my person has an obligation toward you, but I do not owe you my person, and for that reason such contracts are called real, that is, concerning things, even though the obligation is personal. And thus it is proper to call marriage a personal contract, because in a certain way it makes two persons into one, and it has this effect, that the person who has the other person is at the same time in the possession of the other, and vice versa"; Thomas Sanchez (+ 1610), De Sancto matrimonii sacramento, L.II, disp.I, n. 6: "The essence of marriage, or the marriage itself, consists in the bond by which the spouses are formally united, and which arises out of their mutual giving of themselves": Apostolic Signatura, c.Staffa, November 29, 1975.

5. Joseph A. Selling, "A Closer Look on the Doctrine of Gaudium et Spes on Marriage and the Family," in *Bijdragen* 43 (1982) 30–48, here 34; cf Fellhauer, 30; AAS 22 (1930) 547–549.

6. Fellhauer, 108–114; Bernard Häring in *Lexikon fur Theologie und*

Kirche. Das Zweite Vatikanische Konzil, Vol. III, 1968, 429–432; idem, "Fostering the Nobility of Marriage and the Family," in *Commentary on the Documents of Vatican II,* ed. Herbert Vorgrimler, Vol. V, New York-London, 1969, 225–245; Joseph A. Selling, "Twenty Significant Points in the Theology of Marriage and the Family Present in the Teaching of Gaudium et Spes," in *Bijdragen* 43 (1982) 412–441; Peter J. Huizing, "La conception du mariage dans le Code, le Concile et le 'Schema de Sacramentis,' " in *Revue de droit canonique* 27 (Mars-Juin 1977) 135–146.

7. Fellhauer, 125–151.

8. A.M. Arena, "The Jurisprudence of the Sacred Roman Rota: Its Development and Direction after the Second Vatican Council," in *Studia Canonica* 12 (1978) 265–293; idem, "Consenso matrimoniale e giurisprudenza evolutiva nel tribunale della Sacra Romana Rota," in *Monitor Ecclesiasticus* 105 (1980) 486–507; Jean Bernhard, "L'évolution de la jurisprudence matrimoniale: le point de vue d'un canoniste," in *Studia Canonica* 15 (1981) 73–86; idem, "The Evolution of Matrimonial Jurisprudence: The Opinion of a French Canonist," in *The Jurist* 41 (1981) 105–116; P. Branchereau, "Jurisprudence récente en matère matrimoniale," in *L-Année Canonique* 23 (1979) 215–240; C. Candelier, "L' Influence du Concile Vatican II sur les chefs de nullité du mariage," in *Revue de Droit Canonique* 34 (1984) 3–39; Guy Delépine, "*Communio vitae et amoris coniugalis:* le courant personnaliste du mariage dans l'evolution jurisprudentielle de la Rote 1969–1980," in *Revue de Droit Canonique* 33 (1983) 52–80, 293–312; C. J. Hettinger, "Matrimonial Jurisprudence: The Second Post-Conciliar Decade," in *The Jurist* 37 (1977) 358–375; Pierre Hayot, "Conception existentielle du mariage," in *Revue de Droit Canonique* 33 (1983) 9–51; Mario F. Pompedda, "Maturità psichica e matrimonio nei canoni 1095, 1096," in *Apollinaris* 57 (1984) 131–150; Jose M. Serrano Ruiz, "Le droit à la communauté de vie et d'amour conjugal comme objet du consentement matrimonial: aspects juridiques et évolution de la jurisprudence de la S. Rote Romaine," in *Studia Canonica* 10 (1976) 271–301; idem, "Recherches prometteuses en jurisprudence," in *Revue de Droit Canonique* 32 (1982) 109–125; M. Wegan, "L'incapacité d'assumer les obligations du mariage dans la jurisprudence récente du tribunal de la Rote," in *Revue de Droit Canonique* 28 (1978) 134–157; P. Wirth, "Die bisherige Rechtsprechung der römischen Rota zur Frage der psychischen Eheunfähigkeit," in *Archiv für katholisches Kirchenrecht* 147 (1978) 71–98.

9. V. Fagiolo, "Amore conjugale ed essenza del matrimonio," in *L'amore conjugale,* Città del Vaticano (1971) 179–185; *coram* Fagiolo, October 30, 1970 and January 29, 1971.

10. Quoted are sentences c. Pinto, Feb. 12, 1982; Dec. 3, 1983; *c.* Mazzala, April 20, 1982; *c.* Agustoni, Jan. 16, 1982; *c.* Egan, April 22, 1982; Dec. 9, 1982; July 28, 1983; see Canon Law Abstracts, No. 51 (1984, n. 1). It may

seem curious that the same Egan, in his Dec. 9, 1982 decision, concerning a sentence which cited at length decisions from English tribunals, points out that, though these may reflect wisdom and logic, they are not normative in the way that rotal jurisprudence is; where there is a gap in the law, it is not only useless but erroneous to appeal to local jurisprudence. Egan does not specify which rotal jurisprudence is normative.

11. Code of Canon Law. Latin-English Edition, Canon Law Society of America, Washington, D.C. 20064, 1983, p. xiv.

12. Communicationes 3 (1971) 70.

13. Lawrence G. Wrenn, "Canon 1095: A Bird's-Eye View," in *The Jurist* 44 (1984) 220–242, esp. 240–241. Canestri's sentence was written some fifteen years before the present writer used the concept in his manuscript for students "Schema Structurae Iuris Canonici Latini de Matrimonio," Pontificia Università Gregoriana, Rome 1963 (later published in Alphonsus Van Kol, *Theologia Moralis,* Barcelona 1968, Vol. II, 435–683; n. 719, 561–563: "Impotentia moralis"), quoted as having introduced the concept by T. O. Hevia, "Moral Impotence as a Canonical Matrimonial Disability" (*Canon Law Studies,* 488), Washington 1976, and Josef Weber, "'Erfullungsunvermögen' in der Rechtsprechung der Sacra Romana Rota," Regensburg, 1983, 14.

14. Propositions on the Doctrine of Marriage, Dec. 1977, in *Origins* 8 (1978) 235–239, Nr.2.2.,237); the propositions are also published in *Problèmes doctrinaux du mariage chrétien,* Louvain-la-Neuve 1979, with a preface by Cardinal Ratzinger and an introduction by P. Delhaye, general secretary of the group. Cf. P Delhaye, "La dottrina del matrimonio canonico nella formulazione della Commissione Teologica Internazionale," in *Monitor Ecclesiasticus* 105 (1980) 216–233.

15. Jan Grootaers-Joseph A. Selling, "The 1980 Synod of Bishops 'On the Role of the Family.' An Exposition of the Event and an Analysis of Its Texts" (*Bibliotheca Ephemeridum Theologicarum Lovaniensium* 64), Louvain, 1983, 97–99.

16. Pierre Hayot, "Pour plus de vérité au sujet du mariage," in *Revue Théologique de Louvian* 13 (1982) 287–316, here 298–300, referring to Z. Grocholewski, *De exclusione indissolubilitatis ex consensu matrimoniali eiusque probatione. Considerationes super recentiores sententias rotales,* Naples 1973; and O. Fumagalli-Carulli, "La relation dynamique entre les canons 1082 et 1081 du Code de Droit Canonique," in *Revue de Droit Canonique* 29 (1979) 114–139, here 118; Jean Bernhard, "Réflection sur la 'dynamique' de l'engagement matrimonial en droit canonique," in *Revue de Droit Canonique* 27 (1977) 290–303; Jean Lemaire, *Conditions et fondements actuels de la fidélité; le mariage engagement pour la vie? Recherches et débats,* Paris 1971.

17. Pierre Hayot, "La présomption du canon 1086," in *Mélanges Wagnon,* Louvain 1976, 557–575.

18. *l.c.* NN.3.3 and 3.5.

19. *l.c.* N.3.6.

20. Grootaers-Selling, 134–139, 350f.

21. Yves Congar, "La Commission Théologique Internationale (Dec. 1977) et le canon 1012," in *Recherches des Sciences Philosophiques et Théoligiques* 65 (1981) 295–298.

22. M. Ashdowne, "A Study of the Sacramentality of Marriage: When Is Marriage Really Present?" in *Studia Canonica* 9 (1975) 287–303; J. M. Aubert, "Sacramentalité et réalité humaine du mariage," in *Revue de Droit Canonique* 30 (1980) 140–150; W. Aymans, "Gleichsam hausliche Kirche: Ein kanonistischer Beitrag zum Grundverständnis der sakramentalen Ehe als Gottesbund und Vollzugsgestalt kirchlicher Existenz," in *Archiv für katholisches Kirchenrecht* 147 (1978) 424–446; idem, "Die sakramentale Ehe als Gottesbund und Vollzugsgestalt kirchlicher Existenz," in *Theologisches Jahrbuch* (1981) 184–197; J. M. F. Castaño, "De quibusdam difficultatibus contra formulam can. 1012 2, scilicet 'quin sit eo ipso sacramentum,' " in *Periodica de re morali* . . . 67 (1978) 269–281; E. Corecco, "Das Sakrament der Ehe: Eckstein der Kirchenverfassung," in *Archiv für katholisches Kirchenrecht* 148 (1979) 353–369; idem, "Il sacramento del matrimonio; cardine della costituzione della Chiesa," in *Communio* 51 (1980) 46ff.; Richard Cunningham, "Marriage and the Nescient Catholic: Questions of Faith and Sacrament:, in *Studia Canonica* 15 (1980) 263–283; Joseph Duss-Von-Werdt, "Theologie der Ehe. Der sakramentale Charakter der Ehe," in J. Feiner–M. Löhrer, *Mysterium Salutis* Bd.IV,2, Einsiedeln 1973, 422–448; W. Kasper, "Die sakramentale Würde der Ehe," in *Lebendige Seelsorge* 28 (1977) 134–141; idem, *Zur Theologie der christlichen Ehe,* Mainz 1977, 34–54; K. Lehmann, "Die christliche Ehe als Sakrament," in *Communio* 8 (1979) 385–392; idem, "Glaube-Taufe-Ehesakrament. Dogmatische Überlegungen zur Sakramentalität der christlichen Ehe," in *Studia Moralia* 16 (1978) 71–97; J. Manzanares, "Habitudo matrimonium baptizatorum inter et sacramentum: omne matrimonium baptizatorum estne necessario sacramentum?" in *Periodica de re morali* . . . 57 (1978) 35–71; Louis de Naurois, "Le mariage des baptisés de l'Eglise Catholiques qui n'ont pas la foi," in *Revue de Droit Canonique* 30 (1980) 151–174; L. Orsy, "Sacrament, Contract, and Christian Marriage: Disputed Questions," in *Theological Studies* 43 (1982) 379–398; G. B. Varnier, "Deux notes sur le contrat et le sacrement de mariage," in *Recherches de Sciences Philosophiques et Théologiques* 65 (1981) 284–294.

23. Denz.-Schönm. 1807. On Nov. 11, 1563, the council issued two statements on the indissolubility of marriage: canon 5 condemns those who say that the marriage can be dissolved by reason of heresy, domestic incompatibility, or willful desertion by one of the parties; canon 7 condemns those who say that the Church is in error when it has taught and teaches that the marriage

bond cannot be dissolved because of adultery on the part of either spouse (*Sessio* 24, *de matrimonio,* canons 5 and 7). These canons were directed against the new doctrines of the Protestants, especially Luther, the kernel of which was the negation of the sacramental character of Christian marriage, consequently of the Church's jurisdiction over marriage, and the affirmation of the "intrinsic dissolubility" by the spouses themselves. Canon 7 declares that this canonical tradition is a legitimate tradition, in agreement with the teaching of Jesus and St. Paul. The council would not and did not condemn the tradition of the eastern churches nor the contrary doctrine of "Ambrose and others."

24. Propositions N.4.2. P. Fransen, "Die Formel 'si quis dixerit ecclesiam errare' auf der 24.Sitzung des Trienter Konzils," in *Scholastik* 25 (1950) 492–517; 26 (1951) 119–221; idem, "Ehescheidung im Falle von Ehebruch," *ibid.* 27 (1952) 526–556; idem, "Ehescheidung na echtbreuk van een der gehuwden. Het kerkrechlijk dossier van Trente," in *Bijdragen* 14 (1953) 363–387.

25. Proposition N.14.6. See however also N.14.3, confirming the praxis of not admitting divorced remarried to the sacraments.

26. Grootaers-Selling, 274f, note 49.

27. "Unauflöslichkeit der Ehe und kirchliche Ehescheidung in heitiger Problematik," in *Die Ehe: Band oder Bund?* (ed. René Metz und Jean Schlick), Aschaffenbrug 1970, 142–177; French version in *Le lien matrimonial,* Strassbourg 1970, Spanish version in *Matrimonio y divorcio,* Salamanca 1974.

28. Mk 10:9; Mt 19:6.

29. To the author's sources the recent conclusions of two outstanding New Testament scholars may be added.

L. Descamps, "Les textes évangéliques sur le mariage," in *Revue Théologique de Louvain* 9 (1978) 259–286; 11 (1980) 15–50: Jesus' words must be understood in the framework of his radical moral message. Jesus' concern with divorce regards, as so often, the intentions, the inner heart, the obligations of each to assume the responsibility of one's own actions. Jesus' point of view is a moralist's one, rather than of the founder of a "social order" (p. 40 note 85, referring to B. Rigaux, "Le radicalisme du Règne," in J. Dupont (ed.), *La Pauvreté évangélique,* Paris 1971, 135–173). Regarding the hermeneutic import of the apostolic teachings, the last criterion is taking into account the actual conjuncture of Christian marriage. Three points raise questions: the Pauline privilege, Matthew's clause, Matthew's apparent attenuation of indissolubility as attribute of *every* marriage. Regarding this threefold subject, the present-day questions at least must take into account the differentiated conclusions of the historical-critical exegesis and the coefficient of importance given to them by the tradition. This put first, it is in itself legitimate to take also into account the present-day situation and notably the way the breakdown of marriage is felt today in certain families, otherwise sincerely solicitous for living in accordance with the Gospel and the Church [p. 49 and note 105, referring to V. Boulanger (ed), *Mariage: rêve-réalité, Essai théologique,* Montreal 1975 (confrontation of the sources of faith and the experience of Christian spouses) and P. Hayot, "Les procédures matrimoniales et la théologie du mariage," in *Revue Théologique de Louvain* 9 (1978) 33–58 ("interpellation" of the theologues on the basis of marriage procedures from a pastoral point of view)].

The exegete may recall that for Jews the repudiation broke the marriage bond by the initiative of the husband alone, without intervention of any authority—hence by forbiding repudiation and in any case remarriage, Jesus wants *in recto* to oppose every repudiation and every remarriage by the husband, and through extension by the wife. Attributing to itself the right to dissolve certain marriages, the Church confronts new problems which Jesus did not raise. But Paul perhaps—in case he allows remarriage to the Christian spouse persecuted by the pagan partner—would approve of the dissolution of certain marriages. We feel that we must appeal to that faculty of actualization to justify Paul and the Church, and not to the texts on the power of the keys. In those texts "bind and dissolve" cannot, as it seems, be applied to the power over the marriage bond, except only perhaps in a virtual and remote way.

However strong the framework of the principles may be, adaptations do not seem to be excluded a priori; the properly so-called decisions, however, belong to the Church of today and tomorrow (49f).

Rudolf Pesch, *Freie Treue. Die Christen und die Ehescheidung,* Freiburg, 1971, 75f, summarizes the New Testament teaching as follows: Husband and wife are joined together in love and responsibility for each other and bound to partnership in free fidelity. For a Christian divorce is as "impossible" as adultery. The original communities did not interpret Jesus' commandment as a law, but applied it in free fidelity to their different situations (Mt 5:32; Mk 10:11f; I Cor 7:10f). The apparent "exceptions" of "unchastity" (Matthew) and the unbelieving partner who desires to separate (Paul) are neither "legal exceptions" nor "permissions" but exceptional cases brought on by unbelief, by sin, and the answers to these cases are viewed as a protection of the freedom of the Christian, whose fidelity may not be reduced to slavery. The biblical testimony means that the issue of divorce concerns the whole Christian community and not only the spouses, only too often left alone. The faithful Christian is called by the Lord to free fidelity, and does not pharisaically ask for "legal exceptions" which would jeopardize this fidelity. The Church community, however, may well establish that unbelief, infidelity, or adultery has factually broken a marriage or even prevented a relationship from becoming a marriage. It may not transform Jesus' call into a law, imposing on Christians burdens from which Jesus would free them. It must take over Jesus' call to the minds, the hearts, the consciences and love, creating a human climate in which the unity of marriage can be realized and its failure can be born in a human and Christian way, contributing to forgiveness of guilt and the opening to a new, more happy life (74–76). The author is strongly opposed to the interpretation of Jesus' words as establishing a legal indissolubility.

For additional information see John R. Donahue, "Divorce—New Testament Perspectives," in Thomas P. Doyle (ed.), *Marriage Studies II. Reflections in Canon Law and Theology*, Washington, 1982, 1–19; C. Marucci, *Parola di Gesù sul divorzio, Ricerche scritturistiche previe ad un ripensamento theologico, canonistico e pastorale della dottrina cattolica dell'indissolubilità del matrimonio*, Brescia, 1982.

30. *Geschieden und wieder verheiratet. Beurteilung der Ehe von Geschiedenen, die wieder heiraten*, Regensburg, 1983; M. Kaiser, "Geschiedene, die wieder verheiratet sind. Ihre Stellung in der Kirche," in *Stimmen der Zeit*, vol. 203, year 110 (1985) 241–254; "Eine rechtliche ungültige Ehe kann eine sehr glückliche Ehe sei. Ein Gesprach mit Professor Matthäus Kaiser über Fragen des kirchlichen Eherechts," in *Herder Korrespondenz* 40, 1 (January 1986) 20–25; H. Heinemann, "Geschieden un wieder verheiratet. Anmerkungen zu einer Schrift gleichen Titels von Matthäus Kaiser," in *Archiv für katholisches Kirchenrecht* 153 (1984) 113–123; critique of D. S. (eeber) in *Herder Korrespondenz* 38 (1984) 46.

31. "Il principio di indissolubilità nel matrimonio quale stato di vita tra due battezzati," in *Ephemerides Iuris Canonici* 36 (1980) 9–69, esp. 56–59; idem, L'essenza del matrimonio. Contributo allo studio dell'amore coniugale. I. Il momento costitutivo del matrimonio (Pubblicazioni dell'Istituto di Diritto Pubblico della Facoltà di Giurisprudenza, Università degli Studi di Roma Vol. 30), Padova, 1976, 311–313. See the review of this study of U. Navarrette, "Nota bibliografica," in *Periodica* 65 (1976) 743–753.

32. The author refers to Jean-Marie Aubert, "Déclaration de nullité et société moderne," in *Revue de Droit Canonique* 26 (1976) 67–78 (Why or when do people come to the Church with marriage problems? Because they are divorced or on the way to divorce. And what does the Church do? It is not at all interested in the real history of the breakdown of the marriage, but goes to examine things which the people themselves often do not even think have anything to do with their history; the validity of their wedding, their baptisms, the act of consummation of their marriage), and to Louis De Naurois, "Le concept juridique du mariage. Équivoques et ambiguités," in *Revue de Droit Canonique* 26 (1976) 43–66 (one of the ambiguities consists in the often observed discrepancy between the alleged grounds of nullity and the real causes of the breakdown of the marriage).

33. "Ehe im Blick des Glaubens," in *Christlicher Glaube in moderner Gesellschaft*, Teilband 7, Freiburg i.Br. 1981, 8–86, esp. 39–42.

34. Here the author refers to Walter Kasper, *Zur Theologie der christlichen Ehe,* Mainz 77, 84–95; T. Koch, "Ehe und 'nichteheliche Lebensgemeinschaft' als Thema der Ethik," in *Die nichteheliche Lebensgemeinschaft* (G. Landwehr, ed.), Göttingen 1978, treating of juridical problems but easily applicable to canonical questions.

35. This author treated this issue mainly in several articles published in the *Revue de Droit Canonique:* 20 (1970) 181–192; 21 (1971) 243–277; 24 (1974) 334–349; 27 (1977) 290–302.

36. "Die christliche Ehe und die menschliche Realität völliger Ehezerrüttung," in P. Huizing (ed.) *Für eine neue kirchliche Eheordnung. Ein Alternativentwurf,* Düsseldorf 1975, 41–73, esp. 56f.

As Jean Gaudemet, "Les origines historiques de la faculté de rompre le mariage non consommé," in *Sociétés et mariage,* Strasbourg 1980, 210–229, has demonstrated, two "auctoritates" were crucial in this history.

1. The letter of Pope Leo I to Bishop Rusticus (PL 54:1204f), declaring, according to the contemporary Roman laws and customs, that a marriage requires that the parties are free (*ingenui*) and of equal social condition (*aequales*), that the bride receive the dowry (*dotata legitime*), and that she be honored by a public wedding (*publicis nuptiis honestata*). Otherwise the union is a concubinage, not a marriage. Therefore Leo declares legitimate the marriage of a man who previously lived with a concubine, explicitly stating that sexual intercourse is not required for the formation of a legitimate marriage and the "sacrament": "Unde cum societas nuptiarum inde ab initio constituta sit, ut praeter sexuum coniunctionem haberet in se Christi et ecclesiae sacramentum, dubium non est eam mulierem non pertinere ad matrimonium, in qua docetur nuptiale non fuisse mysterium."

2. A canonical treatise of Hincmar of Rheims, written at the end of 860 (MGH, Ep. VI, 87–107), where he, in line with contemporary German customs, first formulated the doctrine that a non-consummated marriage is not a sacrament of Christ and the Church, and not indissoluble. Therefore he interpolated Leo's text and attributed this to St. Augustine's authority: ". . . non habent nuptiae in se Christi et ecclesiae sacramentum, sicut beatus Augustinus dicit, si se nuptialiter non utuntur, id est, si eas non sequitur commixtio sexuum" (*l.c.* 93,1, 6–10).

While Leo's text was received in the medieval canonical collections only about 1130–1140, Hincmar's interpolation with Augustine's authority appear in the collections and the most important one, Gratian's Decree (C.27,q.2,cc.16 and 17). The importance of these canons in the discussion between the schools of Paris and Bologna at the end of the twelfth century and in the decisions of Alexander III is well known. Cf. Jean Dauvillier, *Le mariage dans le droit classique de l'Eglise depuis le Décret de Gratien (1140) jusqu'á la mort de Clément V (1334),* Paris 1933, 285–324. On German law see Hans Dombois, *Kirche und Eherecht. Studien und Abhandlung 1953–1972* (Forschungen und Berichte der Evangelischen Studiengemeinschaft, Band 29), Stuttgart 1974, 26f: the *consummatio,* or the symbolic occupancy of the conjugal bed in the presence of witnesses, signified the public foundation of the community of body and life. Only through this act the bride, as appears e.g. from the "Sachsenspiegel," becomes "companion" of the man, and the bond of fidelity is realized for life; referring to Siegfried Reicke, *Geschichtliche Grundlagen des deutschen Eheschliessungsrecht,* Vol. VI, 33–40.

Consequently the two opposed "theologies" of marriage as "the sacrament of Christ and the Church" and hence indissoluble were based on the "authorities" representing two different juridical cultures, the Roman in which consummation had no juridical value, the German in which it was the essential final element of the wedding process. Would this historical fact have any consequence for the contemporary "theology" of the consummation of a marriage?

Besides, the need for a more appropriate theology of marriage was put forth at the 1980 Synod by Africans and other bishops, who made various suggestions of moving away from the usual symbolic foundation: Grootaers-Selling, 99f.

37. Grootaers-Selling, 28f, 99f.

38. *Propositions* 1.7.

39. Grootaers-Selling 100f.; J. F. Thiel, "Cultural Anthropological Reflections on the Institution of Marriage," in *Concilium* 6 (1970), n.5; Eugene Hillman, "The Development of the Institution of Christian Marriage," ibid.; Adolfo Longhitano, *Il matrimonio fra tradizione e rinnovamento,* Bologna 1985, 10: In the ecclesial community there legitimately exist local churches with their own traditions (*Lumen gentium* 13); the young churches have their own contribution to the other local churches (*Ad gentes* 22). These principles have consequences regarding the conception and the discipline of the marriage law of the Church; Edward Schillebeeckx, "Kerkelijk spreken over sexualiteit en huwelijk," in the collection with the same title, Nijmegen-Baarn 1983, refers to Thomas Aquinas, *Suppl.* q.42, a.2; q.65, a.2: Thomas had no univocal concept of marriage; he was aware of the cultural variety of marriage in different traditions. On May 13, 1983, an African bishop told his audience in San Francisco about some concrete difficulties of the African churches with the common marriage law. What to do if a polygamous man or a woman married to him wants to become a Christian? How can he drive away his wives except one? Who then looks after the children? Should the polygamous state of her husband be an obstacle to her receiving the Christian faith and baptism?: *Origins* 13 (1983) n. 6, June 23, 108f.

40. Lawrence G. Wrenn, "Canon 1095 . . ." 242f.

41. Ombretta Fumagalli Carulli, "Essenza ed esistenza nell'amore con-

iugale: considerazioni canonistiche," in *Ephemerides Iuris Canonici* 36 (1980); 216–218.

42. Eugene C. Kennedy. "Signs of Life in Marriage," in Lawrence G. Wrenn (ed.), *Divorce and Remarriage in the Catholic Church*, New York, 1973, 121–133.

43. Nn. 48 and 49.

44. Piero Antonio Bonnet, "Amor et matrimonium," in *Ephemerides Iuris Canonici* 20 (1974), 60–107; Theodore Mackin, "Conjugal Love and the Magisterium," in *The Jurist* 36 (1976) 263–301; Urbano Navarrete, "Structura iuridica matrimonii secundum Concilium Vaticanum II. Momentum iuridicum amoris coniugalis," in *Periodica de re morali* . . . 56 (1967) 357–383; 554–578; 57 (1968) 131–167; 169–216; idem, "Amor coniugalis et consensus matrimonialis. Quid Paulus VI in allocutione ad praelatos S.R.Rotae 9 Feb. 1976 (AAS 68, 1976, 204–208) doceat?" in *Periodica de re morali* . . . 65 (1976) 619–632; Rudolf Pesch, Freie Treue . . . 75f; José Maria Serrano Ruiz, "Ispirazione conciliare nei principi generali del matrimonio canonico," in Adolfo Longhitano (ed.), *Il matrimonio tra tradizione e rinnovamento* (Il Codice del Vaticano II), Bologna 1985, 13–78, esp. 28, note 33.

45. Thomas J. Green, "Marriage Nullity Procedures in the Schema *De Processibus*," in *The Jurist* 38 (1978) 311–414, esp. 404–410, where some alternatives to the current system are also surveyed.

46. James H. Provost, "Intolerable Marriage Situations Revisited," in *The Jurist* 40 (1980) 141–196, esp. 157–159.

47. Kindly communicated from the not yet published study: Steven Preister and James J. Young, *Catholic Remarriage: Pastoral Issues and Preparation Models*, final draft, June 5, 1985.

48. Andrew M. Greeley, "Church Marriage Procedures and the Contemporary Family," in Lawrence G. Wrenn (ed.) *Divorce and Remarriage in the Catholic Church*, New York 1973, 105–113, esp. 110–113.

49. "Marriage-Indissoluble or Fragile?" in *ibid.* 134–149.

50. "La conception 'existentielle' du mariage et ses répercussions en matière d'erreur," in *Revue de Droit Canonique* 33 (1983) 9–51, esp. 51; idem, "Valeur et limites du jugement prudentiel lors d'un constat de nullité du mariage," in *Revue Théologique de Louvain* 9 (1978) 35–58; Noel Vilain, "Quelques interpellations des sciences humaines comme approches de procédures canoniques matrimoniales," in *Revue de Droit Canonique* 30 (1980) 69–115.

RESPONSES

RAYMOND A. LUCKER

I think that the presentation that we just heard is the kind of presentation that really frees us. We have the fruit of the experience of decades of study and hard work in which Fr. Huizing has been engaged. For him to give the analysis that he does really kind of opens it up and frees us to see the continuity in the tradition and at the same time a whole new development.

Fr. Huizing has shown how a change in a definition really has enormous consequences. We are really not quite sure yet where this is going to lead us.

Perhaps it is difficult for some to accept this kind of change and development in the Church. After all, we grew up in a Church that seemed to give the impression that nothing changes. Thirty years ago anyone who objected to the canonical notion of marriage as a contract would have been thought of as really being beyond the teaching of the Church. Yet now we have an official description of marriage that is more personalist. It is a radical change—quite radical.

We need to admit—and this is hard for us to do apparently—that as a human institution, guided by the Holy Spirit, we have made many mistakes in the past. We need to be able to say that we have been wrong, and that we have changed positions—and usually after tough, hard work on the part of theologians, Scripture scholars, and philosophers. Remember how we used to say that error has no rights! Remember how we used to speak of the union of Church and state, and the state as being one that we would depend on to protect our teaching! Note how we *still* speak of women! Note how we didn't say much about slavery when that was an institution that was accepted in society! Remember how there was reluctance to permit the practice of rhythm! Now natural family planning is to be promoted.

All I am saying is that we live in a time of change. We live in a Church which constantly changes. We need, then, to be open to the authentic developments that Fr. Huizing has so well described for us.

THEODORE MACKIN

I want to make one reflection and out of it bring a question. It is very predictable that diocesan marriage tribunals are going to be in action for a long time for the foreseeable future. It is clear that in rendering their decisions in petitions for nullity, the Catholic courts treat these cases as adversarial actions. Those who are familiar with tribunal procedures know that the marriage is turned into a fictitious person and is the accused defendant. In the language of the courts the marriage is accused of being null, and the one who does the accusing is the petitioner, the one who asks for the annulment. Then there's a judge of the court, the defender of the bond, and the advocate. Now my question is this: Isn't it more accurate to treat petitions for nullity not as adversarial actions but as simple findings of fact, namely whether there is a marriage? So is it necessary to have marriage tribunals in the Church?

PETER J. HUIZING

I am glad that you asked me this question, because I think for the time being we need tribunals—at least, in those relatively few regions of the Church that have them. There has, of course, been a change in the way most tribunals handle marriage cases. This is especially true in the United States and in my own country. Even though formally tribunals have to follow more or less the rules of procedure, they take a much more pastoral approach. I have heard several times that when cases are treated in that way, the concerned persons believe that they have at least found understanding, that they have found a link with the Church, that at least their situation had become bearable. So I think it is necessary that tribunals exist and that they could develop into purely pastoral and freely working organs of the Church. I think that their existence as a link between the old style and new style of approaching marital breakdowns is indispensable.

Part Three
Pastoral Reflections

6.

The Meaning of Marriage in
Women's New Consciousness

Rosemary Haughton

In the last forty years we have seen a collapse of confidence in all the institutions—political, social, religious, scientific—which once shaped the expectations of Western culture. We are two generations whose inherited institutions could find no other answer to conflict than a bomb, no better hope of "peace" than the fear of more bombs. We live in a culture reacting to that loss of confidence, either by letting go of the expectations and values those institutions upheld and symbolized, or by reverting to the most rigid forms of them, in an attempt to deny the reality of the loss.

In this situation, we cannot keep old institutions in being simply by redefining or remodeling them. Marriage can no longer be considered as a "given." We have to have the courage to admit that as an institution it has in practice fallen apart beyond repair. Our task as Christians is to try to discover how the Gospel understanding of human society and relationship is to be applied in the sphere of sexual and intergenerational relationships.

The demographic facts alone impel us to a reassessment: we can no longer ignore the vast numbers of single parent families, split-parent families, "alternative" households, families and relationships.

But the biggest thrust toward a complete rethinking comes from the women's movement—that one among the many movements of liberation coming out of the years since the Second World War, which is calling us to rethink basic assumptions about the mental and emotional orientation of a whole culture.

It is in the light of feminist thinking and feelings of liberation that we look at the experiences of our time and the vision of the Gospel and try to find some basis for judgment and decision in the area of what has been and still may be called "marriage."

I live and work in a house in Gloucester, Massachusetts, which is a place for homeless people to find shelter and support while they begin to repair their shattered lives and take small steps toward a different future. Most of them are women. Many of them are young women, pregnant or with little children, and some are middle-aged or elderly. This preponderance of women is not because it is our policy, but because theirs is the greatest need. They are usually homeless because they have been thrown out by parents or boyfriends, or have themselves escaped from abuse. They have little or no family support and often the family is the root of the problem.

The house is an old house, one of the oldest in the country. For three and a half centuries people have lived in it—have been born in it, grown in it, worked, fought, made love, made bread, dreamed, wept, prayed and died. The bricks of the huge hearth have absorbed many stories of sorrow and love and hate and endurance, and they are absorbing them now—women's stories, not very different from those which were whispered in that house through past generations. But there is a difference, and that difference is the starting point of this paper. The difference is in the consciousness which can develop between some of the women. They share their stories of rejection, abuse, incest, and rape, of the way they learned from infancy that women have no value in themselves, exist only to be used and abused by fathers, brothers, uncles, boyfriends, husbands or sons, and can only be acceptable if they manage to please. But whereas in the past most women told those stories with resignation or apathy, with frustration and anger but little hope, or advised each other how to find comfort in God or in a carefully conducted illicit love affair, now it is different. They begin by telling them in the old way, in the tone of voice that says: "It's terrible but that's life," with the giggle of self-contempt at the end. But as they listen to each other in the setting of a house whose explicit purpose is to give them back their dignity and their hope, something happens: the tone changes, the experiences begin to sound different. They find it possible to feel that that which has been done to them is not God's will (as many have been told) but evil; they become angry, they cry, and they affirm each other as they do so. A spark of self-worth kindles and is gently blown into steady flame by the support of the other. The shared experiences no longer give merely the strength to endure or to comfort in sharing grief, but strong friendships develop and give courage to change, to refuse the old ways and try new ones.

It's a terrifying change. These are not middle-class women with supportive families and good education. They have no role models but mothers and friends who have been abused and later have often become abusive themselves. There are no religious guidelines—the religious teaching goes the opposite way, demanding submission and patience, endlessly excusing the male, talking of reconciliation. The way forward is all new, and it is risky—physically, emotionally, and spiritually risky. Many go a few steps and then draw back to the safety of the known, "the flesh pots of Egypt," which is at least a known territory with the security of the familiar, however unpleasant. But some come out of slavery—if not at the first attempt, or the second, then at the third or even the fourth. The timid, soft-spoken seventeen year old with a four-month-old baby, accustomed to accept abuse from childhood, finds in the group the courage to refuse to spend the rest of her life that way. The girl whose boyfriend uses her to buy his drugs tells him "no," and turns him out. The woman of seventy finally makes the decision to leave forty years of sexual and emotional abuse and begins a new life, against all the advice of her ministers, her friends and her lawyer.

All this has to do with theology, the theology around sexual relationships, marriage and the roles of men and women in God's world, for theology is reflection on real experiences, or it is sounding brass and tinkling cymbal, and this is an experience which cannot be denied. All these women want love, want to be valued, listened to, cared for. Many of them hoped to find love in marriage, and went on hoping and hoping to find it long after reality was telling them there was no hope. Most of them still dream of a happy marriage, a reconciliation or a new relationship one day, though many come to learn it isn't going to happen, and begin painfully to build their lives in other ways. If marriage is ever to be a way of love and fulfillment for women in the future, if the Church is to offer a way forward instead of a way back, then there has to be a better, a more real and honest way of understanding marriage than the one which has allowed and indeed supported as necessary the subordination of women. But something new is indeed happening, and there is hope.

What I see happening in these little groups of women is happening all over the country, all over the world. But it is not, as it might seem, just about the liberation of grossly abused women from hurt and danger. It has to do with a fundamental remaking of the *role* of women in society, and that means the role of women in marriage and family. It is this remaking which makes possible the kind of personal liberation that these women are helping each other to imagine, and then to achieve. It is really different, and it is very powerful, and it is an experience which is forcing Christians and people of other religions to perceive their whole theology differently, or risk seeing that theology gradually emptied of relevance and energy. There is always the option of simply reaffirming the old theologies, laying on the old guilt and cranking out the old thunder-machine to threaten divine wrath, insanity, and communism for those who question, and that option is being worked on by many. Others are trying to rework the old theology of marriage into patterns more acceptable to the new consciousness, but that is not enough. This paper is simply an attempt to say why it is not enough, and to indicate where we might begin the task of discovering a theology of marriage which emerges from and reflects the new consciousness of women, and of many men. I want to ask not only whether the old models are adequate but where we might look for alternative ones, for at present there is a void partly filled with much experimentation, and it is the fear of this void which drives many to cling to old patterns which have ceased to work. In order to do this I need to look first at the way in which theology happens for most of us, and how we react to that as churches and as individuals, and I shall take a little time to touch on the kind of theologizing which has occurred in the past around the issue of sexuality and marriage, not only the what but the why of theological change, in order to put us in a position to understand better the causes and implications of what is happening now.

Because theology is reflection on experience, from a specific religious point of view, it is an ongoing process of discovery which cannot reach an end. And at every stage of discovery we are hampered by the inevitable tendency to absolutize the theological insights which grew from a particular cultural experience in the past. We are aware of this, and most people are now accustomed to the notion of theological development, and even to the rightness of the emergence of radically new theological interpretations springing from specific experience such as that which led to the growth of liberation theologies in Latin America, in Africa, among black people and among women.

In all theological areas this new growth, and even the more low-key theological development, has met with opposition, but it is noticeable that the opposition only reaches panic proportions when the developments are occurring in areas which directly affect the ecclesiastical power structure. There is much greater concern over the threat to clerical control presented by base communities, or the emergence of non-canonical liturgies, than over reevaluation of the inspiration of Scripture or the divinity of Christ. But the greatest resistance to the new insights comes in the area of sexuality, including marriage, and this has been so since the beginning of Christianity, so we should not be surprised at the reaction. The cultural norms in the area of sexuality are so embedded in the fabric of lived Christianity in *all* denominations (with minor variations) that they have become unquestionable. To question them is to question the power structure of the churches because that is based on a patriarchal model and that must not be allowed to happen. As in the beginning it seemed essential to accommodate the Gospel vision to the given social and domestic structure of the patriarchal culture of the time for the sake of acceptance and even survival, so, ever since, the perceived need for stability of possession of land and wealth, including the inheritance of property or power by undoubted male heirs, has been theologized into the fabric of Christian living, feeling and thinking. It created, among other things, the demand that women be virgins at marriage, the notorious double-standard in moral attitudes to women's and men's sexual behavior, and the grounds for annulment of marriage. For the perpetuation of the system it was necessary that women be basically possessions, and the laws of state and Church reflected this. The theology of the Church developed ways to interpret that situation in terms of God's design, and spirituality taught women to look for their salvation within the terms set by the system—a system which is basically a self-perpetuating patriarchal oligarchy whose primary purpose (conscious or not) is not the preaching of the Gospel but precisely that self-perpetuation. Genuine love and mutual respect have always been possible and have redeemed millions of unions within the system, but they did not and could not change it.

If we are to understand why that situation has changed, we need to look first at the ways in which it was never unchallenged. There have always been some Christian voices protesting this sacralization of a cultural imperative; among them I would mention Hroswitha, playwright and feminist of the "dark ages," and Margaret Fell, co-founder with George Fox of the Society of Friends (the Quakers). Margaret's women's liberation theology (for that is what it was) was based firmly in the Gospel teaching, as has been all radical Christian feminism since. The Friends themselves, and a few other smaller movements, sects and communities in the seventeenth, eighteenth and nineteenth centuries, questioned the patriarchal assumptions underlying the huge theological-spiritual construct around norms of sexual relations and behavior. Among these were the Shakers, an offshoot of the Quakers, which grew up in the newly liberated American colonies. They rejected marriage and sex altogether in favor of celibacy, for both sexes, in a community in which there was total sexual equality at all levels. It seemed to them the only appropriate way for the redeemed, and, interestingly, this choice was largely the result of the need of the foundress, Mother Ann, to theologize her own choice to free herself from the atrocious sexual experiences of her marriage.

The Oneida community, with its experiment in organized communal marriage, was another such reaction, and there were others, but the Shaker experience is perhaps especially interesting because its roots (conscious or not) in one person's need to reject the traditional Christian interpretation of women's sexual role, and the enormous attraction the sect had for other married women, help to demonstrate once more how major changes in theological direction and in life-style grow directly from a need to reevaluate personal experience in order to survive spiritually as a person.

This is especially relevant now because most of the demand for the new theological interpretation of sexual relationships in our time has sprung directly from the need of women to know themselves as full persons, as in the little groups of women with whom I work. Many women have recognized that the way they have been regarded and treated by the dominant culture, and by the Church whose job it is to sacralize cultural norms, has made true self-affirmation as a child of God and inheritor of the reign of God nearly impossible. This applies as much to the woman who has been treated, as one woman described it, "like a little princess," as long as she conformed to the desired pattern of patriarchy, as to the woman who has been exploited, abused, raped or driven into prostitution.

The reason why this demand for a reevaluation of the role of women and the moral norms of sexual behavior has occurred so strongly at this time is connected to the huge cultural change in which we are all involved. But cultural change has occurred before—in the examples quoted above, among others. In every case the profound questioning and rethinking of traditional expectations was possible because at a certain historical point those expectations no longer looked as solid as they had once seemed. What had appeared to be part of the fabric of existence, God-given and unchangeable as the phases of the moon, suddenly became questionable simply because the social fabric itself was visibly falling apart. We need to look briefly at what happened before in order to understand our own experience. When, in England, a king would be arrested and executed, the divine authority not only of the king but of the whole structure he symbolized was challenged and dismantled. When a mainly rural economy rapidly gave way to an industrialized urban one on both sides of the Atlantic, then the cultural systems, bonds and obligations which had come to seem as permanent as the patterns of field and pasture, of sowing and reaping (themselves, as it turned out, in their turn intensely vulnerable), were seen to be questionably absolute, no longer touchstones of reality.

In these situations there were two possible responses and they reappear in our situation, in which both the upheavals and the responses are more violent, more widespread and much more conscious and articulate. One was to reassert the absoluteness of the principles on which the traditional ways were founded, therefore to perceive all deviations from them as evil, to denounce and reject them, and so to seek to recreate versions of the old ways in the unavoidable new situation. An example of this was the valiant effort of the Anglican Church to recreate in the new cities the close, supportive community of rural parish. Another less admirable example was the savage suppression of radical Christian sects by both Church and state in the seventeenth and eighteenth centuries in Europe, and the less systematic but just as violent persecution of religious innovations in the New World colonies. In both cases the repression instituted by governing bodies was often both instigated and supported by mob anger and fear.

The other response, which is the one we are chiefly concerned with here, was to question not just the operation but the very religious and social basis of the old order, and therefore to begin to develop alternatives—alternative theologies leading to alternative life-styles, and alternative spiritualities supporting and interpreting both. The visible breakdown of the old gave permission to think new thoughts and try out new ways.

At the very heart of the questioning and the experiment was the issue of relations between the sexes, sex roles in society and of course the institution of marriage, but not all the movements and sects carried their questioning to the point of rethinking the basic patriarchal model of the family. It was easier, as in the case of the Shakers, to reject marriage altogether precisely because it seemed that marriage inevitably meant the dominance of the man over the woman. Some groups made no attempt to liberate women within their liberated communities; others did so in the first flush of Gospel enthusiasm, but soon returned to the more familiar models, just as happened in the early Church.

The Quakers preserved their early sexual equality in the religious sphere, though barely, but in time surrendered it entirely in the domestic sphere. Always sex roles, and especially roles in the family, were the toughest survivors of the old patterns. The roots of patriarchy are deep, and through all the social changes of three centuries on two continents the tough and well-tried old systems endured, with only minor exceptions.

The exceptions were there, however. Questions had been asked and they kept on reverberating. Throughout the nineteenth and early twentieth century the tide of feminism rose. Because there were no other models, feminists developed their thinking and acting in terms of the ''true role of woman'' as traditionally defined, and extending it into new spheres—becoming ''mothers'' and ''sisters'' to the sick, the poor, children in school or the heathen in far-off lands. They structured their new communities of women—in nursing, in education, in religion—on familiar hierarchical models, even in cases where women themselves, rather than males such as doctors or ministers, filled the traditional patriarchal roles. The very experience of working together as women (even within these narrowly defined limits) and the experience of female friendship and autonomy tended to bring into question the absoluteness of the models they tried to live, yet there was no definitive breakthrough in consciousness. In fact the momentum of women's liberation slowed and even reversed in the twenties and thirties of this century, under the onslaught of Freudian stereotyping curiously combined with a tremendous Christian backlash which included the development of a pseudo-mystical role for women as suffering redeemers.

The present rise of feminist questioning and experimenting, of Christian women's radical theology and praxis, had only been possible because of social and cultural changes unimaginably greater than those which brought about earlier theological shifts. The change to a capitalist economy in Europe in the sixteenth century, the experience of colonies seeking independence, the demise of monarchy as real power, the industrial revolution, the rise of the scientific mentality—all these forced theological shifts, though often disguised and always resisted. But none of these—neither the reformation itself, nor the separation of Church and state, nor the floundering of the *ancient régime,* neither the emphasis on urban mission as central, nor the attempt to Christianize scientific disciplines—have even approached in depth and extent the theological reassessment demanded by the experiences of Western culture in the past four decades.

To put briefly what we all know: we are feeling the effects, at all levels—spiritual, social, political, environmental—of a Second World War with its numbing of consciences, the horror of the holocaust, and the incalculable consequences for human society of the fact and possibility of nuclear destruction. This is combined with an exploding technology and the rise of the new colonialism, while old colonies seize autonomy in terms of Western political systems. At the same time we are experiencing the more and more visible destruction of the environment, which means the earth, life-support systems, and the rising tide of famine and war in the third world. Because of these experiences, the last two generations have seen all the old certainties brought into question. The absolutes of religion and culture have become questionable if not totally discredited in a world in which the "final solution" of Nazism did not discourage the democratically elected leaders of progressive nations from deciding that the only solution to conflict was bomb, a solution which all the evidence now shows to have been both unnecessary and counter-productive, and a solution reached through a decision-making process which was dishonest, cynical and callous beyond belief.

That's the world we live in, one in which the use of power, the priorities and methods of leaders of the world (both overt and concealed) successfully live up to the moral standards set by Belsen and Hiroshima. The result is a loss of public confidence and a pervasive fear unparalleled in history. The social and spiritual insecurity that results is expressed in predictable ways. One is denial—a retreat into cynicism or apathy or drugs, but especially the reassertion of old absolutes in their most primitive and unthoughtful forms, just as in the past. This happens because of a need to provide a spiritual refuge for people who feel unable to cope with the appalling theological vacuum created by the dismantling of traditional certainties. The greatest danger to our world, spiritually and physically, springs in fact from this massive denial of the reality of a danger we cannot face. And with the denial, which necessarily demands a whole system of concealment, distortion and evasion, comes the need to persecute and suppress those who refuse to deny. Among the refusers are people in the women's movement and the peace movement, which are closely intertwined; and the strong backlash against the women's movement has its roots in fear that the great lie might be exposed. It is noticeable among the women I work with that a rise in personal self-awareness and pride leads many women

to reexamine their patriotic assumptions and begin to recognize the links between abuse of women, militarism and poverty.

The dismantling of the old consciousness, in the individual and in the society, makes possible the emergence of the new. Women's consciousness of
themselves is inextricably linked to their awareness of the plight of the planet,
even if not all make the connection explicit. That is why the theology of marriage touches the heart of the matter. What a society or a religious system
thinks and does about marriage is bound to be the truest indication of its attitudes in every other sphere. The norms for relations between the sexes govern
attitudes to education, to sex roles in work and home, and in so doing express
the value judgment of a society on the characteristics supposed to belong to
each sex. Whether intellect and power, analysis and control are valued, or
whether wisdom and intuitive grasp, feeling, nurturance and imagination are
highly regarded, shapes decision at every level of social and political life. We
are talking about right- and left-brain functions, and their traditional assign-
ment to women and men respectively. In our culture right-brain functions have
almost always been allocated to women, and to certain men (poets, artists,
mystics) licensed to provide decoration for the lives of the real power-holders;
if at the same time women are regarded as inferior, the right-brain functions
are necessarily regarded as inferior too. To put it the other way around, and
perhaps more truly, in a culture which regards left-brain functions as the only
significant and truly necessary ones for racial survival, right-brain functions
can be dealt with by being assigned to women, as essentially inferior. As long
as women can be regarded as inferior, they may safely exercise right-brain
functions on behalf of the whole social body, without disturbing the left-brain
dominance. Men with obvious right-brain attributes can be allowed to exercise
their gifts within the limits assigned to them, having no "real" power, and it
is even permissible for "normal" men to develop right-brain function to a limited extent, as a safety valve under the stress of the need to be always in control.
In a culture structured in these terms, relations between the sexes, most of all
in marriage, must express very precisely the required characteristics of the two
sexes. This is why over and over again signs of change in the attitudes of married women have been described quite explicitly as "threatening to undermine
the fabric of society." They really do. And, vice versa, when the fabric of
society has been undermined, as ours has, the sexual roles and relations are
affected more deeply than any other aspect of life.

We simply cannot go on pretending that we can put back together the
pieces of a theology of marriage which has been shattered by experience. For
many women, the moment of conversion, the true metanoia, has come when
they reach the decision to seek a divorce. This is not necessarily because the
husband is abusive, but often because he has been cast, willy-nilly, in a role
which he cannot break out of, and which makes it impossible for the relation-

ship to be honest—and therefore impossible for the woman to live with integrity. Such a discovery is very painful, and even involves that loss of family, money, and approval of which the Gospel speaks. To compare the decision to seek a divorce to the choice of discipleship may seem shocking—but that can be what it really is: the choice of life over death, spiritual freedom over bondage. It is, for many, the entrance into a new life, and this example shows very clearly the nature of the development I am talking about. We are looking at the meaning of discipleship in the area of sex relations, and what we are seeing simply cannot be interpreted in terms of the traditional theology of marriage. No reinterpretation even in terms of covenant relationship is enough. When Church law and public expectations around it remain unchanged, a new description is simply the familiar technique of making an unbearably wrong situation more appealing by calling on those involved to exercise virtues of compassion, forbearance and patience within it, and dressing up the result in splendid biblical language.

We can begin the process of identifying a different approach to understanding marriage and sex relationships by looking first at some things which are clearly visible to us, and following those up in rather unexpected ways to come finally to a different view of the whole area of relationships between men and women. Teachers in schools, for instance (including Catholic schools), know that children from single-parent families are no longer exceptional, and may even be the majority in the classroom. We then observe the phenomenon of unmarried or divorced women deciding to live together and bring up their children as one household. Sometimes the relationship may be a sexual one, sometimes not. Men sometimes do the same, and explicitly gay couples of either sex are successfully rearing children who turn out to be, as often as not, comfortably heterosexual. The whole controversy over the fostering of children by gay couples shows that it happens and that these couples are as likely as any others to provide a good home for children in care; at the very least they are less likely to be doing it purely for the money. The ability of people of the same sex (usually women) to make a home and raise children together is not new, and was once easily accepted. (The modern phobia about it stems from the Freudian backlash against women whose ability to be independent threatened male egos.) They are doing it now. "Alternative" households are actually quite common; in fact among the women with whom I work the choice to share home and child care with another woman is often the obvious way to afford the rent and achieve some independence as well as companionship.

These unquestioned demographics and social facts demonstrate from another point of view the need to reevaluate the theology of sexual relationships. The alternative is to label all these households deviant in some way, and attempt to persuade, exhort or blackmail them into returning to more acceptable situations, or consenting to live the rest of their lives regarding themselves as inevitably bad in some way. But they are not obviously different from tradi-tional households in quality of life and relationships. Wounded they may be, often permanently scarred by their experiences, but if we are honest we can see that they are no more (and no less) struggling, loving, failing and suc-ceeding, despairing and hoping, living and partly living than traditional house-holds. We can see these things, and we have to draw conclusions from them, and the conclusions do not support the theology of marriage as we have in-herited it.

Another challenge to traditional attitudes emerges from the observation of relationships in these "alternative" households. I mentioned that some women, and often men too though less often, decide to share their family lives for mainly practical reasons. It is a matter of economic survival and also a protection. But if the arrangement is to succeed there must be a good relation-ship between the women. In fact, close friendships often develop; the sharing of responsibility and memories brings intimacy. In some cases the relationship is, or may become, overtly sexual. It is natural for intimacy and friendship to be experienced physically, and some kinds of physical endearment seem ac-ceptable, but at a certain point they don't seem acceptable anymore. What are we really trying to do? Is it really possible, in terms of moral theology, to draw a line? Of course we have always done so, but if we do, why do we? What is behind the thinking that assumes that any kind of genital contact creates a mor-ally totally different situation from other kinds of physical intimacy? (Whether or not we *approve* of certain kinds of intimacy is not the point.) We really need to ask these questions, and if not to answer them at least to be willing really to look at the quality of the relationships we are trying to reflect on in theo-logical terms. It is in the giving and receiving of life and love that we discern the presence of God. At what point and on what grounds does God suddenly cease to be present?

These observations of what is observably happening around us have to do with people who have chosen, or been forced, to find an alternative to heter-osexual marriage or partnership. But this apparently roundabout route leads me directly to questions about the quality of heterosexual intimacy. Looking at the nature of intimacy of different kinds between people of the same sex naturally raises questions about what happens between happily married people. In a really good marriage, what is it that gives its life-giving quality to the relationship? Can we really define marriage in terms of a sexual contract or covenant? Once more, where do we draw the line? Is it *really* genital sex that makes the difference? Or is it rather that mutual sexual desire can lead to a real expression of love because the couple gives a context to their sexual encounter which supports, enlightens and extends their intimacy? No matter how they decide to define their practical roles in the household, no matter whether both work or one works, whether they have children or not, or how they choose to rear them, there is one thing which makes it possible for couples now to survive the pressures of conflicting opinion about sex and marriage, Church controversy around and over them, economic stress and all the great public anxieties of our time, and to create through all that a relationship which is flexible, realistic, compassionate and hopeful. That one thing is most simply named as friendship. Marital friendship is not an extra. It is the thing that can make marriage possible, when the patriarchal systems no longer work, as it has in the past often made love and mutuality possible within a patriarchal system. If I am right, the presence of divine reality in the relationship has its basis in the quality of friendship, and not in any definition based on sexual intimacy as such. If this is so we have to deal, as suggested, with the fact that such friendship also exists in relationships between people of the same sex, sexual or not; in that case the whole business of defining relationships in terms of their degree or kind of sexual expression immediately begins to look rather primitive, if not downright silly.

Friendship is the heart of the matter, as we observe and experience the obviously good relationships around us, married or not. And friendship is a profound theological category which is discovered at the heart of the Gospel vision of human social and personal relations. But in seeking to root a theology of marriage in the Gospel, as opposed to the Church Fathers' interpretation of the Gospel, we discover that we have, at first sight, precious little to go on. Jesus' few recorded sayings about marriage (apart from a caustic remark about male sexual fantasies) had to do with the custom of getting rid of an unwanted wife as if she were a cow or a coat, and his disapproval of this way of treating a human being was strong. What he might have said about divorce as we experience it we do not know, since such a thing did not exist at the time and nobody was asking about it.

The irony is that Jesus, as the Gospels portray him, far from upholding the sanctity of the marriage bond and family life, was apt to break up marriage and families in a way that dismayed many people. That this was a real and enduring problem for followers in the next generation also is shown by the space the Synoptic writers take to underline Jesus' teaching on the secondary nature of family ties as compared with the call to discipleship. To leave parents, wives, children and land could be a condition of discipleship, if these relationships interfered with the commitment to that new kind of relationship which was discovered in the intimacy of the community which grew up around Jesus. There were many women in this community, and some of them had left their husbands in order to follow the Master, while some husbands and wives came to discipleship together. (If the list given by the male Synoptic writers of relatives to be left did not include husbands, it is evident that, in fact, husbands *were* left, if discipleship required it.)

What was offered to the disciples in return for the family ties they broke? They were offered "alternative" family ties, a close bonding with the new community, but this new "family" was very noticeably different from the old. In it there were to be no "fathers," and no bosses. They were all to serve each other and care for each other. They were to love one another, not dominate each other. They were to be friends.

In all the theological efforts of these last years we have found ourselves turning back to the beginnings, to the Gospel vision itself, in order to discover the categories and insights from our explorations. The Gospel category of friendship is implicit and explicit. It is a description of a kind of relationship which Jesus wanted to put in the place of the existing patriarchal ones, and, in turn, the ways we find him behaving, and asking others to behave, illustrate the concept of friendship itself and give it content and clarity. The double definition of friendship which John gives to Jesus in the context of the Last Supper is in fact a description of what we would like a marriage to exemplify—a profound self-giving to the other, and the sharing of the deepest insights: "Whatever my Father has revealed to me . . ."

We can begin from here. The questions raised are far-reaching. Certainly it is not enough to say that the category of friendship as Jesus lived and demanded it is the theological category with which we can rediscover the meaning of Christian marriage. It is not enough; it is only the beginning. It does not answer the questions which I, and others, have raised, but it does give us a strong basis on which to build our understanding. It gives us a touchstone by which to measure the quality of a relationship, sexual or not. It is also a political definition and has wide social and economic implications, as Jesus clearly intended it to have. It enables us to begin to deal with concepts of fidelity and commitment, in other than sexual or legal categories. It gives us a different way to look at relationships between parents and children, and bears on questions of adoption and inheritance. It does not solve the problems but it reframes them, giving us a whole new vision of the life of God active in the creation of bonds of intimacy and lifelong love not just between two but in a network of support and responsibility which is the Church as Jesus envisioned it.

This paper has attempted to raise profound questions, mainly by looking at what is actually happening and putting those happenings in some kind of historical context. I then suggested a different way to pose those same questions, a biblical theological category which illumines them and enables us to make a new beginning. The vision of the Gospel has always been elusive; it is easier to take bits of Scripture and adapt them to the existing social patterns than to try to grasp the profound practicality of the original vision, and attempt to live it. At this point in history it seems that we have a different perspective:

we take the Gospel possibility seriously, or we perish. At the heart of that possibility live renewed and transformed relationships. If we cannot face the implications of our experience of the real relationships between men and women that we actually see around us, there is not much chance that we shall be honest enough to face any kind of reality at all.

RESPONSES

BERNARD COOKE

I agree with Rosemary that what is taking place is the most profound, healthful shift that has occurred in human history, namely, the beginning of the breakdown of the patriarchal culture. It is a terribly frightening thing, it is a threatening thing. I think, however, when one looks at it, that it is part of the profound revolutionary force that is intrinsic to Christianity. This, I think, indicates that somehow we have to find ways not of causing it, because we won't cause it, but of midwifing it, so as to make it possible for something new to come into existence.

As we do that, there are many different contributions that have to be made, one of them theological. I think that reflecting differently than we have on the theology of marriage is going to be critically important, but I don't think that that is the bottom line. I think that the major contribution of Christianity and of theology within Christianity is to clarify the reality of God. Patriarchal culture has been supported by the presumption that God was what patriarchy wanted it to be, and that has been a fundamental error. The basic name for God is not God the Father, but God the Father of our Lord Jesus Christ. It is an entirely different way of naming God and one that brings into challenge any metaphorical usage of the notion of father as applied to God. I think that ties in with Jesus' word: don't go around calling anyone father.

Having said that, let me make some observations that directly relate to the theology of marriage. First, as Rosemary Haughton indicated, we have to go back to the New Testament and pick up the element of friendship which is emphasized there. The friendship that Jesus gives witness to has a different resonance, a different tonality. He reveals something profound about what this whole mystery of friendship means. That does not challenge at all the sexual relationship, but I think it does challenge our ability to try to understand how profound friendship is a transformative and interpretive element of what human sexuality can be.

Second, in probing how sacraments function, and how they are meant to sanctify us and transform our lives, it becomes clear that it is the reality of God's self-gift that transforms what we experience as human persons. One of the things we have to try to figure out is how does our love relationship with God really enter into and transform our human experience of friendship. How is doing that part of making our human friendships sacramental? It isn't that human friendship just by itself points to God—it does—but as it does, and particularly if there is anything like prayer going on, there is this deeper entry of God into the situation.

ROSEMARY HAUGHTON

To me the category of friendship is a very important context in which we perceive God. In a sense, we let God out of the box. God is really active within the situation between these two people. When we add to that context profound and trusting friendship, we can almost literally feel the presence of God; and when we add to that a sexual intimacy which is truly reciprocal and cooperative and open, then we are, as it were, giving God ever more and more profound opportunity for breakthrough between the couple, and making the divine presence more and more powerful.

I think that what we are dealing with in our kind of society is that we have created between the sexes all kinds of tensions and systems which make it very hard for that sort of breakthrough to happen in the normal sexual context. We have put up barriers of all kinds in the roles which we have required men and women to fulfill in their sexual relationship and in the whole context of their married lives. In a real sense this has cut down many of the channels of communication through which God is perceived and experienced.

What we need to do is to explore how we can recover the uniqueness of the heterosexual relationship as a place for the explosion and celebration of divine energy. The women's new consciousness I have been talking about is part of the attempt to reclaim that uniqueness.

LISA SOWLE CAHILL

First of all, let me say that I really agree that friendship is probably the best definition of marriage or the partnership that marriage requires. In my paper I define love and marriage as a commitment to partnership, which I think is saying a similar sort of thing. My only question is about the sources of the idea. I am starting to feel as though the category ''friendship'' is operating in our views of marriage much like the category ''love'' has operated in the past in the views of Christian ethics, that is, it is a norm that nobody can disagree with, and we all want it to be based in the Bible, so we endorse it and then it means what we want it to mean and we claim that that is what the Gospel had in mind.

I am not sure that friendship as we want to apply it to the relationship of marriage is really what the New Testament is about when it is discussing discipleship or the love that discipleship requires. It is not that those are opposed. It is not that the love of discipleship is against the friendship that we want to endorse in marriage; but to me, it does not include as much. The key thing to me in the friendship which is marriage is that it is mutually satisfying; it is a reciprocal sharing of thoughts, goals, and efforts. That relationship and the fulfillment of the partners of that relationship is an end in itself, whereas love in the New Testament has to do more with self-sacrifice, with partnership in building the community and perhaps goals extrinsic to the relationship of the people who cooperate in doing that. I am not sure, but I just do not like to conflate friendship too easily with love in the New Testament, which to me has a more sacrificial connotation. While sacrifice is always an element in marital love, and that's what the Gospel has to say to marriage, I think that the friendship that marriage requires goes beyond the Christian Gospel and is perhaps a much more universal sort of concept. I want to define marriage as friendship, but I would root the idea more in Aquinas than in the New Testament.

ROSEMARY HAUGHTON

I am not a New Testament scholar, so I cannot go into this all that deeply. Perhaps I am doing what you say most people do, taking an idea and applying it, and trying to imagine it into a New Testament context. This is legitimate, but can be dangerous. It seems to me that what we get out of reading the Synoptic Gospels is an image of people among whom friendship is taking place.

You said that marriage is for its own sake. What I see happening also is that a very happy, fulfilled marriage overflows. It has a sort of mission built into it, whether people actually think about it or not. It reaches out to other people. Therefore, I think that possibly a context of discipleship for friendship is not so foreign to marital oneness as it might seem, because they are both concerned with the sharing of something which they have discovered. I mean that the call to discipleship is a call to discover a different kind of life, a different experience of life, a different understanding of life, and we are meant to share that with other people. And I think that consciously or not that happens with marriage. So maybe marital love and the notion of friendship and discipleship in the New Testament are not that far apart. That is how they come together for me actually.

7.

Christian Marriage

Jack Dominian

Throughout the Judaeo-Christian tradition marriage has been a secular reality taken up in the divine order. In Christianity, marriage has been considered a sacrament, that is to say, that in the relationship between husband and wife, they encounter Christ in each other. It is vital that the secular reality is correctly understood if the divine dimension has justice done to it. Contemporary marriage in Western society is changing rapidly, offering a rich spirituality for Christian marriage. The intimacy and egalitarianism of contemporary marriage offers a rich opportunity for sustaining, healing, and growth. In addition, sexuality is attaining new meaning now that it is no longer primarily concerned with procreation. If properly understood, the sacrament of marriage will play a vital part in the evangelization of Western society.

Old Testament

Marriage has existed before Israel and Christianity came into being. It is a human reality, and it is this secular reality that became a saving mystery in the presence of Yahweh and of Christ.

The Jewish people recognized early in their history the relationship between man and God. In Genesis we find that God created man in the image of himself.

God created man in the image of himself,
in the image of God he created him,
male and female he created them (Gen 1:27).

158

God created man and woman in his image for two purposes: the first was to be in relationship with each other and the second to be fruitful.

> Yahweh God said, "It is not right that man should be alone. I shall make him a helper" (Gen 2:18).
> God blessed them, saying to them, "Be fruitful, multiply, fill the earth and subdue it" (Gen 1:28).

Thus, at the very beginning of their history the Jewish people placed the family in the context of the sacred. They continued to exalt it in this way by its fruitfulness, the ideal but not the reality of permanency and mutual faithfulness.

At a later stage its prophets from the time of Hosea will see in the God-man relationship a symbol of the covenant. Thus, for Israel marriage is a human, secular reality which is taken up in the divine order and becomes a divine mystery.

The New Testament

Our Lord, as we know, remained single, but he held marriage in high esteem. He started his public miracles at the wedding of Cana where he transformed water into wine (Jn 2:1–10). He insisted on the permanency of marriage (Mt 19:12), a standard of sexual conduct which was higher than the mere prohibition of adultery but the avoidance of lust (Mt 5:27–28), and he placed the man-woman relationship in the context of love as he did all other human relationships. Jesus, however, introduced the single state dedicated to God (Mt 19:12) and also revealed that after the resurrection there will be no marriage (Mt 22:30).

Paul wrote a great deal about marriage which at one end of the scale showed some reservation about marriage in his First Letter to the Corinthians, and, at the other end, he gave us the tremendous vision of marriage in the context of Christ and the Church (Eph 5:21–33), and so the covenant idea continues now in the framework of Christ.

The Fathers

We have seen that Christian marriage is a continuity of the Jewish tradition which, in turn, was a human reality. The Fathers continued to do two things for marriage. They ensured its basic goodness against the deterioration of the surrounding Manicheism, but at the same time they downgraded the significance of sex within it. This diminution of the importance of the sexual reached its apotheosis with St. Augustine. A great deal has been written about this great saint and his approach to sexuality, and it would be wrong to place all the subsequent negativity at his door, but he was a major contributor. As far as marriage is concerned he wrote a good deal about it and he left to this day the three permanent marks of Christian marriage, which he called the goods of marriage, children (*proles*), the mutual fidelity of the spouses (*fides*), and permanency of the relationship. These three characteristics, which were to become the ends of marriage in the Middle Ages, have had a profound impact on the character of Christian marriage to this very day.

The Medieval Period

The medieval period starting from the eleventh century onward began to teach the subject of marriage as a sacrament. It is interesting to note that, in the light of contemporary expectations of instant solutions, it took the Church some five centuries to define marriage as a sacrament, the seventh rite, defined as such at the Council of Trent.

Council of Trent to Vatican II

After the Council of Trent, marriage, like so much else in the life of the Church, fell into the hands of canon lawyers and was seen primarily in juridical terms. Emphasis shifted to preserving the minutiae of legal detail with no emphasis whatsoever on the dynamics of the relationship. But the thirty years spanning the 1930's to the 1960's saw an increased discussion and major objections to the traditional views. This debate paid handsome dividends in the declaration on marriage in Vatican II.

Vatican II

Overnight the juridical language was replaced by that of love. Marriage and the family were called a "community of love." The biblical concept of covenant was resurrected and marriage was seen as a relationship. Finally, sexual intercourse was described in the more positive terms of love than in any other previous council. The richness of marriage has been expressed in the most dynamic terms and everyone concerned with marriage should read the original text.

Human Reality and Saving Mystery

Throughout this brief and most incomplete exposition of marriage, I have tried to hold on to the reality that it is the human, secular reality which is taken up and rendered into saving mystery. So, if we are going to make sense of contemporary marriage in its saving capacity, we must understand what is happening to contemporary marriage.

For a very long time there was a given model, which sociologists call instrumental, of what the secular reality of marriage consisted in. This model visualized men and women as playing specific roles in marriage. The man was the provider, the head of the family, the person who took the important decisions, the ambassador of the family to the outside world. The woman was the child-bearer, the person who raised the children, looked after the home, and was the catalyst of love. Provided the couple carried out their respective roles and were fruitful, faithful and had a permanent relationship, then the marriage was considered good.

Today and for some time now, this model of marriage is changing into what has come to be known as the companionship variety. This model demands an equity between the man and the woman, both of whom are likely to be working and providers. The relationship between the spouses is no longer a patriarchal model but one of mutual sharing and decision making. This exchange requires a degree of intimacy which depends on good communication, demonstration of affection and sexual fulfillment. It is this model which is the human reality which has to become the saving mystery.

Sustaining

If this companionship model is increasingly the current form of marriage, then we have to explore how divine grace operates in it. What are the channels through which the couple recognize that good lives in their life? In my writings I have said that there are three ways through which grace operates in contemporary marriage without, of course, excluding other possibilities. These three are sustaining, healing, and growth.

As far as sustaining is concerned the couple continue to support each other materially, providing the fabric of their love and its running cost. This economic sustaining does not alter except that both spouses are now likely to contribute. What does change is that, in addition to economic sustaining, the couple expect from each other emotional sustaining. There are, in fact, two intimate relationships in life: the first is between ourselves and parents and the second between ourselves and our spouse. During the first, we wanted to know and be known in depth. We needed to feel understood and to have our inner needs met, sometimes without even voicing our desires. Contemporary couples find themselves in the same degree of intimacy and they want to know and be known in the same depth and with the same degree of trust as when they were children. When this happens there is a degree of closeness which approaches a sense of oneness and yet the spouses remain separate. It is a closeness that does not obtrude and yet cements the relationship.

Healing

In the midst of this sustaining, couples reveal the depths of their being to each other. This revelation brings out into the open both the strengths and the wounds of each other. The wounds are what concern us here. We all come to marriage with some twenty years of wounds. These wounds come from two sources in our life.

The first source is our genetic makeup. We all know nowadays that part of our anxiety, anger, irritability, moodiness, and depression is genetically determined, so it is in our constitution. The second source is our upbringing. As a psychiatrist, I have to deal with men and women who are markedly insecure, dependent, emotionally deprived and lacking self-esteem. But even the best parents leave a trail of some insecurity, lack of confidence, shyness, anxiety, passivity, and lack of initiative. We are all wounded to a greater or lesser extent. But, happily, this is not the end of the story.

When we marry, the majority of us find someone who complements us. If we are insecure, they may be confident; if we are anxious, they may be more secure; if we lack initiative, they may be more spontaneous; if we feel unloved, they may have an abundance of loving. Whatever our deficiency, we often find partners with the missing components of our personality. That is how, over time, healing takes place. We give to each other, in a reciprocal fashion, a second opportunity to experience what was missing in our life the first time around. Of course, when both partners are extremely wounded, the opportunity for healing becomes remote. But in the vast majority of couples healing takes place. I do not have to stress that healing is at the heart of the Christian faith, and this sacrament probably provides the single most important means for mutual healing in society.

Growth

Beyond sustaining and healing there is growth. The instrumental model was frequently a static one. Provided the couples carried out their responsibilities as spouses and were fruitful and faithful and the marriage was indissoluble, then it was considered a good marriage. But the contemporary marriage lasts forty to fifty years or more. During this time the couple change and grace operates to bring the best out of each other.

At the physical level by the time we have reached marriage age we have attained our mature stature. The only way we are going to change later is by putting a few inches round our waist! Psychologically, we have also reached the limits of our intelligence by the age of marriage. But intelligence is more than an I.Q. As the years pass our ideas filter through the monitoring of our partner who is in the best position to evaluate the best in us and help us to transform our intelligence into wisdom. This does not mean that other people do not contribute to this process—they certainly do—but our spouse probably makes the most important contribution. Like so much else in our life, intelligence is not a static thing. In the course of time we can begin to be influenced by ideas and the desire to bring out something new in our lives. It may be a new recipe, a new book, a new style of thinking, indeed one of a hundred different things. If we lack the confidence to try the new, our spouse can give it to us. Alternatively if we are not sure what we want to try, our partner can help us to clarify our ideas and sometimes render what is unconscious, conscious. In these circumstances our spouse acts as a midwife, bringing out what is latent within us.

Finally, there is no end to the increase of love we show to each other. At this point I have to say something which may stimulate laughter but is very sad indeed. Most of us think we love those close to us by telling them what is wrong with them! We do this to our spouses who are no exception to this negative approach. But most of us know most of the time what is wrong with us. What we need is help and encouragement to overcome our difficulties. We need a great deal of affirmation to reinforce our persistent efforts to overcome our limitations. In this respect we have to learn to remain silent when we want to be critical and to praise abundantly when our partner has done something worthwhile. There is no end to loving which we can do to the last day of our life.

Sexual Love

Reference to love makes me come to the subject of sex. Throughout Christianity sexual intercourse has been linked to procreation. Today we recognize that whatever form of birth regulation we use, ninety-nine percent of sexual intercourse is consciously and deliberately non-procreative. So what is its purpose?

For me sexual intercourse is a body language—a couple using their bodies to speak to each other, with or without words. What are they saying to each other? They are saying at least five things.

In the course of love-making the couple are enjoying the experience, their personal, physical and emotional unity. Like every pleasurable experience they want to give thanks to each other as the person who has contributed to the joy. So intercourse is a recurrent act of thanksgiving.

Second, after successful intercourse, the couple want to repeat it the same night, the next day, the day after. They remain in a state of hopeful anticipation that their partner will make them welcome in a short time. Intercourse is now a recurrent act of hope that we shall be wanted again as a person.

Third, in the course of the day a couple argue and quarrel with each other. Most of the time they forgive and forget quickly, but sometimes the pain does not disappear. It remains long after the event and it needs the deeper love of intercourse to bring relief. Thus intercourse can be an act of reconciliation.

Fourth, coitus is one of the most powerful and economic ways by which a man makes a woman feel a woman and a woman makes a man feel a man. It is therefore a powerful affirmer of the sexual identity.

Fifth, every time a couple make love, they declare to each other that they recognize, want and appreciate the other as a person unique in their life. Coitus is, therefore, a recurrent act of affirming the person.

When sexual intercourse is missing from the life of a couple, we tend to think of the loss in terms of physical pleasure. But it is the existential affirmation of each other that is missing and which the couple find such a void in their life. Thus, at the heart of intercourse is its capacity to give life to the couple and on a few occasions *new* life.

Children

This emphasis on the existential aspect of intercourse may make it appear that I am downgrading the importance of children. I have no desire to do this. Children are precious and vital to the majority of marriages. However, all we have learned from a hundred years of psychology is that the children's stability and happiness depends on the stability and happiness of the parents. There was man-woman relationship before the children arrive; it is vital that it remain healthy during the period when the children are growing up; after they have left the husband-wife relationship continues. Thus, the husband-wife relationship is the primary one, preceding the arrival of children and succeeding their departure. In this husband-wife relationship sex is one of the key activities that maintains the relationship, and its significance cannot be overstated.

Theology

Finally, we want to look at the consequent theory of the model of Christian marriage I have been offering. The first thing to realize is that since Vatican II, we have come to talk of marriage and the family as the domestic church. It is there within the family that its members will meet Christ in each other. It is there that the ordinary experiences of everyday life are transformed into extraordinary events in which the human meets the divine.

As we get up every day, wash, dress, have breakfast, go to work, look after the children, return home, cook our meals, eat, drink, talk and make love to each other, each moment is an opportunity to meet Jesus, in and through each other. Each moment is a challenge to experience God through love. It is in this domestic church that its members form a community of love, where the foundations of love and faith are laid down as the couple experience themselves and their children. The sacrament offers nothing less than a radical activation of the human into the divine. It is a constant transformation that has no end as the members of the family sustain, heal and grow.

In order for this sustaining, healing and growth to take place the continuity of relationship has to be maintained. Permanency is not a prison sentence for the married. It is the means through which the sustaining, healing and growth can take place. When relationships are interrupted, trust, communication and affection are lost and the possibilities of relationship are denied. Thus the primary criterion of permanency is the key through which the members of the family can reap the maximum benefits of the relationship.

The members of the family are people interacting with each other in and through love. That is precisely what the Trinity is—persons interacting with each other in and through love. Thus, here is a sacrament within which the model of the Trinity can be lived to the full.

But that does not exhaust the possibilities of the sacrament, for in many ways this sacrament includes the essential encounters with Christ in other sacraments. Entry into relationship with Christ, baptism is reflected in the entry and sustaining of the relationship of the couple. Confirmation is reflected in the constant affirmation that the couple give to each other and their children. The continuous hurt-forgiveness pattern of marriage anticipates the sacrament of reconciliation. The healing effect of the relationship reflects the healing sacrament. The total oneness-separation unity of marriage gives us an insight into the oneness-separateness unity with Christ in the Eucharist and Communion.

But what about the priesthood? Indeed, many people ask me if marriage is so rich, why pursue the life of celibacy? In all I have said about marriage I have meant no reduction in the importance of the priesthood. What I think unites these apparently disparate sacraments is the sanctity of person in relationship. At the heart of the Christian faith is that we Christians should live our life in a spirit of love in relationship. The ultimate key to being is the Trinity which is the life of persons in relationship of love with each other. So all human beings are called to lead a life in a relationship of love. The married have an exclusive relationship with each other; the priest and the religious also have relationships of love with many. What unites all of us is the sanctity of relationships in love with each other. Marriage is one form of relationship through which eighty percent of society finds its salvation; the single state dedicated to God is another way of being in relationship. But ultimately in heaven we do not have marriage, but relationships of love.

Practical Consequences

What are the practical consequences of such a theology? The theology of the past saw the wedding ceremony as the conclusion of the involvement of the Christian community with the couple. Clearly when marriage is seen as a relationship, the wedding is not the conclusion but the beginning of an unfolding relationship that lasts more than fifty years. The couple have to be prepared for this and supported after the wedding.

The best form of support is being worked out, but it includes discussion groups for the married, new forms of liturgy throughout the year, using the other sacraments such as baptism and confirmation to help the couple see their children against a background of their marital relationship, much more preaching by lay people on marriage, and generally raising the whole status of marriage within the Church.

Summary

Marriage is the sacrament through which eighty percent of the community finds God and Christ. In its depth are to be found sustaining, healing and growth channels through which the love and grace of the sacrament operate. This love is sealed by sexuality, and sexuality in turn needs this love to function with integrity. Most of the time coitus is a body language of love giving life to the couple and occasionally new life which has to be cherished and nurtured. All this is taking place within a model of love between people which is the model of the Trinity.

RESPONSES

ROSEMARY HAUGHTON

There are two comments I would like to make. First, I agree with Jack's point that married people need support from the Christian community. We are making this tremendous transition from what Jack described as the instrumental model of marriage to a companionship model. However, most of the expectations which supported the older ideas of marriage are still in place. This makes it difficult for married couples to make the transition. There is a need to educate the Christian community about the different expectations of married couples so that the community may give them the support they need in dealing with companionship marriage.

The second thing I would like to talk about is the family as friendship. If we are changing the role identity of men and women in marriage, we are also seeing a change in the roles of parents and children with each other. The basic parent-child relationship has to be there, the relationship of support and nurturing toward adulthood, but at a certain point there needs to be affirmation of the possibility of friendship between parents and children. The absence of that is often the reason for the alienation between the generations and the fact that children so often do carry the wounds of their parents into their adult relationships. I think it is tremendously important for people who are marrying to consider right from the beginning the fact that their children are going to be eventually their companions and friends, as well as their children.

PETER J. HUIZING

My question is: What do you think of the approach to divorce in the Church today? Divorced people, especially divorcées, are considered to be guilty. If they are divorced, they have failed before God. It has been my experience that this approach in most cases is absolutely not true. There are human weaknesses, there are failures, yes; but that it is precisely sin and wickedness and guilt, I don't think that's true. From your experience, what is your opinion of this?

JACK DOMINIAN

I think that there is always a certain percentage of marriages that cannot survive. But what we have seen since the early sixties is a huge increase of divorce in Western society. We are witnessing rapidly changing expectations of men and women from each other, but especially from women. It is a demographic fact that seven out of ten petitions in Britain are filed by women.

167

It is really women who are saying that their situation in marriage is not good enough. This is not a question of sin. Sin, as I understand it, is a deliberate violation of one's relationship with God. Nothing as deliberate as this happens in marriage.

Most people who enter marriage want their relationship to last. What happens is that their expectations of love, affection, and companionship are not fulfilled. I know there is a lot of emphasis put on sexuality, but in my experience in dealing with twenty-five years of marital breakdowns, it is the absence of affection which is the key to marital breakdown nowadays—although if your affection breaks down, your sexual involvement also breaks down. It is this lack of affection which gradually creeps into people's lives and overtakes them little by little, due to a variety of reasons. They discover one day that they are no longer in love with one another, they are no longer in relationship with one another. There is no conscious, deliberate, determined rebellion against God. Most of the time you are dealing with tragedy, with human pathos and weakness and suffering. It is not a question of sin. I think that the Church's attempt to protect marriage by punishing the divorced is one of the great injustices of our age. I think what we have to do to counter divorce is not to punish the divorced, not to deny them access to Christ, but to respond to divorce in a positive Christian way.

8.

Catholic Marriage:
An Episcopal Perspective

Raymond A. Lucker

This chapter presents a reflection, from an episcopal perspective, on some of the major themes presented during the symposium and contained in the preceding chapters.

Introduction

We have dealt with difficult issues during this symposium: the nature of marriage, indissolubility, marriage as sacrament, sexuality.

We know also the teaching of the official hierarchical magisterium on these issues. (See for example *Gaudium et Spes, Humanae Vitae, Familiaris Consortio,* and *To Live in Christ Jesus,* NCCB.) The position of the ordinary teaching authority in the Church is clear on matters such as contraception, pre-marital and extra-marital intercourse and the indissolubility of sacramental and consummated marriage. My role here, as I see it, is on one hand to reaffirm these teachings. On the other hand, it is to listen to what theologians, Scripture scholars, ethicists, canonists, counselors and married people are saying and so to translate these teachings for the world of today and the twenty-first century.

We are aware of the development of doctrine. The Dogmatic Constitution on Divine Revelation of the Second Vatican Council says, "This tradition which comes from the apostles develops in the Church with the help of the Holy Spirit. For there is a growth in the understandings of the realities and the words which have been handed down. This happens through the contemplation and study made by believers who treasure these things in their hearts (cf. Lk

2:19, 51), through the intimate understanding of spiritual things they experience, and through the preaching of those who have received through episcopal succession the sure gift of truth. For, as the centuries succeed one another, the Church constantly moves forward toward the fullness of divine truth until the words of God reach their complete fulfillment in it'' (n. 8).

We have new theological methods. One of the most significant is using human experience as a theological source. Historical studies of the Christian sacraments have given us insights into their essential realities, what they are and can be. We have a deeper understanding of human choice, human emotions and human sexuality. We recognize more clearly the impact of culture on our theological formulations. We have become more aware of the emergence of a world Church.

We face ambiguity and recognize that in many areas of human life, issues are not easily separated into clearly good and bad, into black and white, right and wrong. We recognize, for example, ambiguity and the need to make personal choice in issues of war and peace, in business ethics, in the use of power and the accumulation of wealth. Yet the Gospel seems to be clear about the Christian call to non-violence, forgiveness, serving one another, the danger of riches, and the evil of hypocrisy, greed, exploitation and pride.

Yes, we struggle with ambiguity in so many areas of human life. Yet so often we have not been able to accept anything or deal with anything but absolute certainty in the area of human sexuality and sexual activity. We said that there was no such thing as parvity of matter in matters sexual. There are exceptionless moral norms. We knew where we stood. We knew the answers and questions.

Your studies have helped us to recognize the limitations of our knowledge, the difficulties, the ambiguities a Christian must face every day, and the opportunities that a major cultural change will bring. First, I would like to pick out a few issues that you have identified in your papers. You have uncovered valuable insights. You have reached beyond the theological expressions of the nineteenth century manuals. In a few instances your conclusions, sometimes tentative, have gone beyond and even seem to go against papal magisterial teaching. Second, I would like to focus on a few pastoral issues from my own experience as religious educator, pastor and bishop.

Some of the Insights

1. Experience of Married Persons

Almost all of you called us to call on, listen to, and invite reflection on the experience of married persons. This is one of the most significant areas of agreement during this symposium.

This seems to be so obvious since theology is faith seeking understanding (this is widely misunderstood) and theological formulations are culture and time-bound. "Theology," Dr. Haughton says, "is a reflection on experience in the light of faith." This is not to say that a celibate has nothing to say to married people. One of my staff people, a layman, was speaking recently at a small rural parish on the sacraments. During the question period a woman blurted out, "What do priests know about marriage?" Eyes focused on the pastor. The pastor said, "Not much, perhaps. But we do know a lot about history and theology and human experience."

Lisa Cahill, in her paper, said; "A *new* beginning point in the experience of married persons is needed in the Catholic theology and ethics of marriage." "It seems difficult to deny," she concludes, "that the testimony of married persons themselves should have a prerogative in normative evaluations which it thus far has not been granted."

A major theological question arises, of course, on whether or not this experience is revelatory. Does it contribute to the development of doctrine? Is it a tool in helping us understand the word of God? On this point I would probably differ from some of the other members of the symposium.

Dr. Cahill calls for serious dialogue between theology and experience, serious dialogue with married persons, for example, "about the relation of having children to their conjugal commitment and to their sex lives." Archbishop John Quinn called for a similar dialogue and study at a recent synod in Rome.

Fr. Mackin, Dr. Cooke, Dr. Dominian and Dr. Haughton also plead for the reflection of married people.

Fr. Mackin: "I recommend that the examination (of marriage as a sacrament) begin instead with the human matrix and work upward."

Dr. Haughton: especially in her appeal to listen to the stories of women. After summarizing some of these stories she says, "All of this has to do with theology, the theology around sexual relationships, marriage and the roles of men and women in God's world, for theology is reflection on real experiences."

Dr. Cooke says, "Today we are using the life experience of believing Christians . . . as the starting point for our theological reflection. . . . It is the providential action of God in people's lives that provides the immediate 'word' of revelation with which we must deal as theologians."

As a pastor, I welcome and support this appeal to listen to the experience of married people in the Church. All of us, in one way or other, are both teachers and taught.

2. *Sacramentality*

Fr. Mackin brings his long and rich experience into the preparation of his magnificent paper on the sacrament of marriage. A couple of brief quotes cannot do it justice.

"I believe the summary doctrinal formulation would be more true to life if it read not 'Christian marriage is a sacrament,' but 'All Christian spouses can, provided they co-work with the Holy Spirit, make their marriages to be sacraments.' That notion has profound implications on our understanding of marriage as a sacrament, a sign of God's gracious love.

"However many one numbers them, no one of the Christian sacraments was at its beginning a pure innovation in human experience. In every case the scenario of the sacrament, its patterned conduct, was long established in the customs of the ancient peoples.

"This understanding of marriage the human relationship is far more ready to serve as the matrix of the sacrament than any understanding developed hitherto across the centuries of Catholic teaching."

I believe that this approach to the sacramentality of marriage is significant. Human relationship is key. This can say so much more to married couples in pastoral preaching and care.

3. *Women*

Dr. Cahill calls for equal roles for men and women. "It is the union of the two partners which forms the basis of the 'bottom line' of the theological and moral evaluation of marriage."

In analyzing Pope John Paul's teaching about marriage, she says, among other things (some critical), "the Pope seems to present complete and equal freedom and reciprocity of wife and husband, not merely as an ideal to be achieved, but as the very description of a genuine male-female love relationship. He (the Pope) explicitly links 'the equal dignity and responsibility of women with men' to 'reciprocal self-giving' in marriage and family." She concludes that "attention to more equal roles is the *sine qua non* of credibility in twentieth century Western theology." To that I say, "Amen."

Dr. Haughton, drawing from stories of women, also calls for a "fundamental remaking of the role of women in society and that means the role of women in marriage and family." In sharing they learn a new language of liberation. For the ability to articulate oppression is the beginning of liberation.

"This is especially relevant now because most of the demand for a new theological interpretation of sexual relationships in our time has sprung directly from the need of women to know themselves as full persons, as in the little groups of women I work with. Many women have recognized that the way they have been regarded and treated by the dominant culture, and by the Church whose job it is to sacralize cultural norms, has made true self-affirmation as a child of God and inheritor of the reign of God nearly impossible." I need to hear that, listen to it, take it in.

4. *The Beauty, Joy and Sacredness of Sex—and Married Love*

Dr. Cahill has given us a definition of married love: "The love which belongs in marriage is a *commitment to partnership,* that is, a *commitment to achieve* social and domestic cooperation, mutual and equal respect, understanding and support, and the forgiveness which will be necessary to go beyond the inevitable failures in the realization of these ideals." Dr. Haughton gives us friendship as a profound Gospel category.

Dr. Dominian speaks of the sacredness, the beauty, the joy of marital love. He says: "For me sexual intercourse is a body language—a couple using their bodies to speak to each other, with or without words. What are they saying to each other? They are saying at least five things." "Intercourse is a recurrent act of thanksgiving." It is "a recurrent act of hope that we shall be wanted as a person." It "can be an act of reconciliation." "Sexual intercourse is a powerful affirmer of the sexual identity." And, finally, "Every time a couple make love, they declare to each other that they recognize, want and appreciate the other as a person unique in their life. Coitus is, therefore, a recurrent act of affirming the person."

As a pastor, I know that we have not said such things to our people. Maybe we are not the ones to say it. But bishops, priests and pastoral leaders need to affirm others in saying it. This is another reason for listening to the experiences of married people. As a Church we have to proclaim that married love is holy, beautiful, a joy.

Fr. Mackin points out a major leap in the understanding of the hierarchical magisterium of the Church that sexuality in marriage is good. The bishops at the Vatican Council "made one point about it whose significance can be estimated only in the sixteenth-century context of Augustinian pessimism about sexuality. They said that sexual expression including intercourse is in itself good." Fr. Mackin connects it with the sacrament as such: "In sexual lovemaking the sacrament is lived most fully," and God is praised. Let that be proclaimed again and again.

5. *Indissolubility*

Probably the most difficult issue dealt with in this symposium is the one dealt with by Dr. Cooke, Fr. Huizing and others in their discussions of indissolubility. It is a key issue and touches the lives of millions of Catholics. Dr. Cooke raises the question: "Can a person remain committed to the Christian community to live out a sacramental relationship that is existentially impossible?"

"One can, of course," he answers, "give an essentially legal response to this question: we have a law, a law that gives expression to a view of Catholic marriage which we are not free to abandon. Much as it pains us, the overall common good requires that exceptions not be made, so that the indissoluble character of Christian marriage can be safeguarded. But does the presentation of this ideal demand the absolutely universal implementation of this rule?''

Is, then, indissolubility an ideal or a reality? And what is the source of indissolubility? He concludes, ''The source of whatever indissolubility attaches to a particular marriage must be the character of the marriage itself, more specifically its symbolic import as a Christian sacrament.

''It would seem, then, that one should not talk about a marriage as being completely or absolutely indissoluble but as becoming increasingly indissoluble as it becomes increasingly Christian. This is to say quite simply that the more profoundly Christian a marriage relationship becomes, the more inseparable are the two persons as loving human beings and the more does their relationship sacramentalize the absolute indissolubility of the divine-human relationship as it finds expression in the crucified and risen Christ.

''It seems that we need a somewhat new though tradition-respecting look at indissolubility, to discover whether we are justified in applying it as absolutely as we Catholics have done in more recent centuries. It strikes me that a more flexible and individualized approach will continue to honor the teaching that Christian marriage is of its nature indissoluble.''

A Few Pastoral Issues

All of the theological, ethical, scriptural, canonical, psychological issues dealt with this week touch on the daily lives of men and women in the Church. Some of them strike me as especially relevant to pastoral care.

I am committed to the implementation of the notion of shared responsibility in the Church. I continually seek ways to call people to participate actively in the life and ministry in the Church. Diocesan pastoral planning is a starting point to all that we do as a staff to serve the parishes and people in the diocese. Essential to the Second Vatican Council's vision of the Church is the call of the laity to transform the world. This is the first pastoral issue that I would like to touch on.

We believe that the mission of the Church, its very purpose, must be the same as the mission of Jesus. The Church has no other purpose for its existence than to extend the kingdom of God to people of every nation, of every age, of every social and economic condition.

The kingdom is wherever God reigns, wherever God's will is done. The Lord, by the power of the Spirit and by our free choice, is to rule over our mind, our heart and our actions. And we are to work to bring a rule of God's love, justice, peace, truth, fidelity, patience and the rest to our society.

Jesus invites us to continue his life and work. He gives us gifts to share in ministries of the word, of worship and spiritual life, and of service. Pope John Paul II said one time, "Jesus alone is the solution to all your problems. He alone is the way, the truth, the life. He alone is the real salvation of the world. He alone is the hope of salvation." With all my heart I believe this.

In parishes throughout the diocese of New Ulm I have said over and over again to the people I serve, "All of us are called by God to extend the kingdom of God. We are to be a community of praying, believing, worshiping, loving people. Jesus invites us to take an active part in his mission."

In the diocese and throughout the world there has been a veritable explosion of people accepting the call and the challenge to exercise ministries of all kinds within the ecclesial community. Where we have not done so well is in recognizing, affirming, encouraging, supporting people in the transformation of the world, which is essentially the ministry of the laity, of all of God's people. By "we" here I speak especially of bishops and Church leaders. We have encouraged people in teaching ministries, youth work, pastoral care, some liturgical ministries, spiritual direction, ministries of concern for the poor, the widow, peace and justice—but all of this within the Church and under Church leadership and control.

Yet the Second Vatican Council said, "The laity, by their vocation, seek the kingdom of God by engaging in temporal affairs, and by ordering them according to the plan of God" (*Lumen Gentium,* 31). It is especially in the family and in society, in sexuality and economics, in marriage and in work that this transformation must take place.

We are going through a rural crisis of serious proportions. This crisis has helped me to understand a similar crisis in our attitude toward and our treatment of sexuality. There is a parallel in history between the way we (white males, especially) treat the land (and sea and sky) and the way we treat women. I use land to include the whole field of economics, the *world.* And I use the word "women" here to include sexuality, fertility, sexual relationship.

Land is looked upon as a commodity to be used, owned, exploited, dominated. Women are similarly considered. Land could be bought, sold, discarded. Land is an object of our greed, our covetousness. Women also. When women are degraded and exploited, sexuality is rejected as sacred, good, beautiful, powerful, to be treated with respect and responsibility.

Our land, our water, our air is being contaminated, used up, polluted through greed and exploitation and contaminated by chemicals and nuclear fallout. Economic injustice results when a few can lay claim to absolute ownership and exploitation of the goods of the earth. Human sexuality is degraded when it is trivialized, when people treat one another as sex objects, when there is little commitment.

I see so many connections between pollution of soil, water and land, and sexual exploitation; between economic repression and preparations for war; between the rejection of God in the world of work and the rejection of God in human sexuality.

Yes, every member of the Church is called to transform the world. That is particularly needed in economics and sexuality, in the world of work and in the family.

This brings me to my second concern. There is need for a positive theology of sexuality. The contributions of the speakers to this are invaluable. All of us need to proclaim to the housetops the words of the Second Vatican Council that sexual intercourse in marriage is good. "Hence the acts by which spouses join to one another intimately and chastely are good and honorable" (*Gaudium et Spes,* 48).

Fr. Mackin developed this point so well and reminded us of the pessimism of the past. Men and women are created equal and in the likeness of God. We are God-like in our very sexuality. Married people worship God in their sexual lovemaking.

As a bishop, I need to help free people to rejoice in their sexuality. But I need to listen to married people and encourage them, support them in sharing their insights with others in small groups, with their children, with couples preparing for marriage.

Jack Dominian's article on "Chastity" in this week's London *Tablet* does the kind of thing I have in mind. He says, "Christianity emphasizes that sex is a precious gift of God, that its full potential is realized only when it is embedded in personal relationships of love and that only chastity can preserve the essence of these relationships. . . . Every act of intercourse is a body language of pleasure which is a form of personal communication. This unitive feature is undoubtedly the principal meaning of sex, for, without it, the marital bond can disintegrate, which is the greatest catastrophe that can befall a marriage."

"Sexual intercourse," he continues, "needs a continuous reliable relationship to express its potential. Transient and incomplete experiences, which are the essence of fornication, do not permit the full existential growth of a personal relationship. Thus sex is deprived of its true potential.

"The same applies to adultery. Intercourse where a relationship is adulterous deprives the married couple of what belongs to them and threatens their marriage, and as in the case of fornication does not allow a full realization of the potential of sex."

More of us, and especially more married people, need to speak of human sexuality and especially conjugal sexual relationships as a precious gift of God, a joy, and the basis of life and love.

My last two points are brief. We have learned so much in recent years of the importance of small groups, basic Christian communities, and the strength of shared prayer, shared faith, and a reflection on experience in building such communities.

As a pastoral leader there is nothing to me more important or more needed in the Church than committed faith-filled adults. I see the total communion of life and love of married people as essential in this development.

Finally, married people, and all of us, are called to holiness. "Lay men and women hear the call of holiness in the very web of their existence (*Lumen Gentium,* 31) in and through the events of the world, the pluralism of modern living, the complex decisions and conflicting values they must struggle with, the richness and fragility of sexual relationships, the delicate balance between activity and stillness, presence and privacy, love and loss" (*Called and Gifted,* 13).

Holiness is nourished by prayer, by listening to the Lord. Let me tell you about Lela. She is a friend, a widow living on social security. She has experienced great hardship, suffering and grief in her life. Forty-five years ago she and her husband, who were at that time going through a particularly stormy time in their marriage, came to know the importance of daily Scripture reading, meditation and sharing in their lives.

Lela says, "God has a plan for us and we can know that plan." Almost every day for over forty-five years she and her husband spent some quiet time each morning, twenty minutes or so, reading a Scripture passage and then quietly, prayerfully listening. After their meditation they jotted down their thoughts. They would then share these thoughts with each other. They became convinced that it was during these times that God guided them, spoke to them. No major decision or activity was begun without this "guidance."

Marriage is a total union of persons, physical, sexual, psychological, spiritual. It is my belief that this symposium has advanced that vision of married life and so has promoted the kingdom of God.

Epilogue
Toward the Twenty-First Century
A Future Agenda

William P. Roberts

The chapters in this book have challenged several assumptions and raised important questions in regard to the present situation of marriage in the Catholic Church. They have been written with a respect for history and tradition, and with appreciation for the new direction taken by Vatican II toward a more positive understanding of marriage and sexuality. They have also been written with sensitivity to the suffering of many people, and with concern for the Gospel demand to minister to that pain.

What is of special significance about this volume is that the central questions and ideas raised by the authors are not theirs alone, but are representative of the kind of deep questioning that has emerged over the past few decades among the majority of Catholic theologians, canon lawyers, pastoral workers and the faithful at large. While such questioning does not demand blind agreement, it does deserve serious attention and consideration.

On the closing morning of the symposium one of the participants came forward to the microphone to urge Bishop Lucker to utilize his influence and do what he could to lead his fellow American bishops to involve themselves with the American Church in the same kind of serious, widespread dialogue on the issues of marriage and sexuality that they had engaged in regarding the topics of peace and the economy. It is essential, I believe, for the well-being of the Church, that this kind of dialogue take place soon. There are at least two reasons for this. First the kind of questioning that has arisen about marriage and sexuality will not go away by being ignored. A continued official ignoring of the questions will only further divide the Church. Second, as Vatican II made clear, the Spirit speaks through the entire people of God. Is it not preposterous to think that we can discover what the Spirit is saying to the Church

178

about marriage and sexuality, if official statements on these topics do not seriously consider and reflect the faith-filled experience of women and married people?

Hopefully, such a dialogue between bishops and the rest of the Church in America would inspire national dialogues elsewhere. It would be further hoped that these dialogues would be a prelude to a worldwide meeting of the Catholic episcopacy to give serious attention to the questions raised, and to provide further reformulation of the way the Church expresses in word and practice its teaching on marriage and sexuality.

While it is not the purpose here to write a complete agenda for such dialogues, I would like to indicate several of the kinds of questions and issues that would deserve serious consideration. Many of these have been either suggested or hinted at in the various chapters of this book.

1. If marriage is an intimate partnership of life and love, are mutual love, compassion, concern, respect and intimate communication essential components of marriage, or are they merely desirable qualities that a couple will hopefully work toward? Put another way, if these components are missing, is the marriage a valid one? Going further, if these components cease to exist in a marriage that was at one time valid, has the marriage ceased to exist?

2. Is every marriage between two baptized persons automatically a sacrament? Or is some degree of living faith in Jesus Christ required in the couple for their marriage to become a sacrament? What degree of life-giving love between the spouses is necessary for their marriage to be sacramental, and, hence, a sign of Christ's love? If a baptized couple are qualified to enter the married state, but do not have the necessary faith to participate in the sacrament of marriage, should not the Church still recognize their right to marry, even if their marriage is not a sacrament? Can such couples later be admitted to the sacrament if they become converted to Christian faith?

3. Is marriage automatically consummated by the first act of post-marital intercourse? What quality of marital relationship needs to be present before we can say that a marriage has been consummated by sexual intercourse? What quality of sexual intercourse is required?

4. Is Jesus' saying that humans ought not separate what God has joined in marriage a statement of the existential impossibility of dissolving a marriage, or is it a prophetic proclamation of a moral ideal toward which we are commanded to strive? When love and all of the other characteristics that human experience associates with marriage are no longer present, does the "bond of marriage" continue to exist? If so, in what does this "bond" consist? Put another way, when a marital relationship has been irrevocably destroyed, what is there left to which one must remain faithful?

5. Can marriage be reduced to a juridical reality? If not, is a tribunal proc-

ess the best way to judge marriage cases? Could the tribunal approach be better replaced by a pastoral approach in dealing with broken marriages?

6. Has the Church's ethical teachings on marriage been too preoccupied with sex and the biological and procreational aspects of intercourse, and not concerned nearly enough with marriage as intimate relationship and the significant role of sexual intercourse in nurturing the uniqueness of the marital relationship? If so, how can this be corrected? If marriage is a sacrament, is there something uniquely sacramental about marital intercourse? How would an appropriate concentration on the relational and sacramental aspects of marital intercourse affect the way the Church expresses its teaching in regard to marital sexuality and particularly birth control?

7. Does an inconsistency exist between the Church's teaching about the sacramentality and goodness of marriage on the one hand, and its insistence, on the other hand, that marriage is an obstacle to priestly orders? Along the same lines, is there a similar inconsistency between the Church's teaching, on the one hand, that women and men are equal in human dignity and hence there is no place for discrimination on the basis of gender, and, on the other hand, the Church's prohibition of women's entrance into certain ministerial roles?

Obviously, the above list of questions does not pretend to be an exhaustive one. But might it serve as a start for putting together an agenda of topics relating to marriage and sexuality that deserve entirely open, honest and un-intimidated discussion throughout a Spirit-filled Church? In this way may it be hoped that all of us will be enabled to perceive and live more fully the good news as it relates to sexuality and marriage, existing, as they do, at the core of the human experience!

Authors

LISA SOWLE CAHILL

Lisa Sowle Cahill pursued her undergraduate studies at the University of Santa Clara. She received her M.A. and Ph.D. in theological studies from the University of Chicago Divinity School, and taught theology at Concordia College in Minnesota. Since 1976 she has been Professor of Theology at Boston College. Her areas of academic speciality include method in theological ethics, medical ethics, and sexual ethics.

Professor Cahill is associate editor of *Logos* and *Journal of Religious Ethics*. She is editor for ethics for *Religious Studies Review* and is a member of the editorial advisory boards for *Horizons* and the *Journal of Law and Religion*. She serves on the Board of Directors for the Society of Christian Ethics and as ethicist on the Institutional Review Board of the Harvard Community Health Plan. She is a member of the American Academy of Religion, the Catholic Theological Society of America and the College Theology Society, and an associate member of the Hastings Institute of Society, Ethics and the Life Sciences.

Lisa Cahill has authored a number of scholarly articles. Her recently published book is entitled *Between the Sexes: A Study of Method in Christian Ethics*.

She is married to Lawrence Cahill, an attorney, and is the mother of Charlotte Mary and James Donald.

BERNARD COOKE

Bernard Cooke received his M.A. in philosophy at St. Louis University, his Licentiate in Sacred Theology at St. Mary's College, Kansas, and his S.T.D. at Institut Catholique de Paris. For eleven years he was chairperson of the Department of Theology at Marquette University. He has been Professor of Religious Studies at the University of Windsor and the University of Calgary. He has also been Bernard Hanley Visiting Professor at the University of Santa Clara. Bernard Cooke is presently chairperson of the Department of Religious Studies and Professor of Systematic Theology at Holy Cross College, Worcester, Massachusetts.

Cooke has published fourteen books and dozens of articles. Among his most significant books are *Christian Sacrament, and Christian Personality, Ministry to Word and Sacrament,* and *Sacraments and Sacramentality.* His latest book *Reconciled Sinners* is on the sacrament of reconciliation.

He has given numerous lectures, workshops, and summer courses in the United States, Canada, France, Spain, Switzerland, Japan, Korea, Ireland and East Africa. He is former president of the College Theology Society and the Catholic Theological Society of America.

The University of Detroit bestowed on Bernard Cooke an honorary doctorate (Litt.D.). From 1968–70 he pursued a post-doctoral research fellowship at Yale Divinity School. During 1983–84 academic year he was Fellow at the Wilson Center in Washington, D.C. At its 1979 annual convention, the Catholic Theological Society of America bestowed on Cooke its highest honor, the John Courtney Murray award.

JACK DOMINIAN

Dr. Jack Dominian was born in Athens and educated in India and England. He trained in Cambridge and Oxford, and qualified as a doctor in 1955 and as a psychiatrist in 1961. He is a Senior Consultant Psychiatrist at the Central Middlesex Hospital. In 1971 he established the Marriage Research Centre, of which he is director. His books include *Marital Breakdown, Christian Marriage, Cycles of Affirmation, Proposals for a New Sexual Ethic, From Cosmos to Love* (with A. R. Peacocke), *Marital Pathology,* and *Marriage, Faith and Love.*

ROSEMARY HAUGHTON

Rosemary Haughton was born in England. She is married and the mother of ten children and a number of foster children. In 1974 she and her husband, Algy, founded a community called *Lothlorien* to work with mentally troubled people in southwest Scotland.

Her writing and lecture schedules drew her to the United States and to her involvement with the growing movement of "Basic Christian Communities" in North America. She now spends most of each year in America, out of a desire to be part of the new growth of the Church whose form resembles that of the earliest churches.

She is part of a small community at Wellspring House in Gloucester, Massachusetts, a place of hospitality for those in crisis. Also based in Wellspring is a work she co-directs called *The Movement for North American Mission.* This program provides a two and a half year training for Christians of any age or denomination who feel called to serve the poor in North America, especially in places where there is little or no Christian presence.

Haughton is a well-known author and lecturer. Among her books are

Married Love in Christian Life, The Theology of Marriage, The Transformation of Man, The Catholic Thing, and *The Passionate God.* Her latest book is entitled *The Re-Creation of Eve.*

She received an honorary Doctor of Divinity degree from the University of Notre Dame and several other degrees and awards.

PETER J. HUIZING, S.J.

Fr. Huizing was born in Haarlam, Holland. He entered the Society of Jesus in 1931, and pursued his philosophical and theological studies in Jesuit schools. He studied Dutch civil law in Amsterdam and Nijmegen, and canon law in Rome and Louvain.

Peter Huizing has been Professor of Canon Law at a variety of Jesuit universities in Rome, Nijmegen, Louvain and Washington. He has authored numerous articles, and was director of the section on canon law of *Concilium.* He was also consultor of the commission for the revision of the Code of Canon Law.

RAYMOND A. LUCKER

Raymond Lucker is Bishop of New Ulm, Minnesota. He was ordained in 1952 for the Archdiocese of St. Paul/Minneapolis. He received his M.A. in History from St. Paul Seminary, his S.T.D. from the University of St. Thomas in Rome, and his Ph.D. in Education from the University of Minnesota.

For eleven years Bishop Lucker was Professor of Catechetics at St. Paul Seminary. He also served the Archdiocese of St. Paul/Minneapolis as Director of the Confraternity of Christian Doctrine, and as Superintendent of Schools. In January 1969 he became Director of the Department of Education for the United States Catholic Conference in Washington, D.C.

In 1971 Raymond Lucker was ordained a bishop and appointed as Auxiliary to the Archbishop of St. Paul/Minneapolis. During the next five years he also served as pastor of two urban parishes in that archdiocese. On February 19, 1976 he was installed as Bishop of New Ulm.

Lucker is the author of books on the aims of religious education and on the released time controversy. He has also written articles on religious education, evangelization, mission and ministry in the Church. He has been active on the National Council of Catholic Bishops' Committees on the Catechetical Directory, the Laity, the Permanent Diaconate and Charismatic Renewal.

THEODORE MACKIN, S.J.

Fr. Mackin is a member of the California Province of the Society of Jesus. He received his B.A. and M.A. in philosophy at Gonzaga University, Spokane, and his S.T.D. from Gregorian University. His doctoral dissertation treated the topic: "The Instrumental-Dispositive Causality in the Sacraments According to the Early Writings of Thomas Aquinas."

Since 1958 Theodore Mackin has been a member of the faculty of Religious Studies at Santa Clara University, where he specializes in sacramental theology, and where he is presently John Nobili Professor of Religious Studies.

For almost three decades Mackin has been preparing a monumental trilogy on Catholic marriage. Paulist Press has already published the first two volumes: *Marriage in the Catholic Church: What Is Marriage?* and *Marriage in the Catholic Church: Divorce and Remarriage*. The third volume, *Marriage, the Sacrament* is currently in production.

PHEME PERKINS

Pheme Perkins was educated as an undergraduate in the Great Books program of St. John's College, Annapolis, Maryland. She received her Ph.D. degree in "New Testament and Christian Origins" from Harvard University in 1971 for work on the "Gnostic Revelation Dialogues." She is currently Professor of New Testament at Boston College where she has taught since 1972.

Professor Perkins has authored thirteen books and over forty articles. Some of her best known books are *Reading the New Testament, Hearing the Parables of Jesus, Love Commands in the New Testament,* and *Resurrection*.

She also serves on the editorial boards of a number of journals and monograph series, among them *Catholic Biblical Quarterly, Journal of Biblical Literature, Interpretation, Horizons,* and *College Teaching*. She lectures extensively in the United States and Canada and conducts workshops for updating clergy and religious educators. She is a trustee of the Massachusetts Bible Society and a member of the USCC Committee to draft a pastoral letter on women in the Church.

WILLIAM P. ROBERTS

William P. Roberts received his Licentiate in Theology from Weston School of Theology and his Ph.D. from Marquette University. He teaches theology at the University of Dayton where one of his specialties is the theology of marriage. He is the author of several books including *Touchstones for Prayer, Marriage: Sacrament of Hope and Challenge,* and *Encounters with Christ: An Introduction to the Sacraments*.